LATER-LIFE SOCIAL SUPPORT AND SERVICE PROVISION IN DIVERSE AND VULNERABLE POPULATIONS

Later-Life Social Support and Service Provision in Diverse and Vulnerable Populations offers current, multidisciplinary perspectives on social support and service provision to older Americans. The chapters trace how our understanding of social support among older adults has developed over the past 40 years and explore current gerontological research in the area. They consider how informal care arrangements articulate with formal long-term care policies and programs to provide support to the diverse population of older Americans. They also emphasize heterogeneity in the composition of support networks, particularly in relation to gender, sexual orientation, race/ethnicity, and immigrant status. Collectively, the chapters provide insight into the complexity of older adult's social support networks that can be used to improve the services provided to caregivers and care recipients as well as the policies that promote high-quality support to people of all ages who are in need of assistance.

Janet M. Wilmoth, PhD, is professor of sociology at Syracuse University. She has authored over 50 publications that examine older adult migration, living arrangements, and health status, and explore how military service shapes various life-course outcomes.

Merril Silverstein, PhD, is the Cantor Professor of Aging Studies at Syracuse University. He has authored over 150 publications focused on aging in the context of family life, with an emphasis on life course and international perspectives.

SOCIETY AND AGING

Madonna Harrington Meyer, PhD, and
Jennifer Karas Montez, PhD, Series Editors

For a complete list of all books in this series, please visit the series page at:
https://www.routledge.com/Society-and-Aging-Series/book-series/SAS

**Later-Life Social Support and Service Provision in
Diverse and Vulnerable Populations**
Understanding Networks of Care
Edited by Janet M. Wilmoth and Merril Silverstein

LATER-LIFE SOCIAL SUPPORT AND SERVICE PROVISION IN DIVERSE AND VULNERABLE POPULATIONS

Understanding Networks of Care

Edited by Janet M. Wilmoth
and Merril Silverstein

NEW YORK AND LONDON

First published 2017
by Routledge
711 Third Avenue, New York, NY 10017

and by Routledge
2 Park Square, Milton Park, Abingdon, Oxon, OX14 4RN

Routledge is an imprint of the Taylor & Francis Group, an informa business

© 2017 Taylor & Francis

The right of Janet M. Wilmoth and Merril Silverstein to be identified as the authors of the editorial material, and of the authors for their individual chapters, has been asserted in accordance with sections 77 and 78 of the Copyright, Designs and Patents Act 1988.

All rights reserved. No part of this book may be reprinted or reproduced or utilized in any form or by any electronic, mechanical, or other means, now known or hereafter invented, including photocopying and recording, or in any information storage or retrieval system, without permission in writing from the publishers.

Trademark notice: Product or corporate names may be trademarks or registered trademarks, and are used only for identification and explanation without intent to infringe.

Library of Congress Cataloging in Publication Data
Names: Wilmoth, Janet M. (Janet May), editor. | Silverstein, Merril, editor.
Title: Later-life social support and service provision in diverse and vulnerable populations / edited by Janet M. Wilmoth and Merril Silverstein.
Description: New York: Routledge, 2017. | Includes bibliographical references and index.
Identifiers: LCCN 2016052589 | ISBN 9780415788304 (hardback) | ISBN 9780415788311 (pbk.)
Subjects: LCSH: Older people–Services for. | Older people–Social conditions. | Older people–Social networks. | Social service.
Classification: LCC HV1451 .L385 2017 | DDC 362.6–dc23LC
record available at https://lccn.loc.gov/2016052589

ISBN: 978-0-415-78830-4 (hbk)
ISBN: 978-0-415-78831-1 (pbk)
ISBN: 978-1-315-22295-0 (ebk)

Typeset in ITC Legacy Serif
by Deanta Global Publishing Services, Chennai, India

This edited volume is dedicated to Marjorie Cantor, whose pioneering research on older adults continues to shape the field of gerontology and influence scholars of later-life social support.

J. M. Wilmoth and M. Silverstein

CONTENTS

Series Foreword by Madonna Harrington Meyer   ix
Foreword by Monsignor Charles Fahey   xi
List of Contributors   xiii

1   Social Support and Service Provision to Older
Adults: An Introduction and Overview   1
Janet M. Wilmoth and Merril Silverstein

2   Social Relations and Social Support: Understanding
Group and Individual Differences   8
Toni C. Antonucci and Jasmine A. Manalel

3   The Aging and Latinization of the United States:
Opportunities and Investments   27
Fernando M. Torres-Gil and Courtney M. Demko

4   The Role of the Latino Family in Late-Life Caregiving   38
Jacqueline L. Angel, Sunshine Rote, and Kyriakos Markides

5   Social Networks and Supports among Older Gay
and Bisexual Men: The Impact of HIV   54
*Mark Brennan-Ing, Liz Seidel, Britta Larson,
and Stephen E. Karpiak*

6   Preparations for Later Life Care among LGBT Older Adults   77
Brian de Vries

7   LGBT Older Adults Emerging from the Shadows:
Health Disparities, Risk & Resilience   95
Karen I. Fredriksen-Goldsen and Charles P. Hoy-Ellis

8   Caregiving in Later Life: Challenges and Policies   118
Carole Cox

CONTENTS

9 Long-Distance Caregiving: Unique Challenges
   and Service Needs   136
   Amy Horowitz and Kathrin Boerner

10 Improving Access to Geriatrics Care for Rural Veterans:
   A Successful Partnership Between Urban Medical Centers
   and Rural Clinics   155
   *Judith L. Howe, Jennifer L. Griffith, William W. Hung,
   and B. Josea Kramer*

11 The Synergistic Interplay of Philosophy, Place, Program,
   and Policy: Learning the Art of the Possible from
   Small-House Nursing Homes   173
   Rosalie A. Kane and Lois J. Cutler

Index   209

SERIES FOREWORD

We all need care, at times. Babies, certainly, and the sick, often, need care. So do many with disabilities and many who are aging. That care may be provided by a wide array of care workers including family, friends, nurses, and attendants, and it may be unpaid or paid via a wide array of social programs. In 1979, Marjorie Cantor published an article in *Research on Aging* that laid out the classic hierarchical–compensatory theory of social supports, which addressed the complexity, preferences, and responsiveness of care networks. She wrote, "The social support system of an older person is comprised of an amalgam of basic entitlements and services provided by large scale bureaucratic organizations, both governmental and voluntary, and more personal idiosyncratic assistance received from kin and significant others" (Cantor 1979:434). Her work, based on support networks in New York City, helped to reformulate the ways we think, and talk, about care work. Support networks tend to be created in hierarchical patterns that are predictable. For example, those in need of care tend to rely on daughters before sons. Support networks also vary dramatically with respect to size, complexity, sustainability, resilience, and durability. Indeed, some in need of long-term care are well tended, while others need much more support than they are receiving.

In the decades since Cantor's landmark article, scholars have employed data sets from around the world to systematically examine how hierarchies of care vary by time, diagnosis, country, and key socio-demographic variables such as gender, race, class, age, marital status, and sexual orientation. With *Later-Life Social Support and Service Provision in Diverse and Vulnerable Populations*, Janet Wilmoth and Merril Silverstein have drawn together leading sociology, social work, and health scholars to analyze informal and formal support networks for those in need of long-term care. What are the lingering and newly emerging challenges to social support networks in societies with growing numbers of aged and disabled residents? What types of policies and programs best assist support networks as they face these challenges? The authors cover a broad scope of long-term care needs and responses, with some focusing particularly on subgroups that were close to Cantor's heart, including older Latinos; lesbian, gay, bisexual, and transgender individuals (LGBTs); and veterans.

Taken together, the authors summarize decades of scholarly research and lay out a clear course for research to come. They provide important insights into the strengths, and vulnerabilities, of various social support network patterns, social policies, and government programs. The authors contribute to discussions about best practices, policy reforms, and basic human rights. They increase our understanding of what works, and what does not; what we need more, and less, of as our nation continues to age. They lay out frameworks for developing policies, programs, and networks that will provide appropriate care, maximize independence, and assure dignity in the lives of persons of all ages in need of care.

Madonna Harrington Meyer
Syracuse University

REFERENCE

Cantor, Marjorie H. 1979. "Neighbors and Friends: An Overlooked Resource in the Informal Support System." *Research on Aging* 1(4):434–63.

FOREWORD
Monsignor Charles Fahey

This volume is but one of several tributes to Marjorie Cantor (1921–2009), who was the distinguished Brookdale Professor Emerita at Fordham University's Graduate School of Social Service.

Her daughter, Nancy Cantor, former chancellor of Syracuse University, now the chancellor of Rutgers University-Newark, and her son Richard Cantor established the Marjorie Cantor Endowed Professorship in Aging at Syracuse University. The initial chair holder, Merril Silverstein, and Janet Wilmoth, Director of the Aging Studies Institute at Syracuse, were the principals in organizing the 2014 convening that occasioned the papers in this collection.

The decade of the sixties marked a dramatic change in our understanding of aging and the care of the frail elderly. Marjorie Cantor was an early and continuing leader in society's efforts to integrate formal professional services in a facet of the life's journey which heretofore had been the exclusive domain of informal supports; family, friend, coreligionists, and private philanthropy. Such efforts have proceeded with unevenness, uncertainties, and controversies up to the present moment.

Marjorie's central interests and concerns coincided with the recognition of dramatic demographic and epidemiological developments. The 1961 White House Conference on Aging was the first time that the country focused on these realities and began to lay the groundwork for societal responses, including the enactment of Medicare, Medicaid, and the Older Americans Act, along with age discrimination statues and the evolution of Supplementary Security Income. Individually and col-

xi

lectively these developments and efforts to implement them brought opportunities and challenges to meet widely varying needs without compromising the substantial efforts of family, friends, and neighbors. Marjorie's pioneering activities were directed at identifying and relieving the needs of various subgroups within the overall aging population, as well as supporting those caring for them.

The various contributors in this collection of papers are for the most part collaborators, fellow investigators, students and friends of Marjorie's. Fittingly their articles reflect further explorations around the themes and methodologies central to her pioneering work. They explore the special needs and vulnerable subgroups distinguished by culture, ethnicity, race, and financial resources. They too recognize the needs of groups whose "newness" and size, such as Latinos and others, and whose relative lack of visibility, such as LGBT elders, call for special attention.

Fittingly, for an inveterate New York City person having been borne, raised, and educated there (Hunter College and Columbia's University Teacher's College), her initial entry into the field was with the New York City Department of the Aging. She served as Director of Research and Evaluation. She directed its activities in trying to better understand the needs of older New Yorkers and those who would serve them. She was principal investigator of a landmark cross-ethnic study "The Elderly in the Inner City of New York." It proved to be the first of some nine other large-scale studies during her forty years in the field.

After a stint at Hunter College she spent the rest of her distinguished career at Fordham University's School of Social service. While at Fordham she proved to be not only a recognized scholar and respected researcher but also excelled as a mentor and professional colleague. Her connection with students often extend beyond the classroom, even to her apartment, which became known to many as Fordham at Central Park South.

Marjorie exercised leadership and insights in various venues, organizations, and roles. Perhaps symbolic of this facet of her professional activities and leadership was her election as president of the Gerontological Society of America. It is important to note that in addition to being a significant leader at a moment of great social change she was a loving wife, sister, mother, grandmother, and friend.

The entries in this important book reflect many of the facets of Marjorie Cantor's career in the field of aging. It has provided one more opportunity for those of us who not only respected and cared for her to acknowledge her importance to society and to us.

LIST OF CONTRIBUTORS

Jacqueline L. Angel, PhD, is Professor of Public Affairs and Sociology at the University of Texas at Austin. Her research addresses the relationships linking family structures, inequality, and health across the life course, including a special focus on the Hispanic population and Mexican American families in particular. She is author/coauthor/editor of 80 journal articles, 30 book chapters, and 10 books. Some of her recent publications include *Latinos in an Aging World* (with Ronald Angel), *Challenges of Latino Aging in the Americas* (coedited with William Vega, Kyriakos Markides, and Fernando Torres-Gil), and *Handbook of the Sociology of Aging* (with Rick Settersten).

Toni C. Antonucci, PhD, is the Douvan Collegiate Professor of Psychology and Program Director of the Life Course Development Program at the Institute for Social Research at the University of Michigan. Professor Antonucci's research focuses, nationally and internationally, on social relations and health across the life span among individuals and families and across generations. Her work has involved populations in the United States, Europe, Asia, and the Middle East. She is particularly interested in how social relations optimize or jeopardize an individual's ability to face life's challenges.

Kathrin Boerner, PhD, is Associate Professor of Gerontology at the McCormack Graduate School of Policy and Global Studies, University of Massachusetts, Boston. Her research expertise is in adult development and aging, with a focus on coping with chronic illness, end of life, and bereavement. Dr. Boerner has a strong publication and funding record (over 80 journal articles/book chapters; U.S. and international funding). Dr. Boerner's research program aims at increasing preparation for the final phase of life in patients, family caregivers, and health-care staff alike, both by developing strategies to strengthen caregiver preparedness and by identifying barriers to high-quality end-of-life care.

Mark Brennan-Ing, PhD, is Director for Research and Evaluation at ACRIA and an adjunct assistant professor at New York University's College of Nursing. His research focuses on psychosocial issues of aging among people with HIV and LGBT individuals, including coping with chronic illness, mental health, sexuality, and social care resources. He has published over 100 peer-reviewed articles, books, chapters, and reports, and was an editor of the seminal volume, *Older Adults with HIV: An In-Depth Examination of an Emerging Population*. He is the 2016 Chair of the American Psychological Association's Committee on Sexual Orientation and Gender Diversity.

Carole Cox, MSW, PhD, is Professor in the Graduate School of Social Services, Fordham University. She is a fellow of the Gerontological Society of America and a Fulbright Scholar. She is the author of eight books and over 60 chapters and published articles. Her research includes studies on and the empowerment of grandparent caregivers, ethnicity and aging, and caregiving for persons with Alzheimer's disease.

Lois J. Cutler, PhD, now with Cutler Consulting in Stillwater, Minnesota, is recognized nationally for her expertise on how physical environments affect the behavior and well-being of older people, their families, and caregivers. As a research associate at the University of Minnesota, she investigated aspects of the physical environment in a series of studies in nursing homes and assisted living. She developed practical self-assessment tools for care providers to examine their own environments, and conducted numerous post-occupancy evaluation studies of the built environment, and she has analyzed regulations pertaining to construction and physical environments in long-term care.

LIST OF CONTRIBUTORS

Brian de Vries, PhD, is Professor of Gerontology at San Francisco State University. Professor de Vries has written or cowritten over 100 chapters, journal articles, and other publications and has edited or coedited five books, most recently *Community-Based Research on LGBT Aging* (with Cathy Croghan). His research examines the social lives and well-being of LGBT older adults, including the ongoing legacy and costs of discrimination and the prominent role of friendship.

Courtney M. Demko, BA, MSW, is a doctoral student in Social Welfare at UCLA. She also holds a BA in political science from Davidson College and an MSW from UCLA. Courtney currently serves as the Associate Director of UCLA's Center for Policy Research on Aging. Her research interests include dementia, family caregiving, long-term care, and intergenerational aspects of aging.

Karen I. Fredriksen-Goldsen, PhD, is Professor and Director of Healthy Generations Hartford Center of Excellence at the University of Washington. Specializing in innovations in cross-generational health, aging, and well-being, she has conducted extensive research within diverse and historically disadvantaged communities. She is leading the National Health, Aging and Sexuality Study: Aging with Pride, the first longitudinal study to address aging and health in sexual and gender minority communities, which is funded by the National Institutes of Health and the National Institute on Aging. She is the author of more than 75 peer-reviewed publications and three books.

Jennifer L. Griffith, MA, is Grant Writer at SmartStart Evaluation and Research. Previous to this position, she was the Executive Director of SCIRE Veterans Biomedical Research Foundation associated with the Department of Veterans Affairs and the University of California, Irvine. Formerly, she was the Administrator at the USC Southern California Research Center for ALPD & Cirrhosis, Program Manager for the Consortium of NY Geriatrics Education Centers based at the Icahn School of Medicine at Mount Sinai, and adjunct faculty at Fordham University, Graduate School for Social Service.

Amy Horowitz, PhD, is the Nicholas J. Langenfeld Chair in Social Research and Professor at Fordham University Graduate School of Social

Service. Dr. Horowitz has been the principal investigator on numerous NIH research grants on aging, family relations, disability, and visual impairment, and has published widely on topics relating to family caregiving for the disabled elderly, adaptation to disability, and the interrelationships between late-life disability, depression, and rehabilitation. Her research on long-distance caregiving has been recently funded by a grant from the National Institute on Aging (2016–2018)

Judith L. Howe, PhD, is Professor at Brookdale Department of Geriatrics and Palliative Medicine, Icahn School of Medicine at Mount Sinai, and Associate Director of Education and Evaluation and Deputy Director at Bronx VAMC GRECC. She has presented at numerous national meetings and regional meetings, has published widely in books and journals, and is Editor-in-Chief of *Gerontology and Geriatrics Education*, the official journal of the Association of Gerontology in Higher Education (AGHE). She has served as an elected member of the Executive Committee of AGHE, was President of the State Society on Aging of New York, and is past President of the National Association of Geriatric Education Centers/ National Association for Geriatric Education. She is a Fellow of the New York Academy of Medicine, Association for Gerontology in Higher Education, and the Gerontological Society of America.

Charles P. Hoy-Ellis, PhD, is Assistant Professor in Social Welfare in the College of Social Work at the University of Utah. He has authored or coauthored 21 articles and book chapters and has presented his research at 18 peer-reviewed regional, national, and international conferences. His scholarship focuses on health and mental health disparities among LGBT older adults and how these are informed by the intersections of identity and aging in a heteronormative society.

William W. Hung, MD, MPH, is Associate Professor of Geriatrics and Palliative Medicine at the Brookdale Department of Geriatrics at the Icahn School of Medicine at Mount Sinai, NY. He is also a physician-investigator at the Geriatric Research Education and Clinical Center at the James J. Peters VA Medical Center in Bronx, NY. His research examines the impact of geriatric models of care to improve care delivery for older adults. He has also developed and led clinical geriatric programs which aim to improve transitions of care for older adults and geriatric care in rural areas.

List of Contributors

Rosalie A. Kane, PhD, is a social worker and Professor of Health Policy and Management in the School of Public Health at the University of Minnesota. She has authored or coauthored more than a dozen books and hundreds of articles and book chapters. She is the past editor-in-chief of both *Health and Social Work* and *The Gerontologist*. Her research deals with both practice and policy for long-term services and supports in all settings—nursing homes, assisted living, and home care, and the measurement and promotion of quality of life and quality of care.

Stephen E. Karpiak, PhD, was on the faculty of Columbia University Medical School for 25 years. He is Senior Director for Research at ACRIA's *Center on HIV and Aging* and on the faculty of NYU College of Nursing. In 2005, he launched *ROAH* (Research on Older Adults with HIV), which received recognition from the U.S. Surgeon General. He is a member of the *American Academy of HIV Medicine* and the *American Geriatrics Society* HIV-AGE effort. He has over 120 peer-reviewed publications.

B. Josea Kramer, PhD, is Associate Director for Education/Evaluation at the Geriatric Research Education and Clinical Center at the Veterans Affairs (VA) Greater Los Angeles Healthcare System and the director of the national VA Geriatric Scholars Program, which is a continuing professional development program designed to integrate geriatrics into VA primary care practices. As a health services researcher, she has a long-standing interest in improving access to quality health care in rural areas.

Britta Larson, MNA, is Senior Services Director at Center on Halsted, the Midwest's most comprehensive community center for the Lesbian, Gay, Bisexual, Transgender, and Queer (LGBTQ) community. Ms. Larson is responsible for overseeing the older adult programs at Center on Halsted and the provision of case management services to the residents of Town Hall apartments, Chicago's first LGBT-friendly senior housing. She has coauthored articles on the social care networks of older LGBT adults in the *Journal of Homosexuality* and on religious participation among older LGBT adults in the *Journal of Religion*.

Jasmine A. Manalel, MS, is a doctoral candidate in Developmental Psychology at the University of Michigan. She studies social relations

xvii

across the life span and their links to individual health and well-being. Her current work examines spousal and intergenerational relationships in adulthood, and the developmental contexts, processes, and outcomes associated with the positive and negative aspects of these relationships.

Kyriakos Markides, PhD, is currently the Annie and John Gnitzinger Distinguished Professor of Aging in the Department of Preventive Medicine and Community Health at the University of Texas Medical Branch in Galveston. Dr. Markides is the editor of the *Journal of Aging and Health*, which he founded in 1989. He is the author or coauthor of over 250 publications, most of which are on aging and health issues in the Mexican American population as well as on minority aging issues in general. He is currently Principal Investigator of the Hispanic EPESE (Established Population for the Epidemiological Study of the Elder), a longitudinal study of the health of older Mexican Americans from the five southwestern states.

Sunshine Rote, PhD, is Assistant Professor in the Kent School of Social Work at the University of Louisville. Dr. Rote's research examines the role of social relationships for the psychological well-being of older adults, especially older Latinos.

Liz Seidel, MSW, is Manager for Research and Evaluation at ACRIA's Center on HIV and Aging. Ms. Seidel's research focuses on the psychosocial challenges faced by many older adults with HIV, including stigma, depression, and social isolation. Additionally, Ms. Seidel serves as the evaluator of ACRIA's National Training Center. She is a board member of the State Society on Aging of New York and an instructor at Fordham University's Graduate School of Social Service.

Merril Silverstein, PhD, is the inaugural holder of the Marjorie Cantor Chair in Aging Studies at Syracuse University in the Maxwell School Department of Sociology and School of Social Work. He received his doctorate in Sociology from Columbia University. In over 150 research publications, he has focused on aging in the context of family life, with an emphasis on life course and international perspectives. He serves as principal investigator of the Longitudinal Study of Generations and has had projects in China, Sweden, the Netherlands, and Israel. He is a

Brookdale Fellow and Fulbright Senior Scholar and between 2010–2014 served as editor-in-chief of *Journal of Gerontology: Social Sciences.*

Fernando M. Torres-Gil, PhD, is Professor of Social Welfare and Public Policy, and Director of the Center for Policy Research on Aging at the University of California, Los Angeles (UCLA). He has authored over 100 articles and book chapters and six books addressing issues on the politics of aging, diversity, and minority aging and the policy implications of an aging society. His current research on the emerging Latino population is reflected in his book—*Aging, Health and Longevity in the Mexican-Origin Population* (edited with J. Angel, F. Torres-Gil, and K. Markides). He is a board member of the AARP and has served in multiple governmental positions related to aging, disability, and health care.

Janet M. Wilmoth, PhD, is Professor of Sociology and Director of the Aging Studies Institute at Syracuse University. Professor Wilmoth has authored over 50 articles and book chapters, and coedited *Gerontology: Perspectives and Issues* (2nd and 3rd editions) and *Life Course Perspectives on Military Service*. Her research examines older adult migration, living arrangements, and health status, and explores how military service shapes various life-course outcomes related to marriage and family, economic well-being, and disability.

CHAPTER 1

SOCIAL SUPPORT AND SERVICE PROVISION TO OLDER ADULTS

An Introduction and Overview

Janet M. Wilmoth and Merril Silverstein

Older adults rely on a complex network of social supports to cope with the challenges of aging, although the particular composition of those support networks varies substantially by age, gender, sexual orientation, race/ethnicity, and immigrant status. In welfare states like the United States, the family, the market, and the state are involved in the provision and financing of services to older adults (Soldo 1994). Over the past 40 years, there has been considerable discussion among gerontologists regarding the reliance of older adults on sources of support and the extent to which the composition and configuration of social support networks follows a structured pattern and varies by sociodemographic characteristics. During this time, theories describing and explaining social support networks of older adults have also evolved.

Theories of support to older adults have variously emphasized preferences and constraints in the support-seeking process. An influential theory emphasizing preferences for support and care was advanced by Cantor (1979) in her *hierarchical–compensatory model of social supports*, which posits an ordered selection of caregivers that starts with spouses, daughters, and sons, then extends to more distant family members, friends, and neighbors. This perspective countered competing perspectives seeking to understand the social principles underlying the organization of informal support. For instance, Litwak's (1985) *task-specific model* emphasized

1

mixed functions among network members who provide specialized types of support based on their emotional connection, geographic proximity, and level of commitment to the care recipient. While not entirely antagonistic, these two theories reflect the tension between the importance of preferences and structured differentiation in the support choices made by older adults and their social network members.

More recently, scholars have used Antonucci's (1985) *convoy model* and Carstensen's (1993) *socio-emotional selectivity theory* to study how social support networks change over the life course. These perspectives focus on gains and losses in the roster of potential support providers, as well as changes in the salience of particular social ties. Scholarly contributions by Fingerman (2001) and Lüscher and Pillemer (1998) have highlighted *mixed feelings* in supportive relationships, recognizing emotional complexity in support provision and helping fuel the emergence of the ambivalence paradigm in family gerontology. Connidis and McMullin (2002), examining the construct of ambivalence through a sociological lens, consider how wider social forces, particularly the absence of formal resources, shape the motives and emotions of informal support providers. Taken together, these contemporary theories and models enrich and extend earlier considerations of support networks of older adults by formally incorporating dynamic, conflicting, and societal elements in the support process.

The ability to test the propositions of these theoretical constructs has been facilitated by the development of several high-quality, longitudinal surveys of older adults and their families, including the Health and Retirement Study and its international "sister studies," the National Health and Aging Trends Study, the National Survey of Families and Households, Americans' Changing Lives, Midlife Development in the United States, the Wisconsin Longitudinal Study, the Longitudinal Study of Generations, and the Within-Family Differences Study. These studies have yielded important knowledge about how families and larger social networks are mobilized (or not) in support of frail older adults. Currently available data sources, consisting of both regional, national, and multinational samples, have provided the capacity to examine micro-family dynamics in supportive behaviors as well as processes by which sources of support are broadly shaped by national welfare regimes. In addition to enabling comparative research, large national samples often have sufficient over-samplings of at-risk groups to investigate how disadvantages related to minority, immigrant, and low socioeconomic status have compromised the health and well-being of older adults and elevated demands on their caregivers.

At the same time, advanced statistical techniques such as multi-level models, growth curve models, and structural equation models have become more readily available in statistical software packages. This has allowed researchers to specify models that better approximate the changing complexity of older adults' social supports over time. Several studies have been collecting data on the same individuals for more than two decades and over multiple cohorts and generations. These design features have enabled the investigation of long-term trends in social support over the adult life span as well as historical changes in family structure and the supply and mix of informal care providers. Our understanding of this complexity has also been enhanced by the increased use of qualitative methods, including participant observations, in-depth interviewing, life history and narrative analysis, and ethnographies.

These methodological advances have led gerontologists to ask increasingly nuanced questions about later-life social support. Much of this research is driven by the fundamental question of whether the support older adults receive is sufficient to meet their needs. Although the majority of older adults report that they receive an adequate amount of social support, the percentage reporting they "never" or "rarely" receive adequate support increases with age, is higher among men than women, and is higher among minority elders than non-Hispanic white elders (Centers for Disease Control 2008). Inadequate support is problematic because it represents unmet needs that can place vulnerable older adults at risk of adverse consequences such as dehydration, falls, and hospitalization (LaPlante et al. 2004; Xu et al. 2012).

Recent demographic and social changes may increase the level of inadequate support in later life. Longer life expectancies coupled with lower fertility rates have changed the structure of American families from two or three generations with a broad array of members to three or more generations with fewer members. Consequently, there are fewer members of the younger generations who can provide care to the older generations (Himes 2002; Wilmoth and Longino 2006). These trends will be compounded as the baby boomers, who have higher rates of childlessness than prior cohorts, move into their eighties, when caregiving needs are greatest (Uhlenberg and Cheuk 2008). At the same time, divorce, remarriage, cohabitation, and new union forms have created substantial heterogeneity in family forms that has implications for informal and formal care provision (Manning and Brown 2011), while the increasing diversity of the American population is changing the dynamics between older adults and care providers (Torres-Gil and Treas 2008). Furthermore, the retrenchment of the welfare state and associated emergence of market-friendly policies are shifting the costs associated with age-related risks from the government to families and individuals in ways that entrench old age inequality (Quadagno and Street 2004; Harrington Meyer 2010; Harrington Meyer and Herd 2007). Given these trends, it is timely to examine the current state of social support and service provision to the diverse population of older adults in the United States.

There has not been a book that systematically addresses these issues since the publication of Cantor and Brennan's *Social Care of the Elderly: The Effects of Ethnicity, Class, and Culture* in 2000. The present edited volume builds on the legacy of Marjorie Cantor's contributions to gerontology by offering current, multidisciplinary perspectives on social support and service provision to older Americans. It begins with Toni Antonucci and Jasmine A. Manalel providing an overview of the developments in the field in recognition of Marjorie's contribution and enduring legacy in Chapter 2. They underscore one of Marjorie Cantor's primary contributions, which is the recognition that individual and group differences are critically important to the study of social relations and social support.

Chapters 3 and 4 examine the implications of increasing ethnic diversity among the older adult population. In Chapter 3, Fernando Torres Gil and Courtney M. Demko explore the demographic changes associated with the upcoming doubling of the older population as baby boomers move into later life and result in a majority–minority nation as Latinos become the largest minority group. The chapter addresses the implications and unintended consequences of these trends, as well as the ultimate opportunities it provides for a reinvigorated society. Chapter 4, by Jacqueline L. Angel, Sunshine Rote, and Kyriakos Markides, builds upon this legacy by examining sources of support for Hispanic elders who were born in the United States, early-life immigrants, and late-life immigrants. Using data from wave 7 of the Hispanic Established Population of the Epidemiologic Study of the Elderly (H-EPESE, 2010/2011), they find that late-life immigrants are at high risk of dependency on family, especially one close, focal family member, for personal care and financial tasks. They also discuss the implications of their findings for future research and policy in light of recent health-care reform.

The next three chapters focus on a range of issues related to caregiving among lesbian, gay, bisexual, and transgender (LGBT) older adults. In Chapter 5, Mark Brennan-Ing, Liz Seidel, Britta Larson, and Stephen Karpiak examine the impact of HIV on the social support among older gay and bisexual men. The friend-centric social networks among this population have been undermined by HIV/AIDS, while those living with HIV/AIDS experience numerous comorbid conditions that increase caregiving needs. This chapter compares the social networks, supports, and care needs of HIV-positive and -negative gay and bisexual men over 50 to better understand how policies and programs can best be tailored to address this aging population. Chapter 6, by Brian deVries, uses findings from three studies to understand the future concerns, hopes, and preparations of LGBT persons in the second half of life. These analyses underscore the importance of later-life care discussions amongst those who are likely to age outside of traditional family structures. In Chapter 7, Karen Fredriksen-Goldsen and Charles Hoy-Ellis share findings from the first federally funded groundbreaking study of LGBT health and aging that contains 2,560 demographically diverse LGBT adults aged 50 and older. They explore how social positions and the structural and environmental context intersect with adverse and health-promoting mechanisms to influence health outcomes in LGBT communities. The research highlights the importance of understanding how social determinants, and risks and opportunities, relate to optimal aging in our increasingly diverse society.

The last four chapters consider policy and program needs related to the provision of informal and formal support. Chapter 8, by Carole Cox, discusses the challenges faced by caregivers, with a focus on family caregivers who are providing care to older persons in need of assistance and grandparents who are raising their grandchildren. The major policies that can assist caregivers are discussed, as well as the gaps that are barriers to their effectiveness. In Chapter 9, Amy Horowitz and Kathrin Boerner provide an overview of current knowledge about long-distance caregiving. They present results of a pilot study of long-distance caregivers to elders in long-term care that provide insight into the challenges these caregivers face and a foundation for future research on the topic. In Chapter 10, Judith Howe, Jennifer Leigh Griffith, William W. Hung, and B. Josea Kramer describe a multifaceted program involving stake-holders from Veterans Health Administration (VHA) and non-VHA urban medical centers and VHA rural outpatient clinics. The program provides face-to-face individual and team-based didactic and clinical education, quality improvement education and guidance, mentoring opportunities, virtual learning, and case-based education and direct clinical consultation via tele-health modalities. Data are presented that demonstrate the program impact on provider knowledge and skills in geriatrics. Chapter 11, by Rosalie Kane and Lois J. Cutler, summarizes a systematic study of 50 small-house nursing homes, which are licensed and certified skilled facilities with about 7–16 residents who live in self-contained houses, cottages, or urban apartments. The chapter describes in detail the environmental changes (designs, layouts, furnishings, and fixtures) and the transformed staff roles, and discusses the implications for various long-term care residential facilities.

Collectively, these chapters build on the contributions of Cantor's (1979) classic *hierarchical–compensatory theory of social supports* by tracing how our understanding of social support among older adults has developed over the past 40 years and highlighting current gerontological research in the area. They move beyond the relatively narrow caregiving lens by considering how informal care arrangements articulate with formal long-term care policies and programs to provide support to the diverse population of older Americas. The chapters also emphasize heterogeneity in the composition of support networks, particularly in relation to gender, sexual orientation, race/ethnicity, and immigrant status. In doing so, they provide insight into the complexity of older adults' social support networks that can be used to improve the services provided to caregivers and care recipients as well as the policies that promote high-quality support to people of all ages who are in need of assistance.

REFERENCES

Antonucci, Toni C. 1985. Personal Characteristics, Social Support, and Social Behavior. P. 94–128 in Robert H. Binstock (ed.) *Handbook of Aging and the Social Sciences* (2nd ed.), New York: Academic Press.

Cantor, Majorie. H. 1979. "Neighbors and Friends: An Overlooked Resource in the Informal Support System." *Research on Aging* 1:434–63.

Carstensen, Lauren L. 1993. Motivation for Social Contact Across the Life Span: A Theory of Socioemotional Selectivity. P. 209–54 in J. E. Jacobs (ed.) *Nebraska*

Symposium on Motivation: 1992, Developmental Perspectives on Motivation (Vol. 40), Lincoln: University of Nebraska Press.

Centers for Disease Control. 2008. "The State of Mental Health and Aging in America." Retrieved October 18, 2016 from http://www.cdc.gov/aging/pdf/mental_health.pdf.

Connidis, Ingrid A. and Julie A. McMullin. 2002. "Sociological Ambivalence and Family Ties: A Critical Perspective." *Journal of Marriage and Family* 64(3):558–67.

Fingerman, Karen. 2001. *Aging Mothers and their Adult Daughters: A Study in Mixed Emotions.* New York: Springer.

Harrington Meyer, Madonna. 2010. Shifting Risk and Responsibility: The State and Inequality in Old Age. P. 21–41 in Robert B. Hudson (ed.) *The New Politics of Old Age Policy* 2nd ed.), Baltimore, MD: Johns Hopkins Press.

Harrington Meyer, Madonna and Pamela Herd. 2007. *Market Friendly or Family Friendly? The State and Gender Inequality in Old Age.* New York: Russell Sage.

Himes, Christine. 2002. "Elderly Americans." *Population Bulletin 4 (June).* Washington, DC: U.S. Bureau of the Census.

LaPlante, Mitchell P., H. Stephen Kaye, Taewoon Kang, and Charlene Harrington. 2004. "Unmet Need for Personal Assistance Services: Estimating the Shortfall in Hours of Health and Adverse Consequences." *Journals of Gerontology: Social Sciences* 29(2):S98–S108.

Litwak, Eugene. 1985. *The Complementary Roles of Informal Networks and Formal Systems.* New York: Guilford Press.

Lüscher, Kurt and Karl Pillemer. 1998. "Intergenerational Ambivalence: A New Approach to the Study of Parent-Child Relations in Later Life." *Journal of Marriage and the Family* 60(2):413–25.

Manning, Wendy and Susan Brown. 2011. The Demography of Unions Among Older Americans, 1990-Present: A Family Change Approach. P. 193–210 in Richard A. Settersten and Jacqueline L. Angel (eds.) *Handbook of Sociology of Aging.* New York: Springer.

Quadagno, Jill and Debra Street. 2004. "Recent Trends in US Social Welfare Policy: Minor Retrenchment or Major Transformation?" *Research on Aging* 28(3):303–16.

Soldo, Beth. 1994. Care of the Elderly: Division of Labor Among the Family, the Market, and the State. P. 195–216 in Linda G. Martin and Samuel H. Preston (eds.) *Demography of Aging,* Washington, DC: National Academy Press.

Torres-Gil, Fernando and Judith Treas. 2008. "Immigration and Aging: The Nexus of Complexity and Promise." *Generations* 32(4):6–10.

Uhlenberg, Peter and Michelle Cheuk. 2008. Demographic Change and the Future of Informal Caregiving. P. 9–23 in Maximiliane E. Szinovacz and Adam Davey (eds.) *Caregiving Contexts: Cultural, Familial and Societal Impacts.* New York: Springer.

Wilmoth, Janet M. and Charles F. Longino Jr. 2006. "Demographic Trends That Will Shape U.S. Policy in the 21st Century." *Research on Aging* 28(3):269–88.

Xu, Huiping, Kenneth E. Covinsky, Eric Stallard, Joseph Thomas III, and Laura P. Sands. 2012. "Insufficient Help for Activity of Daily Living Disabilities and Risk for All-Cause Hospitalization." *Journal of the American Geriatrics Society* 60(5):927–33.

CHAPTER 2

SOCIAL RELATIONS AND SOCIAL SUPPORT

Understanding Group and Individual Differences

Toni C. Antonucci and Jasmine A. Manalel

INTRODUCTION

In this chapter, we review the recent evolution of research and its implications for practice in the areas of social relations and social support. We organize the chapter around one of Marjorie Cantor's enduring legacies, the recognition that individual and group differences exist and are critically important to the study of social relations. She taught us that individuals and groups differ in their specific needs and norms regarding social relations. For example, some groups expect intense intimate relations while for others minimal interaction is acceptable. Finally, looking toward the future, we note Marjorie Cantor's influence on the future of the field and how her theoretical views are now being confirmed through increasingly sophisticated methods and measures.

Social Relations—Early Perspectives

The 1960s and 1970s could be described as the period of early modern exploration of the field of social relations, especially among adults and older people. At that time, there was very little high-quality empirical evidence using representative samples or advanced analytical strategies. Nevertheless, it was widely believed that social relations, in the form of family relationships and friendships, were a positive resource available to all. It was expected that research should help identify the optimal expression of social relations. Although it was originally thought that all such social relations were positive, it was eventually understood that these same close social relations could actually be negative. For example, Silverstein and his colleagues, using the Longitudinal Study of Generations (LSOG), were able to empirically demonstrate the existence of conflict within many intergenerational families (Silverstein et al. 2010; Silverstein 1997). Based on this work and the work of others (e.g., Rook and Pietromonaco 1987; Kahn and Antonucci 1980), it eventually came to be widely accepted that social relations could be positive or negative, beneficial or detrimental (Antonucci, Akiyama, and Lansford 1998; Ingersoll-Dayton, Morgan, and Antonucci 1997). Nevertheless, it was generally believed that 'one size fits all.' It was assumed that the best or most illustrative expression of positive relations, as well as the worst and most illustrative expressions of negative relations, would be the same for everyone. The job of science was to identify the specific characteristics of beneficial and detrimental social relations.

At that time, individual and group differences were assessed by comparison with an accepted norm. Of course, that norm was overwhelmingly white and middle class. If one differed from this norm, it was assumed that the individual or group was wrong, divergent, maladapted, or disadvantaged. Thus, if one's network was larger or smaller, or characterized by less positive or more negative interactions than the white, middle-class norm, then that network was considered deficient or nonnormal. Gradually it came to be understood, largely through work by people like Marjorie Cantor, that differences could and should be identified and celebrated. Similarly, it came to be understood that different did not necessarily mean wrong and that people could be different without being disadvantaged or inferior. As empirical evidence increasingly became available indicating that people could function well and feel supported under a variety of circumstances, differences have come to be acknowledged as potentially viable alternatives to the accepted norm. The edict that one size fits all has gradually been abandoned.

As the field came to recognize differences as potentially equally beneficial, it eventually came to the realization that differences should also be celebrated for what they might teach us. This was, indeed, a significant step and has brought us a great influx of new knowledge. If people experiencing different patterns of social relations can be equally successful, it suggests that our understanding of the basic concepts should be modified.

THE EMERGING FIELD OF SOCIAL SUPPORT

At the same time, in what might be considered a corollary to the field of social relations, there was emerging new research focused on social support. This field identified how social relations translated into support for and from others. The field emerged from a convergence of other disciplines such as developmental psychology, social work, and sociology. Developmental psychologists considered it an extension of the burgeoning field of attachment that focused primarily on the mother–child relationship (Ainsworth et al. 1978; Bowlby 1969). Researchers, especially in the United States, argued that the early mother–infant relationship was the basis for all later social relationships. It thus became the focus of a voluminous amount of research (Cassidy and Shaver 1999; Ainsworth et al. 1978). Although it was not at first widely recognized, Bowlby's (1969) original articulation of the theory was, in fact, the life span in nature. The theory was meant to describe relationships from infancy through adulthood. Eventually, attachment as a life-span concept (Antonucci 1976) was more widely accepted and became the focus of a great deal of research in its own right (Rholes and Simpson 2006; Simpson and Rholes 1998; Koski and Shaver 1997; Bartholomew 1993; Collins and Read 1990; Troll and Smith 1976).

The extension of this theoretical perspective based on empirical findings is illustrative. The original research on middle-class white American samples identified three categories of attachment: secure, insecure, and ambivalent. Although the specifics of these categories are not central here, the important point is that these three categories assumed that one category was the standard, or best, form of attachment and all others were divergent or less optimal. Clearly, this perspective was consistent with the one-size-fits-all approach. As additional attachment research was conducted on other samples in the United States, such as working-class or poor families and ethnic or racial minorities, divergent attachment behaviors were identified. These divergent behaviors were considered indicative of disadvantaged or not secure attachment. However, as attachment research became international, it became clear that attachment categories, at least as assessed by the now widely accepted Ainsworth Strange Situation, a series of increasingly stressful separation episodes (Ainsworth and Bell 1970), were not appropriate for all children. It was eventually ascertained that cultural differences in parenting led to differences in attachment behaviors and hence in attachment categorization if these differences were not taken into account during assessment (e.g., Van Ijzendoorn and Kroonenberg 1988; Takahashi 1986; Grossmann et al. 1985). Upon reflection, this makes sense. Children who spend their entire day strapped to their mother's back will react quite differently to the separation episodes of the Strange Situation than children who regularly separate from her to sleep, be cared for by others, or play. Eventually, it became clear that although the theory of attachment might apply across cultures, attachment behaviors, resulting from cultural differences in parenting practices, might be different. If not taken into account, inaccurate and inappropriate attachment classifications would be assessed. In sum, this research represented another important recognition that one size does not fit all.

Sociologists also recognized the importance of social relations: in this case viewing the examination of social relations as a means of understanding interactions within families, communities, and organizations. For example, Elizabeth Bott (1957) studied social networks in several neighborhoods of East London. As a result of her careful and systematic qualitative study of marital roles and relationships, she was able to document how various network types influenced gender role segregation within marriage. Similarly, Helena Lopata (1979) studied the experience of widows both in the Chicago area and in other parts of the world. Many say she coined the term social support to describe the way in which social relations helped widows manage their bereavement and life after spousal loss. Her comparative work identified the ways in which women's roles were different throughout the world and enabled her to document the different ways women's social relations allowed them to receive support. Some illustrative early evidence was also provided by the LSOG (Bengtson 2001; Richards, Bengtson, and Miller 1989; Bengtson 1975; Bengtson 1971). The study began as a three-generation study in the early 1970s. Using data collected from each generation, Bengtson and his colleagues (1975; Silverstein and Long 1998) were able to demonstrate patterns of social relations within families and across generations. Among the most interesting findings was the somewhat counterintuitive finding that relations were more positive among non-adjacent generations, such as grandparents and grandchildren, than adjacent generations, such as parents and children (see Bengtson 1971). In other words, grandchildren and grandparents had more positive feelings and less negative feelings toward each other than either parents and grandparents or parents and children. This conflicted with general assumptions that adjacent generations would be more similar and therefore have a greater affinity for each other. However, upon reflection, one might argue that the nonadjacent generations had the luxury of closeness without the responsibilities or rebelliousness of the parent–child relationships to discipline, set boundaries, establish independence, and the like.

As noted, later research on the LSOG longitudinal sample identified patterns of both positive and negative relations, specifically conflict within and across generations. As one might expect, higher levels of conflict were associated with lower levels of well-being. At the same time, individual and group differences were identified; hence some individuals were uniquely different from their family members while in other cases general patterns of relationships could be found among different families. The most recent work in this area has empirically demonstrated the importance of ambivalence (Connidis and McMullin 2002; Pillemer and Suitor 2002; Lüscher and Pillemer 1998). Empirical evidence now available (Fingerman, Sechrist, and Birditt 2013; Birditt et al. 2012) has established the relatively common state of ambivalence in close relationships, the presence of both positive and negative feelings toward the same person. This level of relationship complexity empirically verifies what social workers have observed in practice and offers insight on how to cope with such relationships within families.

Social Relations from a Practical/Practice Perspective

Social workers experience social relations from a slightly different perspective. One might argue that theirs is a more practical approach. Frequently engaged with individuals and families who have specific needs, social workers often must consider how social relations might translate into useful resources. Marjorie Cantor had a social work background, which clearly influenced the practicality of her work. She demonstrated how social relations could translate into help for people in need—be they aging adults, people with disabilities, minority group members, or individuals struggling with HIV/AIDS (Shippy, Cantor, and Brennan 2004; Cantor and Brennan 2000; Cantor 1979). In each case, her work pointed to both the unique and universal aspects of social relations that might translate into helpful or supportive relationships.

In her groundbreaking study of older people from multiple cultures living in different neighborhoods in New York City, Cantor (1979) examined aid preferences of older individuals. She found that while almost everyone revealed the same priority of preferences, that is, spouse first, then children and other family members, many relied on an impressive network of friends and neighbors. She labeled this the hierarchical–compensatory model of social relations. Again, the crossing of disciplines and perspectives allowed for a much more reasonable and practical understanding of individual circumstances. Thus, while married people preferred their spouse as a primary caregiver and parents next preferred their children as caregivers, if there was no spouse or child available, when the need arose, friends and neighbors were acceptable substitutes.

Some Classic Findings

Classic findings on social relations and social support provide insight concerning how best to conceptualize these relationships. As increasingly better quality data became available, it was possible to identify consistent patterns of relationships. There were fairly standard and replicable age and gender differences. Advances included identifying characteristics associated with close relations. Perhaps the most exciting finding was the identified link between social relations and health, notably mortality; for example, people with more social ties were less likely to die over 9 years (Berkman and Syme 1979). Next, we selectively consider developments in these areas, as well as notable new findings to show how this early work laid the groundwork for future research.

AGE AND CLOSENESS

It was widely believed that older people had many fewer social relations and were predominantly lonely and isolated (Cumming and Henry 1979). As Cantor found in her study of older people in New York City neighborhoods, older people actually were fairly well connected, especially if they had lived in the same neighborhood for some time. In the early 1980s, we (Antonucci and Akiyama 1987) reported on findings from a nationally representative sample of people over 50 years of age, focusing on structural aspects of social networks, for example network size, age, and gender of network members. More recently, in 2005, we (Antonucci, 2016) were able to replicate that study with a regionally representative sample of people the same age. There were a number of parallel findings, although there were also some noteworthy differences. These are summarized next, and in Table 2.1.

First, we examined age differences and closeness patterns of social relations among older people. We examined three groups of older people: people aged 50–64, 65–74, and over 75; and three levels of closeness: closest, closer, and less close. Interestingly, in 1987, there were no age differences in the size of an individual's social network, while in 2005 younger people reported having more people in their networks. This age difference is not because older people's networks became smaller but rather because younger people's networks became larger (see Table 2.1).

We also examined age differences in feelings of closeness. Here, the findings in the two different time periods paralleled each other in that, at both times, people of all ages reported more people to whom they felt closest or closer compared with those to whom they felt less close. Interestingly, there was no age × closeness interaction in either year. Next, we examined differences in the ages of the network members. In both samples, network members of older respondents were significantly older but there was also a significant age × closeness interaction in both samples. The patterns of these interactions, however, were different in the 2 years. In 1980, the people nominated as closer were younger than those nominated as closest and less close. However, in 2005, the difference was evident in the youngest group, who reported that the people to whom they felt closer were older than those to whom they felt closest or less

Table 2.1: Network size and average age of network members by age group and closeness in 1980 and 2005

	1980			2005		
	Young (50–64)	Middle (65–74)	Old (75+)	Young (50–64)	Middle (65–74)	Old (75+)
Total network size	9.4	8.5	8.7	13.2	11.0	8.7
Mean age (years)	46.9	50.9	53.2	48.9	52.4	55.7
Close	2.0	1.8	2.0	3.6	2.7	2.0
Mean age (years)	53.7	54.9	59.3	50.6	58.0	58.6
Closer	3.9	3.2	3.2	4.8	4.0	2.8
Mean age (years)	49.8	53.0	49.2	53.7	54.0	56.3
Closest	3.5	3.5	3.5	4.8	4.3	3.9
Mean age (years)	42.4	48.3	54.6	44.1	49.2	54.4

close. Finally, we examined age and closeness in the gender distribution of social networks. Here, there were no significant differences. People of all ages and all levels of closeness reported more women than men in their networks in both years.

With increased awareness of and respect for differences in social networks, we can objectively evaluate the implications of these reported differences in size, age, and gender of network members. These findings suggest that older people are not, simply by virtue of age, disadvantaged. It also appears to be the case that gender equity in network membership is not the norm, that is, most people have more women than men in their networks. We turn next to network composition, that is, whether there are age or closeness differences in who is mentioned as a network member (see Table 2.2).

As one would predict in both 1980 and 2005, the spouse is most likely to be mentioned as the closest network member. There are no age or closeness differences in this. People are also very likely to name their children as among their closest relationships but in 2005 this was less true of the youngest age group, perhaps because of the general increase in age of childbearing. There were no age × closeness interactions in either year. Turning next to siblings, age and closeness interacted in both years.

Table 2.2: Percentage composition of network by age group and closeness in 1980 and 2005

	Closeness	1980			2005		
		Young (50–64)	*Middle (65–74)*	*Old (75+)*	*Young (50–64)*	*Middle (65–74)*	*Old (75+)*
Spouse	Close	0.6	0	0	0.8	0	0
	Closer	0.8	0.3	0	1.4	1.5	1.3
	Closest	18.2	13.4	13.6	17.5	15.2	14.3
Children	Close	2.8	6.2	6.3	5.6	6.6	10.3
	Closer	20.4	16.7	20.1	9.6	28.4	24.2
	Closest	50.9	48.7	47.3	47.1	59.7	60.4
Siblings	Close	17.2	16.0	8.2	21.0	19.3	10.3
	Closer	27.3	20.8	14.4	36.5	19.6	17.3
	Closest	10.9	9.2	8.9	17.7	9.5	7.0
Other family	Close	28.7	32.4	33.3	22.2	22.3	34.2
	Closer	31.6	34.2	44.7	23.2	22.0	31.4
	Closest	14.5	18.8	22.9	11.1	11.3	15.5
Friends	Close	50.7	45.3	52.2	50.4	51.8	45.2
	Closer	19.9	28.0	20.8	29.4	28.4	25.8
	Closest	5.5	10.0	7.2	6.6	4.0	2.8

Generally, siblings were more likely to be considered closer (although not closest or less close), but among people aged 65-74, siblings were equally likely to be considered either closer or less close. The reported pattern of network composition for other family members, which included grandparents, in-laws, and cousins, was the same in both years. Older people included a greater number of other family members in their networks than younger people, and other family members were more likely to be mentioned as closer and less close than as closest. And finally, there were some differences in feelings of closeness toward friends. In 1980, an age × closeness interaction indicated that the people in the oldest (over 75) and youngest (50-64) age groups included fewer friends in their networks than people in the middle (65-74) age group. In 2005, this interaction did not occur. There were no age differences in the number of friends in the network, and friends were more likely to be considered closer or less close. Generally speaking, friends were rated most similarly to other family members, that is, more likely to be in the less close and closer categories than in the closest category.

This empirical evidence describing social networks is presented in some detail because it is so clearly consistent with Cantor's compensatory hierarchy of social support. People feel closest to their spouse and children but also include siblings, other family, and friends as close. In times of need and when closer network members are not available, the hierarchy of whom one would turn to is consistent with these data. While Cantor's hierarchy model was developed in the 1970s based on data collected that decade in New York City, national data collected in the 1980s and regional data collected 25 years later are consistent with the theory. Impressively, more recent research has taken the examination of social networks an additional step to consider when and whether social networks might impact known associations such as that between health and socioeconomic status. We turn to those findings next.

Social Support and the SES-Health Model

It is well established that socioeconomic status (SES) is positively associated with health, such that people with lower incomes, lower occupation levels, and lower levels of education tend to have poorer health. This finding has been widely replicated (House, Kessler, and Herzog 1990; Haan, Kaplan, and Syme 1989). Given the role of social relations as a vehicle for helping people cope with stress, Antonucci, Ajrouch, and Janevic (2003) explored whether positive social relations could offset the negative SES-Health association. In a study of middle-aged and older men, they demonstrated that men with lower levels of education who had larger, closer networks had better health and that men who felt more supported by their children had health similar to that of people with higher levels of education. In other words, support from key others erased the low SES-poor health association. At a practical level, this means that men of low SES, who might ordinarily be considered at risk for significant health problems, would be no more at risk than men at high SES levels if key social supports are present. Clearly, this finding has practical implications for clinicians and case workers addressing the needs of vulnerable populations. We turn next to recent developments concerning the association between social support and mortality.

MORE RECENT AND MORE NUANCED FINDINGS

As noted, some of the most impressive early findings in the field demonstrated that positive social ties could reduce mortality and help people cope with stress (Lyyra and Heikkinin 2006; Uchino 2004; Bowling and Grundy 1998; House, Landis, and Umberson 1988; Blazer 1982; House, Robbins, and Metzner 1982; Berkman and Syme 1979). New findings have provided a more nuanced view of these associations. For example, in a recent study by Antonucci, Birditt, and Webster (2010), negative social relations were found to be associated with decreased mortality but only under certain conditions. People with life-threatening illnesses were less likely to die if they reported negative relations with their close significant others. While this finding appears to be inconsistent with findings such as those of Berkman and Syme (1979), Antonucci et al. (2010) offer two possible explanations. They hypothesized that the presence of a life-threatening or serious illness changed the role of social relations and significant others. On the one hand, under these circumstances, the support role of close others may become one of helping to provide support and to persuade the ill person to engage in the appropriate medical regimen. These interactions may be perceived as nagging or negative. Another possible interpretation is that people may somehow be energized by negative relationships and use that energy to fight the disease and stay alive. An early, more clinically based finding found that people with life-threatening illnesses who had positive social relations died sooner than those with less positive relations. Antonucci et al. (2010) interpreted these findings as indicating that people with good relations were more at peace and less willing to have their support networks suffer through a long, drawn-out death. They also suggested that how social relations operate varies by time, place, and circumstance. The next set of findings concerns enacted support and provides another example of how support may vary by relationship and circumstance.

Birditt, Antonucci, and Tighe (2012) interviewed people who had previously reported experiencing high levels of stress. They were asked to identify who in their social network was helpful to them as they faced these difficult life circumstances. They asked all parties, that is, principal and core network members, about the stress, how they evaluated the quality of their support relationship, and how much support had been provided to help with the stress. Everyone agreed that high levels of support were provided by these core network members during conditions of high stress. However, support was enacted only by people reporting high-quality relationships irrespective of high or low-stress appraisals. That is to say, under conditions of high stress, everyone provided support regardless of whether the relationship was deemed positive or negative. Under conditions of low-stress appraisal, support was provided only by those who reported a high relationship quality.

These findings are both useful and cautionary to the practitioner. Yes, support relations can be helpful under difficult conditions of stress or illness but this cannot universally be assumed or sustained. In some cases, negative relations can have a positive effect, and in others, quality of relationship and stress levels determine whether and when support can be expected.

Individual and Group Differences

As noted, Marjorie Cantor recognized the importance of documenting individual and group differences. It is a tribute, at least in part to her efforts, that these differences have been documented and are increasingly considered as scientifically important to our understanding of basic concepts and to the provision of care by clinicians. In several reports prepared at the request of the Gerontological Society of America (Antonucci and Cantor 1994, 1991), she helped document race, ethnic background, and culture differences for the field. These findings were important in demonstrating that individuals from different backgrounds may differ in their expectations and experiences of social relations. Examples of these now widely recognized findings include the strong family ties of African Americans and different patterns/expectations of support among immigrant groups, such as Mexican Americans or Asian Americans. Such differences continue to be as, if not more, important as ever. We turn next to recent research that has expanded on these differences, specifically identifying the role of social relations among three ethnic/racial groups in forgiveness and health.

Antonucci, Ajrouch, and Birditt (2011) examined social relations and patterns of forgiveness among non-Hispanic whites, African Americans, and Arab Americans in the metropolitan Detroit area using both focus groups and telephone surveys. There were subgroup differences in the quality of social relations, although to be clear, everyone reported quite positive relations with the people to whom they felt most close. Subgroup differences, however, indicated that Arab Americans reported the highest positive quality relations and non-Hispanic whites the lowest, while African Americans reported a middle level of positive quality relations. The findings for negative relationship quality were similar, though not exactly so. Arab Americans and African Americans reported equally high negative relationship quality while non-Hispanic whites reported the least negative relationship quality. Results also indicated that, in general, people who reported more positive social relations within family were also more forgiving. Interestingly, this association was only present for Arab Americans and African Americans. There was no such association among non-Hispanic whites (Antonucci et al. 2011). Lastly, and once again pointing to the practical implications of this type of research, they examined the association between forgiveness and health. Here, the price of minority group status and forgiveness is evident. Among Arab Americans, those most and least likely to forgive reported the lowest levels of self-rated health. However, being forgiving was not related to depression or life satisfaction for Arab Americans (Antonucci and Ajrouch 2012). Among African Americans, being forgiving was related both to self-rated health and to depression but not to life satisfaction. More forgiving African Americans also had higher self-rated health and fewer depressive symptoms, although there was no association with life satisfaction. Finally, and perhaps most informative, is that there were no associations between forgiveness and health among non-Hispanic whites. These findings point both to the far-reaching effects of social relations on forgiveness as well as the related association between forgiveness and health. They once again highlight the importance of individual and group differences.

Another area of evolving individual and group differences concerns the family (Silverstein and Giarrusso 2010). It is widely recognized that the nature and structure of the family is changing, with many people facing old age in blended families. Relatedly, caregivers and care recipients have long been groups of concern to gerontologists. This is especially true in light of changing demographic trends (Szinovacz and Davey 2007). Ryan et al. (2012) examined the availability of caregivers among the baby boomer cohort compared with their own parents and cohorts from the Great Depression and World War II. Using longitudinal data from the Health and Retirement Study, they found that, compared with these previous cohorts, baby boomers were less likely to be married and less likely to have children. Given the tendency for caregivers to be a spouse or child, these demographic trends are cause for concern. Hence, it is critical that individuals, families, and service providers anticipate these changes and create alternate sources of caregiving.

Not all potential alternate sources of caregiving, however, are optimal. New family forms, such as stepfamilies and blended families, raise concerns. Recent studies reported by Sherman, Webster, and Antonucci (2013) investigated caregiver burden in families with late-life remarried spousal caregivers of Alzheimer's patients. They examined the quality of support experienced by the caregiver and the influence of that quality on the spousal caregiver burden. The findings are alarming, given the changing trends in family demography. They are also more nuanced. Sherman and colleagues assessed two types of care-related networks: positive and negative supports from their networks, especially biological and stepfamily members. Among positive care-related support networks, burden was associated with controlling types of instrumental support. Among negative care-related networks, burden was most highly associated with larger negative networks and with interactions that were more conflictual. Caregiver burden and depressive symptomatology were also high if the caregiver reported a high number of disagreements with stepfamily members but was not associated with family disagreements if the disagreement was with members of their own biological family rather than stepfamily members. As this new subgroup of families, that is, those in late-life remarriages, increases, these findings may be especially helpful for those facing caregiving responsibilities. Fortunately (or unfortunately), caregiving, especially among Alzheimer's patients, is neither a sudden nor short-lived event. Hence, professionals working with such families can advise them to anticipate these circumstances and intervene with prevention or intervention caregiving planning to maximize the effectiveness and minimize the unpleasantness of these experiences.

Where We Are Now and Where We Are Going

As this brief and selected review indicates, the field has made some significant strides in identifying individual and group differences in social relations. Recent methodological and measurement developments suggest that there is even more potential to advance the field in the future. A brief summary of several new tools helps to make this point. It has often been hypothesized that there is a physical and psychological synchrony, that is to say, bidirectionality, of influence and association. With the increased availability of relatively simple and portable biomeasures, it has been possible to test and establish these associations. Examples of new biomeasures include measures of blood pressure, cortisol, c-reactive protein, and genes. Assessments can now be achieved through portable blood pressure cuffs, saliva and urine samples, dried blood spots, and hair samples. These have already made it possible to assess cardiovascular risk factors, hypothalamic neural activity and stress, inflammation, and the predisposition to or presence of chronic illnesses. Since social relations have been hypothesized to influence and be influenced by health, these biomeasures are proving to be especially useful. Researchers are now documenting associations between these biomeasures and various characteristics of social relations.

In addition, there have been important new developments in how we collect data from individuals. These range from personal digital assistants such as palm pilots or smartphones, which permit more individual and exact data collections, to the Internet, allowing for quick and cost-effective data collection from a wide array of individuals and groups. Other technical breakthroughs permit the examination of changes in the brain resulting, for example, from exposure to different social stresses or experiences through magnetic resonance imaging. We have also developed new and unique styles of data collection, including, for example, daily diaries and data bursts. The former allow for daily data collections, thus permitting a more detailed examination of change within relatively brief periods of time. The latter, data bursts, offer still another method for intense data collection. Usually interspersed with longitudinal data collections over longer periods of time, data bursts include brief, intense periods of data collection. Examples include a long-term study with monthly data collections complimented by a data burst of five successive days of data collection. Research in the field of social relations has benefited and will continue to benefit from these considerable breakthroughs. They offer ever more opportunities to learn about individual and group differences.

As we look to the future, there are several important new directions in the biopsychosocial science of social relations that will further our understanding of individual and group differences. For example, the identification of the human genome and advances in genetics are increasing our awareness of the role of human genetics in health and wellness. However, whereas it was once thought that genes determined health and wellness, it is now widely recognized that genes and environment mutually influence each other. Gene-environment interplay refers to the bidirectionality of influence and represents an entirely new way of understanding behavior. Thus, individuals are not only influenced by their genetic makeup but also by the environment within which they live and the group or groups to which they belong, which is known to influence the expression or suppression of their genes. The newly developing field of epigenetics takes the issue a step further and indicates that environments can actually change genes. Whereas genes were once thought to be immutable, now it is increasingly clear that not only can the expression of genes be affected by the environment to which they are exposed but that very same environment can change the gene itself and do so transgenerationally. These are exciting developments for multiple reasons. First, the ability to measure and thereby establish the physiological link to what had previously been considered 'only' social phenomena lends credence for many to the importance of these social life circumstances. Second, recognition that the environment, including social relations, can have such a profound effect on individuals as to influence or change their genetic makeup suggests that the inquiring scientist and the conscientious clinician are wise to attend to the environment to which each individual and group is exposed. Doing so is very likely to improve our knowledge and understanding as well as offer insightful prevention and intervention strategies.

In Summary

Following Marjorie Cantor's lead, the field of social relations has evolved and advanced in the study of both individuals and the groups to which they belong. We are increasingly able to document individual characteristics of social relations as well as group differences in the structure, function, and expression of social relations. We have built upon data based on generalized circumstances to explore individual and group differences in specific situations. New developments in methods and measures have advanced the level of sophistication we have been able to achieve and show every promise of continuing to do so in the future. Of special note is the fact that these new and developing areas of inquiry do not necessarily change what Marjorie Cantor taught us but rather provide more grounding and greater specificity to these lessons. For example, we not only know that different groups may be exposed to different stresses and resources but can now examine how these experiences influence their health at a biological and genetic level. These are indeed exciting times. What remains to be seen is if we will be able to continue in the direction Marjorie Cantor has led us: to acquire the knowledge and then use it to improve the lives of the people we serve.

References

Ainsworth, Mary D. Salter and Silvia M. Bell. 1970. "Attachment, Exploration, and Separation: Illustrated by the Behavior of One-Year-Olds in a Strange Situation." *Child Development* 49-67.

Ainsworth, Mary D. Salter, Mary C. Blehar, Everett Waters, and Sally N. Wall. 1978. *Patterns of Attachment: A Psychological Study of the Strange Situation*. Hillsdale, NJ: Erlbaum.

Antonucci, Toni C. 1976. "Attachment: A Life-Span Concept." *Human Development* 19(3):135-42.

Antonucci, Toni C. and Kristine J. Ajrouch. 2012. "Forgiveness, Social Relations and Health." *Final report*.

Antonucci, Toni C., Kristine J. Ajrouch, and Kira S. Birditt "Social relationships and forgiveness." Presented at the *Annual Meetings of the Gerontological Society of America, Atlanta, Georgia* November 18-22, 2011.

Antonucci, Toni C., Kristine J. Ajrouch, and Mary R. Janevic. 2003. "The Effect of Social Relations with Children on the Education-Health Link in Men and Women Aged 40 and Over." *Social Science & Medicine* 56(5):949-60.

Antonucci, Toni. "Convoys of Social Relations Over Time." Presented at the Annual Meetings of the Gerontological Society of America, New Orleans, Louisiana November 16-20, 2016.

Antonucci, Toni C., and Hiroko Akiyama. 1987. "Social Networks in Adult Life and a Preliminary Examination of the Convoy Model." *Journal of Gerontology* 42(5):519–27.

Antonucci, Toni C., Hiroko Akiyama, and Jennifer E. Lansford. 1998. "The Negative Effects of Close Social Relations among Older Adults." *Family Relations* 47:379–84.

Antonucci, Toni C., Kira S. Birditt, and Noah Webster. 2010. "Social Relations and Mortality: A More Nuanced Approach." *Journal of Health Psychology* 15(5):649–59.

Antonucci, Toni C. and Marjorie H. Cantor. 1991. Strengthening the Family Support System for Older Minority Persons. P. xii–xiv in *Minority Elders: Longevity, Economics, and Health*, Washington, DC: Gerontological Society of America.

Antonucci, Toni C. and Marjorie H. Cantor. 1994. Strengthening the Family's Support System for Older Minority Persons. P. xii–xiv in *Minority Elders: Longevity, Economics, and Health* (2nd ed.), Washington, DC: Gerontological Society of America.

Bartholomew, Kim. 1993. From Childhood to Adult Relationships: Attachment Theory and Research. P. 30-62 in Steve Duck (ed.) *Learning about Relationships. Understanding Relationship Processes Series* (Vol. 2), Thousand Oaks, CA: Sage Publications, Inc.

Bengtson, Vern L. 2001. "Beyond the Nuclear Family: The Increasing Importance of Multigenerational Relationships in American Society." *Journal of Marriage and Family* 63(1):1-16.

Bengtson, Vern L. 1975. "Generation and Family Effects in Value Socialization." *American Sociological Review* 40(June):358-71.

Bengtson, Vern L. 1971. "Inter-Age Perceptions and the Generation Gap." *The Gerontologist* 11(4): 85-9.

Berkman, Lisa F. and S. Leonard Syme. 1979. "Social Networks, Host Resistance, and Mortality: A Nine-Year Follow-Up Study of Alameda County Residents." *American Journal of Epidemiology* 109(2):186-204.

Birditt, Kira S., Toni C. Antonucci, and Lauren Tighe. 2012. "Enacted Support during Stressful Life Events in Middle and Older Adulthood: An Examination of the Interpersonal Context." *Psychology and Aging* 27(3):728-41.

Birditt, Kira S., Lauren A. Tighe, Karen L. Fingerman, and Steven H. Zarit. 2012. "Intergenerational Relationship Quality across Three Generations." *The Journals of Gerontology, Series B: Psychological Sciences and Social Sciences* 67(5):627-38.

Blazer, Dan G. 1982. "Social Support and Mortality in an Elderly Community Population." *American Journal of Epidemiology* 115(5):684-94.

Bott, Elizabeth. 1957. *Family and Social Network: Roles, Norms, and External Relationships in Ordinary Urban Families*. London: Tavistock Publications.

Bowlby, John. 1969. *Attachment and Loss: Vol. 1*. New York: Basic Books.

Bowling, Ann and Emily Grundy. 1998. "The Association between Social Networks and Mortality in Later Life." *Reviews in Clinical Gerontology* 8:353-61.

Cantor, Marjorie H. 1979. "Neighbors and Friends: An Overlooked Resource in the Informal Support System." *Research on Aging* 1:434-63.

Cantor, Marjorie H. and Mark G. Brennan. 2000. *Social Care of the Elderly: The Effects of Ethnicity, Class, and Culture*. New York: Springer.

Cassidy, Jude and Phillip R. Shaver, editors. 1999. *Handbook of Attachment: Theory, Research, and Clinical Applications*. New York: The Guilford Press.

Collins, Nancy L. and Stephen J. Read. 1990. "Adult Attachment, Working Models, and Relationship Quality in Dating Couples." *Journal of Personality and Social Psychology* 58(4):644.

Connidis, Ingrid Arnet and Julie Ann McMullin. 2002. "Sociological Ambivalence and Family Ties: A Critical Perspective." *Journal of Marriage and Family* 64(3):558–67.

Cumming, Elaine and William Earl Henry. 1979. *Growing Old*. New York: Arno Press.

Fingerman, Karen L., Jori Sechrist, and Kira Birditt. 2013. "Changing Views on Intergenerational Ties." *Gerontology* 59(1):64–70.

Grossmann, Karin, Klaus E. Grossmann, Gottfried Spangler, Gerhard Suess, and Lothar Unzner. 1985. "Maternal Sensitivity and Newborns' Orientation Responses as Related to Quality of Attachment in Northern Germany." P. 233–56 in *Monographs of the Society for Research in Child Development*.

Haan, Mary N., George A. Kaplan, and S. Leonard Syme. 1989. Socioeconomic Status and Health: Old Observations and New Thoughts. P. 76–135 in John P. Bunker, Deanna S. Gomby, and Barbara H. Kehrer (eds.) *Pathways to Health*. Menlo Park, CA: The Henry Kaiser Family Foundation.

House, James S., Ronald C. Kessler, and A. Regula Herzog. 1990. "Age, Socio-Economic Status, and Health." *Millbank Quarterly* 68:383–411.

House, James S., Karl R. Landis, and Debra Umberson. 1988. "Social Relationships and Health." *Science* 241(4865):540–5.

House, James S., Cynthia Robbins, and Helen L. Metzner. 1982. "The Association of Social Relationships and Activities with Mortality: Prospective Evidence from the Tecumseh Community Health Study." *American Journal of Epidemiology* 116(1):123–40.

Ingersoll-Dayton, Berit, David Morgan, and Toni Antonucci. 1997. "The Effects of Positive and Negative Social Exchanges on Aging Adults." *Journal of Gerontology: Social Sciences* 52B(4):S190–99.

Kahn, Robert L. and Toni C. Antonucci. 1980. Convoys over the Life Course: Attachment, Roles, and Social Support. P. 81–102 in Paul B. Baltes and Orville Brim (eds.) *Life-Span Development and Behavior* (Vol. 3). New York: Academic Press. Reprinted 1989 in Joep Munnichs and Gwenyth Uildris (eds.) *Psychogerontologie*. Van Loghum Slaterus.

Koski, Lilah Raynor and Phillip R. Shaver. 1997. Attachment and Relationship Satisfaction across the Lifespan. P. 26–55 in Robert J. Sternberg & Mahzad Hojjat (eds.) *Satisfaction in Close Relationships*. New York: Guilford Press.

Lopata, Helena Z. 1979. *Women as Widows: Support Systems*. New York: Elsevier Science.

Lüscher, Kurt and Karl Pillemer. 1998. "Intergenerational Ambivalence: A New Approach to the Study of Parent-Child Relations in Later Life." *Journal of Marriage and the Family* 60(2):413–25.

Lyyra, Tiina-Mari and Riitta-Liisa Heikkinen. 2006. "Perceived Social Support and Mortality in Older People." *Journals of Gerontology: Social Sciences* 61B:S147–S152.

Pillemer, Karl and J. Jill Suitor. 2002. "Explaining Mothers' Ambivalence toward Their Adult Children." *Journal of Marriage and Family* 64(3):602–13.

Rholes, W. Steven and Jeffry A. Simpson, editors. 2006. *Adult Attachment: Theory, Research, and Clinical Implication*. New York: The Guilford Press.

Richards, Leslie N., Vern L. Bengtson, and Robert B. Miller. 1989. The "Generation in the Middle": Perceptions of Changes in Adults' Intergenerational Relationships. P. 341-366 in Kurt Kreppner and Richard M. Lerner (eds.) *Family Systems and Life-Span Development*. Hillsdale, NJ: Erlbaum.

Rook, Karen S. and Paula Pietromonaco. 1987. Close Relationships: Ties that Heal or Ties that Bind. P. 1-35 in Warren H. Jones and Daniel Perlman (eds.) *Advances in Personal Relationships* (Vol 1). Greenwich, CT: JAI Press.

Ryan, Lindsay H., Jacqui Smith, Toni C. Antonucci, and James S. Jackson. 2012. "Cohort Differences in the Availability of Informal Caregivers: Are the Boomers at Risk?" *The Gerontologist* 52:177-88.

Sherman, Carey Wexler, Noah J. Webster, and Toni C. Antonucci. 2013. "Dementia Caregiving in the Context of Late-Life Remarriage: Support Networks, Relationship Quality, and Well-Being." *Journal of Marriage and Family* 75(5):1149-63.

Shippy, R. Andrew, Marjorie H. Cantor, and Mark Brennan. 2004. "Social Networks of Aging Gay Men." *The Journal of Men's Studies* 13(1):107-20.

Silverstein, Merril. 1997. Emerging Theoretical and Empirical Issues in the Study of Social Support and Competence in Later Life. P. 223-31 in Sherry Willis and Klaus W. Schaie (eds.) *Societal Mechanisms for Maintaining Competence in Old Age*. New York: Springer.

Silverstein, Merril, Daphna Gans, Ariela Lowenstein, Roseann Giarrusso, and Vern L. Bengtson. 2010. "Older Parent-Child Relationships in Six Nations: The Intersection of Affection and Conflict." *Journal of Marriage and Family* 72(4):1006-21.

Silverstein, Merril and Roseann Giarrusso. 2010. "Aging and Family Life: A Decade Review." *Journal of Marriage and Family* 72(5):1039-58.

Silverstein, Merril and Jeffrey D. Long. 1998. "Trajectories of Grandparents' Perceived Solidarity with Adult Grandchildren: A Growth Curve Analysis over 23 Years." *Journal of Marriage and the Family* 60(4):912-23.

Simpson, Jeffry A. and W. Steven Rholes, editors. 1998. *Attachment Theory and Close Relationships*. New York: Guilford Press.

Szinovacz, Maximiliane E. and Adam Davey, editors. 2007. *Caregiving Contexts: Cultural, Familial, and Societal Implications*. New York: Springer Pub.

Takahashi, Keiko. 1986. "Examining the Strange-Situation Procedure with Japanese Mothers and 12-Month-Old Infants." *Developmental Psychology* 22(2):265-70.

Troll, Lillian E. and Jean Smith. 1976. "Attachment through the Life Span: Some Questions about Dyadic Bonds among Adults." *Human Development* 19(3):156-70.

Uchino, Bert N. 2004. *Social Support and Physical Health: Understanding the Health Consequences of Relationships*. New Haven, CT: Yale University Press.

Van Ijzendoorn, Marinus H. and Pieter M. Kroonenberg. 1988. "Cross-Cultural Patterns of Attachment: A Meta-Analysis of the Strange Situation." *Child Development*: 147-56.

CHAPTER 3

THE AGING AND LATINIZATION OF THE UNITED STATES

Opportunities and Investments

Fernando M. Torres-Gil and
Courtney M. Demko

INTRODUCTION

The United States is undergoing a dramatic demographic transformation, spanning from 2010 to 2050—an event not unlike those of previous eras but with an element unique to this century. While the population of older persons doubles as the baby boom cohort ages, the United States will become a majority–minority nation composed of several demographic groups. The largest of these groups, Hispanics and Latinos, will permeate all aspects of American society. These demographic changes will test the historic resiliency of the United States and its 300-year history of adapting, integrating, and acculturating waves of immigrant, ethnic, racial, and minority groups. In addition, with this transformation will come opportunities to invest in the future workforce of the United States and to provide all persons with an opportunity to benefit from an increasingly multiethnic society, as they enjoy increased longevity.

Latinos are just one component of a majority–minority nation. Collectively, they, along with blacks, Asians and Pacific Islanders, Native Americans, and immigrant groups, will overshadow the non-Hispanic, white population. Yet, this Hispanic population provides a prism through which to uncover the opportunities and the importance of investing in a diverse population. Puerto Ricans, Mexican Americans, Cubans, and Central and South Americans will compose the largest minority group by the year 2050. In parts of the United States, they are now the majority. While each racial and ethnic group will be impacted by aging, Latinos will face a particular set of circumstances related to the politics of immigration and the outsized importance of older persons in the electorate.

Why might the aging and the Latinization of the United States matter to those who may not be older or members of a Hispanic community? What lessons might this nexus provide to the future of the United States? And why might it be opportune for us to focus on these two groups—the elderly and Latinos—as the United States faces its demographic destiny in the twenty-first century?

Many changes—social, demographic, technological, economic— will occur during the last quarter of life for the large, post-World War II cohort whose members were born between 1946 and 1964. Their aging and longevity have taken center stage in popular culture and in politics. In fact, in the year 2014, every member of that cohort will be 50 years of age and over. Thus, how to meet their economic and retirement security is of paramount concern in public policy. What awaits them, however, may be revealed in part by a proverbial canary in the mine shaft: a subgroup whose evolution in this country may provide important clues about how the United States responds not just to the aging of the population but to its ultimate transformation as a majority-minority nation. That canary comprises the fast-growing Hispanic population, as well as the growing bilateral dependence of the United States with Mexico, Central America, and South America. What occurs between now and 2050 in the aging and Latinization of the United States will provide important indicators about the future profile and conditions of all who expect to be part of this nation in the middle of the twenty-first century.

THE BROWNING OF THE DEMOGRAPHIC DESTINY

Aging and Baby Boomers

That the United States is aging is no longer a mystery, or even a surprise. Recent data show that the United States is both aging—enjoying increased longevity—and that persons aged 65 years and over will soon account for a significant portion of the overall population (UN Population Prospects 2008). By 2050, persons aged 85 and older will increase significantly compared with 2010, due in large part to the aging of the baby boomer cohort (U.S. Census Bureau 2012).

Diversity and Latinos

Within this overall aging and growth in numbers of older persons will arise growing diversity, with increases among blacks, Asians and Pacific Islanders, Native Americans, immigrants, and Latinos. This latter group will become the largest of these diverse populations, and Asians will enjoy the fastest rate of growth. Figure 3.1 illustrates this increase in diversity, showing the population by race and Hispanic origin in 2012 and 2060. Even with this increase in diversity, the older adult population will remain majority white non-Hispanic.

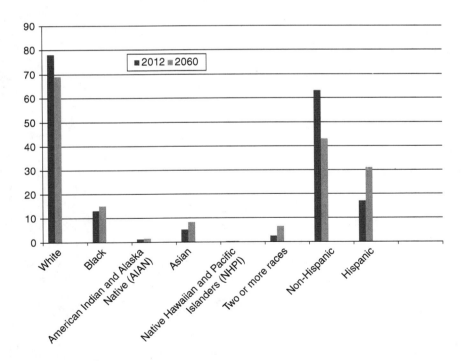

Figure 3.1: *Population by Race and Hispanic Origin:
2012 and 2060 (percent of total population)*

Replacement Rates

However, the fact that the United States is getting older and more diverse and that Latinos will become the largest minority group masks a more profound demographic destiny: changes in who will be having children and replacing those who pass away. The replacement, or fertility, rates describe the ultimate consequence of changing demographic profiles and give clues about the relevance of aging and Latinization to the particular issues that the Cantor conference will address including social supports, caregiving, and health care as well as to the larger macro and policy implications of aging, diversity, and Latinization.

Only one group will have a replacement rate of about the required 2:1 (the ratio required for births to equal deaths): Hispanics at 2:4; whites are below replacement rates (1:8) while blacks are now at a status quo and their fertility rate is expected to drop further (Pew Research Center 2012). One can see on any public-school playground in cities such as Los Angeles, Denver, Miami, Chicago, and New York City that future; the majority of children are Hispanics. Of course, these fertility rates can and do change; by the second and third generation we can expect Latinos to be assimilated and with education and economic advancements, their fertility rates may drop. For now, however, with the continued influx of Latino immigrants, legal and illegal, and the 2 4 replacement rate of native-born Hispanics, this group will be the future workforce of the United States (Pew Research Center 2012).

Latino Baby Boomers: The Canary

One subgroup of a set of subgroups represents the "canary in the mine shaft": Latino boomers. While much attention is given in the popular press and among scholars to the baby boomer cohort, and increased attention among politicians and advocates is given to the growing Hispanic population, little attention has been given to a subgroup of both populations: Latinos who were born between 1946 and 1964. Why is this subgroup important, and what might it tell us about the aging and Latinization of the United States?

As Figure 3.2 demonstrates, Latino boomers occupy a pivotal overlap among baby boomers and the Hispanic population. They are the glue that binds both groups. This relatively small subgroup has outsized importance in terms of the future implications and consequences for the

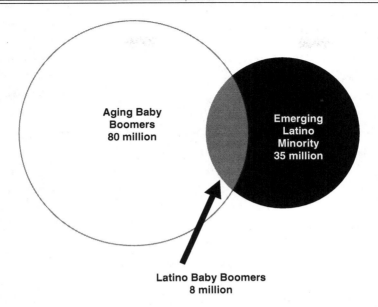

Figure 3.2: Latino Baby Boomers as a Portion of the Aging Baby Boomers and Emerging Latino Minority

Source: Gassoumis et al. 2008.

aging and Latinization of the United States. In part, Latino baby boomers comprise the current leadership of the Hispanic population, and they are the first generation to age in the New America. Today's Latino boomers are the offspring of immigrant parents—those who came from Mexico after the Mexican Revolution, migrated from the island of Puerto Rico in the last midcentury, or were refugees from Cuba when it was liberated by Castro. They benefited from their parents' and grandparents' sacrifices (including the World War II and Korean War military service of their fathers and uncles) and promoted the civil rights advancement of the Chicano movement and political aspirations during the 1960s and 1970s. And they became the nuclei of the expanding Latino middle class and educated professionals. Today, Latino leadership and achievements in the artistic, cultural, economic, social, educational, and political arenas come largely from this group. Moreover, Latino boomers will become the next generation of Hispanic elders and will age with a different set of expectations than that of their parents and grandparents. And Latino boomers have become an important political force, as politicians and as an electorate. Thus, Latino boomers are the subgroup to watch as we move closer to 2050.

The Big Picture: Unintended Consequences

So what does all of this information mean in terms of the changing demographics and the rise of senior citizens and Hispanics in this century? What are the implications of these demographic events, and what might be the consequences of responding to, or not acting on, these changes?

A seminal article published in 2010 foretold the future of aging and Latinization. In "The Gray and the Brown," Brownstein (2010) noted that older persons and Hispanics were the two groups that will constitute the great growth of the U.S. population in the first half of the twenty-first century. He wondered whether the public and the political arena were prepared for these new changes and gave a rather dire prediction of what would happen should we ignore these trends. In short, he suggested that we are on the verge of interracial and intergenerational tensions. He used examples of places like Arizona and the Sunbelt where Hispanics are becoming a majority yet where there are growing populations of white and English-speaking retirees.

This generational mismatch raises tensions and potential conflicts over voting power, priorities, and aspirations. White retirees expect a life of leisure and service and want taxes kept low and streets kept safe. Young Latino families want better schools, public services, and opportunities for their children to get good jobs with good wages. Ironically, in places like Arizona, the Southwest, and the Sunbelt, older white retirees look to the Hispanic community as a low-wage, amenable, and needed workforce to trim their lawns, wash their cars, serve them in restaurants, and assist them with personal services such as caregiving. Yet, the ultimate irony is that these same older, white retirees utilize their conservative voting patterns to minimize taxation, reduce governmental benefits and programs, and focus on law-and-order concerns.

These generational and ethnic tensions are most vivid with immigration reform. The efforts to create a path to citizenship for the estimated 11 million undocumented persons, including children who were brought to this country illegally, have been blocked by the efforts of tea-party politicians and the conservative tendency of older, white voters. Arizona has been most visible as a state with punitive law enforcement practices against undocumented immigrants and resistance to immigration reform measures, including the Dream Act, which would at least provide a pathway to citizenship for undocumented children who are educated in this country.

Admittedly, this is a bleak scenario, potentially pitting older whites and aging baby boomers against young Latinos and potential Latino baby boomers. Yet this scenario illustrates that inaction may not be an option, as we look to the aging and Latinization of the United States.

AN ALTERNATIVE SCENARIO: COMMON CONCERNS AND INVESTMENTS

There is an alternate scenario—one that's more proactive and optimistic. This approach recognizes that diversity, aging, and immigration are what keep the United States young and vibrant. *The Economist* (2015) notes that the United States, unlike Europe, has a demographic dividend: youthful, energetic, and engaged minority and immigrant groups that believe in the "American Dream." Yet, *The Economist* also raised a profound question: "Will the U.S. recognize this demographic opportunity or will it squander it (as seen in the 2016 Presidential Debates?"

Thus, we can presume that, with sufficient perseverance and foresightedness, we can also respond in a progressive and active manner to the aging and Latinization of the United States. How might this be done? Hayes-Bautista, in his seminal book *The Burden of Support*, alerted us to the specter of young Latinos assuming the burden of supporting older whites (Hayes-Bautista et al. 1990). This admittedly dire prophecy assumed that resentment and conflict would stem from the growing Latino population in California having to be the workforce for an aging white population and a political group whose electoral influence would be to the disadvantage of a striving, young, diverse population. Since then, others have provided a more optimistic set of scenarios. Myers (2008), in particular, has expanded on the Hayes-Bautista vision and posed the opportunities of a new intergenerational social contract, one that recognizes the common agenda among young Latinos and older whites. Both groups desire security and civic stability, whether it is safe streets and decent public education or sustaining Social Security and Medicare, which, incidentally, Hispanic elders rely on heavily. And both groups are, in their own ways, marginalized by society—one through nativism and the other through ageism. Lynch (2011) takes this view even further. He suggests that the politics of aging is such that the inherent political clout of the AARP can be brought to the political benefit of emerging Latinos, with their own growing political influence, and that, in turn, each group, recognizing common political agendas, can become a powerful coalition in electoral politics.

The Future of a New America: Aging and Latinization

What might this mean for the future of the United States at the pivotal halfway mark of the twenty-first century? A select set of issues illustrates the relevance of aging and Latinization to all who hope to grow older in the United States, irrespective of gender, race, ethnicity, and socioeconomic status.

Long-Term Care and Caregiving

A contemporary issue, relevant to all who expect to grow older, is the addressing of an intimate question: Who will take care of us as we get older and need assistance? The answer: increasingly, immigrants and minorities, with an added bonus of those groups who still consider it a noble occupation to care for elders. With the decline in fertility rates among whites, they can expect fewer or no children to be available for caregiving. And, given that most persons, especially those who have ambitions for their children to be successful in status occupations such as lawyer, doctor, or Google executive, children are not raised to be home-care workers or to be In-Home Supportive Services managers. Thus, the job of providing activities of daily living (ADLs) care to older (and younger disabled) persons increasingly falls to those with the least professional and employment opportunities, those who are part of the low-wage workforce. Given that Americans do not value long-term care workers or caregivers (even family members must make sacrifices), baby boomers will find, as they get older and face the vicissitudes of aging such as mobility limitations and chronic conditions, that, increasingly, Latinos, poor blacks, Filipinos, Pakistanis, and other immigrants will provide the intimate care for their old age. Thus, to the extent that we wonder who will take care of us in old age, we may find reason to value the groups that, combined, will become the majority population of this country.

Taxpayers and Entitlements

Relevant to the long-term care concerns is the question: Who will be the workers who provide the taxes to sustain the Social Security and Medicare pay-as-you-go systems? Given that fertility rates have dropped among non-Hispanic whites and are about to break even for blacks, we must look to the emerging populations with larger families—Hispanics and immigrants—for the future taxpayers. This is not just about a workforce that can provide the payroll taxes for the large entitlement programs; it's also about a workforce that is able and willing to generate federal and state taxes. If we will expect federal and state governments to provide an array of social services and a safety net such as disability insurance, workman's compensation, In-Home Supportive Services, and education revenues then we must ask: Who will be those future taxpayers? And, more importantly, will those future taxpayers be able and willing to pay those taxes?

Economics, Assets, and Investments

If the answers to these rhetorical questions are emerging populations with higher birth rates, then we must ask: Will they have the education, training, and health care to be productive, educated workers, and will they receive the appropriate skills for the new economies? Lynch (2011) capsulizes this question by asking a follow-up hypothetical: Who will buy our houses? The policy scribes in this arena—Brownstein (2010), Hayes-Bautista et al. (1990), Lynch (2011), Myers (2008), Torres-Gil—have pointed out in various ways that the answer is simply that the next generation of home buyers will be largely Hispanics, immigrants, and Asians and Pacific Islanders. Thus, if today's baby boomers, who are largely white, all over 50 years of age, and all moving toward a hopeful retirement, are expecting that their homes will be their primary assets to fund their retirements (not to mention their second homes, boutique ranches, RVs, and other properties), then they must look to Hispanics, immigrants, and Asians and Pacific Islanders to be able and willing to pay inflated prices for these homes and to have the income, savings, and wages to afford the down payments and meet more stringent loan requirements.

National Security

One last example, and one not usually considered among social scientists, academics, advocates, or the politically correct crowd, is a profound and disturbing question: Who will fight America's wars? Or, more palatable: Who will serve in our nation's military and volunteer to protect us from our enemies? The reality is that the United States will always need a strong military and, unless we decide to become a second-tier power like France and Great Britain or withdraw unilaterally from the world, our economic and national interests will require a strong national defense. With that requirement, we must insure that an all-volunteer force is staffed by men and women who are willing to protect this nation. Again, who will be those future volunteers? The same answer: With declining fertility rates among whites, those volunteers will increasingly need to be immigrants, Hispanics, and Asians and Pacific Islanders. Thus, there is a need to find ways to entice such men and women from these emerging communities. Fortunately for this great nation, these very populations have proven to be the most patriotic and tend to exhibit old-school American values: they are religious, family-oriented, conservative, and patriotic, and they have a strong work ethic. They also have a renowned history of serving this nation bravely and honorably such as the Nisei combat battalions of World War II and Hispanics receiving the largest number of Medal of Honor awards. But will we value their aspirations, or will the constant scapegoating of immigrants and minorities by tea-party politicians alienate these emerging ethnic groups?

INCLUSIVENESS AND ACCEPTANCE

This article has sought to examine the relevance of twin phenomena—aging and Latinization—to the fields of gerontology and social policy. The greatness of this nation and its ability to ultimately overcome the barriers of discrimination and unequal opportunities is enshrined in the Declaration of Independence and the U.S. Constitution, and the hope that we can bring out the better angels of our human nature would enable the United States to be the one nation in the world that is most able to incorporate and acculturate constant waves of immigration and migration. In the expectation that we will continue this 300-year pattern, we will hope and strive to incorporate and acculturate the next waves of groups that will make us a majority-minority nation by 2050. At the same time, we will strive to fully enable the next generation of elders—the largest group of senior citizens in the twenty-first century—to be partners in an intergenerational and interethnic coalition to pursue the progressive policies that will draw from the untapped potential of elders, Hispanics, and all other populations.

REFERENCES

Brownstein, Ronald. 2010. "The Gray and the Brown: The Generational Mismatch." *National Journal* 24:14–22.

Gassoumis, Zachary D., Kate Wilbur, Max Benavidez, and Chon Noriega. 2008. "Latino Baby Boomers: A Hidden Population." *Latinos and Economic Security Policy Brief* 3.

The Economist. 2015. "Firing up America: A Special Report on America's Latinos." March 14–20.

Hayes-Bautista, David, Werner Schink, and Jorge Chapa. 1990. *The Burden of Support: Young Latinos in an Aging Society*. Stanford University Press.

Lynch, Frederick. 2011. *One Nation Under AARP: The Fight Over Medicare, Social Security and America's Future*. Berkeley, CA: University of California Press.

Myers, Dowell. 2008. "Aging Baby Boomers and the Effect of Immigration: Rediscovering the Intergenerational Social Contract." *Generations: Immigration in an Aging Society*, 18–23.

Pew Research Center. 2012. "Explaining Why Minority Births Now Outnumber White Births." Retrieved from http://www.pewsocialtrends.org/2012/05/17/explaining-why-minority-births-now-outnumber-white-births/.

U.S. Census Bureau. 2012. U.S. Census Bureau "Projections Show a Slower Growing, Older, More Diverse Nation a Half Century from Now." U.S. Census Bureau. Retrieved from https://www.census.gov/newsroom/releases/archives/population/cb12-243.html.

UN Population Prospects. 2008. Retrieved from http://commons.wikimedia.org/wiki/File:Life_Expectancy_at_Birth_for_Males_and_Females_-_USA_-_1950-2050.png.

CHAPTER 4

THE ROLE OF THE LATINO FAMILY IN LATE-LIFE CAREGIVING

Jacqueline L. Angel, Sunshine Rote, and Kyriakos Markides

INTRODUCTION

The growing number of elderly persons presents all developed nations with problems that are unprecedented in human history. For older adults with fragile social support systems and meager resources, longer life may bring protracted periods of poor functioning and dependency. In the United States, the aging of the population creates unique challenges for social policy and the institutions that are charged with their support. More than one-quarter of the nation's population is expected to be 65 and older by 2030, and more than one-third will be living into their eighth, ninth, and tenth decades of life (Passel and Cohn 2008). Equally important, an ever-larger fraction of this older population will consist of Latinos (Arias 2012). Additional trends such as the long life expectancy and disproportionate burden of chronic disease and disability among elderly Latinos have important implications for Latino families and for relations among generations, as well as for the future of programs such as Social Security and Medicare.

A large portion of elderly Latinos are immigrants. While immigrant Latinos tend to have more favorable mortality than U.S.-born Latinos, they become more disabled in middle and old age than the non-Latino white population (Markides and Gerst 2011). For many immigrant Latinos now in their mid-80s, a severe lack of resources and serious health limitations introduce major uncertainties into their own and their families' futures. Among the oldest-old, Latinos have a higher likelihood of serious physical and cognitive decline than other ethnic groups but tend to be highly resistant to nursing homes, especially among immigrant elderly Latinos. Those over age 80 are likely to make increasing demands on health and informal and formal support services (Lee and Mason 2011). For this group, long-term care needs and preferences in care and living arrangements may differ significantly from those of the majority (Dilworth-Anderson, Williams, and Gibson 2002). Yet, Latino families, like other families, are undergoing changes that will affect their ability to continue caring for their elders (Herrera et al. 2008). The movement away from traditional family and residential arrangements that results from neoliberal market reforms, international migration, and other global forces means that norms and practices related to intergenerational relations and exchanges will inevitably change. As a result, the use of formal caregiving systems will increase in a period of fiscal austerity (Meyer and Parker 2011). The possibility of an increased number of years characterized by poor health and material hardship raises serious questions about the potential burden on government and family that such dependency implies (Stone 2011).

In this chapter, we use a unique data set of Mexican-origin family caregivers and their parents to explore these issues. We first examine the extent to which migration history, socioeconomic status, and other factors account for differences in social network and support, defined in the terms of the distribution of responsibility in caring for aging parents. Migration history or life course stage of migration is the key independent variable. Immigrants who arrive early in life have similar educational and cultural experiences as the native born, and are more flexible and have an easier time adapting to learning a new language and culture and creating a larger extended kinship network. People who arrive in midlife tend to be healthy and migrate for economic reasons and this is when migration is the most selective. Late-life immigrants have more difficulty learning the culture, are more dependent on others, and have less time to save money, develop a career, and integrate culturally into the destination country's culture, leaving a smaller network of potential support structures. We then present new data that allow us to shed light on the validity of the common claim that the Latino family is uniformly solid, unified, and altruistic. Next, we discuss the consequences of lower fertility combined with an increase in the number of women working outside the home on the Mexican-origin family's capacity to provide care in the future. The chapter ends with a discussion of the implications of the variable patterns of family care for health and social policy.

BACKGROUND

In the United States, families are the primary source of care for the elderly and, in most cases, the responsibility for the care of aging parents and parents-in-law falls to daughters (Angel et al. 1996; Herrera et al. 2012). Latino family members currently provide nearly 80 percent of at-home long-term care, a higher percentage than for African Americans and non-Latino whites (Torres-Gil 2005). A large fraction (36 percent) of Latinos provide care for an older person, normally a relative (Evercare 2008). They are clearly in a midlife cycle squeeze in juggling family and work. Results from a nationwide survey of the sandwich generation in 2012 show that nearly one-third of Latino adults have an elderly parent and a dependent child in comparison to one-quarter of non-Latino whites and 20 percent of African Americans (Parker and Patten 2013a).

Three key factors are making it increasingly difficult for Latinos to maintain this cultural tradition of nearly exclusive informal care of elders. First, Latino women must work today because their income is vital to the household maintenance (Harrington Meyer and Pavalko 1996; Singley 2008). For family caregivers, considerable time must be spent caring for elderly parents, often resulting in reduced paid hours (Johnson and Sasso 2006; Kane, Kane, and Ladd 1998). This is especially observed in the Mexican-origin population, whose members comprise a disproportionate share of the poor. For Latinos and other racial and ethnic groups, an average of almost seven days was lost due to caregiver responsibilities in 2011, totaling about 126 million missed work days (Witters 2011). Moreover, full-time employed caregivers suffer an average of $5,625 in pre-tax lost wages per year in 2007 (Evercare 2007). Over a caregiver's lifetime, lost retirement savings averages $238,716 for men and $303,880 for women (MetLife Mature Market Institute 2011). Recent evidence indicates that there is a disproportionate share of the burden for out-of-pocket costs for dementia in minority elders and their family members (Kelley et al. 2015). In addition to the economic costs, caregiving takes a toll on physical and mental well-being: three of five individuals report health problems due to caregiving (Ho et al. 2005).

The second factor affecting the ability to provide care is geographic mobility. Latino family caregivers have become less available as family members have dispersed across the United States. Adult Latinos, including children of elderly Mexican Americans, are defying conventional migration patterns associated with the Latino population which assume spatial concentration in a few key states and regions, such as Texas and California (Durand, Telles, and Flashman 2006). These changing migration patterns are age-graded and predominantly found in the working-age and baby boomer populations. On the positive side, the redistribution of Hispanics enables the development of ethnic enclaves, new social networks, and labor-market opportunities. However, such incentives for settling permanently in an area may strain intergenerational opportunities for caregiving in Hispanic families. Enhanced economic opportunities may have negative consequences for those left behind. Inevitably, migration or geographic mobility of any distance undermines adult children's ability to interact with and provide even limited care for aging parents (Van Hook and Glick 2007). In many cases, elderly parents do not tend to follow their adult children.

Third, socioeconomic resources, including education, assets, and retirement income, constrain choices. A parent's lack of income no doubt influences the degree of perceived burden and stress and the ultimate decision on whether to institutionalize a dependent parent (Luppa et al. 2010). That decision especially affects Hispanics and Mexican Americans, given their relatively low levels of income and wealth as well as education (Angel and Angel 2009). As we discuss next, the capacity of family members to care for elderly Mexican-origin parents to meet the changing needs for assistance is likely to differ by cultural factors associated with immigration, including life course stage at migration (Angel et al. 2014; Crist, Garcia-Smith, and Phillips 2006; Van Hook and Glick 2007).

Culture and Family Caregiving

Hispanic families generally, and individuals of Mexican origin particularly, benefit from aspects of their culture that have been shown to be socially protective. They engender a strong family orientation and commitment to a system of informal support that is qualitatively distinct from that of non-Hispanic whites (Landale, Schoen, and Daniels 2010). The Pew Research Center found that Hispanics are the most likely of

41

these groups to expect to care for an aging family member in the future. Almost two-thirds of Hispanic respondents aged between 40 and 59 are caring for at least one elderly parent aged 65 and older and stated that they are very likely to provide elder care compared with 48 percent of blacks and 43 percent of non-Hispanic whites (Parker and Patten 2013b). Researchers found that the idea of taking care of our own remains a strongly held belief among Hispanic families in rural America (Magilvy et al. 2000). However, this high value placed on the traditions and customs of the past conflicts with the broader social realities of contemporary gender roles and the construct of caregiving (Stone 2011).

The presence of strong social support may offset economic disadvantage. Financial security offers the oldest-old elderly improved access to health services and preventive care and helps caregivers, especially in relation to elders with dementia (Flores et al. 2009). On the other hand, social support networks, particularly involving family members, will protect elderly persons' health security in numerous ways. Members of the network contribute support by assisting with caregiving, housing, food, transportation, and health-care expenditures, especially when the older adults have exhausted their own financial resources. In all cases, children's ability to contribute to the social and financial support of a dependent parent is influenced by their income, employment obligations, and other financial responsibilities, including those for their own children as well as cultural preferences in care arrangements.

Although Hispanics as a group are strongly tied to their families and place high value on intergenerational bonds, protracted periods of poor functioning and dependency in elderly parents may undermine greater family involvement (Angel et al. 2010). Conversely, an abundance of literature demonstrates the important role that chronic disabling physical and mental illness plays in the availability of family members as potential social supports (for a review, see Dilworth-Anderson, Gardner, and Lubell 2002). Larger social networks may lower the use of formal mental health services for the most seriously cognitively impaired (Pescosolido, Gardner, and Lubell1998).

The types of stressors range from the nature of the disability, type of task, and time dedicated to caregiving. For example, caring for a loved one with incontinence, dementia, or both requires constant supervision. Problematic behaviors related to cognitive decline are especially burdensome (Rote, Angel, and Markides 2014). The time devoted to assistance with activities of daily living such as bathing, dressing, and grooming may restrict time for social activities and isolate the caregiver, leading to depression and exhaustion. Caregivers' lack of awareness of the expectations and obligations associated with the caregiver role can also create strain. For example, managing the tasks prior to impending death may give rise to anticipatory grief and anxiety. Data on the caregivers of individuals with Alzheimer's disease indicate that over 60 percent report emotional stress and over 40 percent report physical stress associated with caregiving (Alzheimer's Association 2013).

Contributions to family caregiving for elderly parents invariably depend on assessments of the older parent's (care receiver's) health condition. As physical and cognitive abilities of older adults decrease, reliance on caregivers and others for assistance, such as with the management of medication, increases (Schulz and Martire 2004). Moreover, the severity of illness interacts with social networks and continuously shapes the lives of caregivers (Pescosolido, Brooks Gardner, and Lubell 1998). Dementia symptoms, for example, are often first recognized by close family, friends, and neighbors, suggesting the importance of social networks in the early phases of the care trajectory (Carpentier, Bernard, Grenier, and Guberman 2010). Caregivers with low levels of education, low rates of health insurance coverage, low incomes, and little wealth place additional strain on already fragile social support networks (Angel and Angel 2009). The resulting strain in social ties then creates a need to seek help from outside the family network (Pavalko 2011).

It is also important to understand the role of life course stage at migration in caregiving, given its potentially critical role in stratifying resources and opportunities for supportive networks within the Mexican-origin population in the United States. Caregiving is greatly increased in the presence of family resources, which are themselves a function of immigration-related factors (Burr and Mutchler 2003). Labor force Mexican-origin immigrants may differ considerably in kin reliance because of differences in the strength of norms regarding family responsibilities, which are often prescribed by indicators of acculturation such as nativity, language proficiency, and age at migration (Flores et al. 2009).

DATA AND METHODS

We employ a new survey of caregivers of native and foreign-born individuals of Mexican origin aged 80 and older in the United States, the

Hispanic Established Population for Epidemiologic Study of the Elderly (H-EPESE), to address limitations in past research on the role of immigrant families in late-life caregiving. The H-EPESE is the first large-scale epidemiologic investigation of the health and care experiences of elderly Mexican origins in five southwestern states: Texas, California, New Mexico, Arizona, and Colorado. The landmark study includes the original cohort of 3,050, aged 65 and older, who were surveyed in their homes in 1993–94 and reinterviewed in 1995–96, 1998–99, 2000–01, 2004–05, 2006–07, and 2010–11 for a total of seven observation waves. At wave five, 902 new subjects aged 75 and older were added to the cohort.

A caregiver supplement was appended to the H-EPESE in 2010–11. Elderly subjects were asked to provide the name and contact information of the person they were closest to or they depended on the most for help. These informants (n = 925), many of whom were children of the elderly subject (n = 629), were interviewed regarding the health, finances, and general situation of the elderly subjects. Questions of familial obligation were asked to the elderly subject in wave 2, leaving 308 caregiver and care recipient dyads with complete information on all study variables.

The survey provides rich information on physical and cognitive function as well as detailed information on social support, caregiver burden, and the distribution of responsibilities across family members that will allow us to examine these issues about which we know very little and which are of major policy relevance. We include elderly subjects' sociodemographic characteristics (age, gender, education, marital status), disability (ADLs), cognitive functioning (Mini-Mental State Examination [MMSE]), gait and balance (Performance Oriented Mobility Assessment [POMA]), health insurance coverage, and traditional values. Traditional values are gauged by the level of agreement with seven statements about attitudes toward traditional family structure and sex-role organization. Examples include *knowing your family ancestry and language is an important part of family life, it is important to know your cousins, aunts, and uncles, and to have a close relationship with them*, and *brothers have a responsibility to protect their sisters while they are growing up* (Hazuda et al. 1988).

These data help us to understand the character of social capital, particularly the norm for the elderly to be cared for by kin, which is particularly strong in Hispanic populations. The data also illuminate the role that Mexican-origin families play in providing for themselves or paying for the care that older family members need over time. We also explore the influence of life course stage at migration on dispersion of responsibility for caregiving duties. Specifically, the analyses examine different patterns of the family-care structure (personal, instrumental, and financial), and explore the sociodemographic migration processes and other individual-level characteristics that are associated with different patterns.

RESULTS

Table 4.1 shows the sample characteristics by life course stage of migration. We observe significant differences in caregivers' household income by their elderly parents' life course stage of migration. The income distributions among caregivers of U.S.-born elderly and early-life immigrants are similar, with about 26 percent reporting a household income less than $15,000. On the other hand, about 36 percent of caregivers of late-life immigrants report this level of income. In addition to income, there are significant differences in care recipient educational attainment by life course stage of migration with late-life immigrants reporting lower mean educational levels than U.S.-born or early-life immigrants.

For health and functioning of the care recipient, late-life immigrants tend to report more limitations in activities of daily living (ADLs) and instrumental activities of daily living (IADLs). A larger percentage of late-life immigrants (77 percent) report Medicare and Medicaid coverage than early-life immigrants (60 percent) and the U.S.-born elderly (51 percent). We also find significant differences in the mean score on cultural values by life course stage of migration. Cultural values reflect how strongly the elderly subject identifies with attitudes toward traditional family structure, family closeness, filial obligation and reciprocity, and sex-role organization. We find the U.S.-born report less traditional values than early-life immigrants and late-life immigrants report on average the most traditional values. These descriptive statistics show that caregiving burden may be especially concentrated in families of late-life immigrants due to differences in access to resources and health and functioning; however, it says little about how caregiving tasks are navigated by family members.

Figure 4.1 shows the distribution of household care tasks by life course stage of migration. More than half of the sample is reliant on a focal child or other family member for help with household tasks like meal prepara-

ANGEL, ROTE, AND MARKIDES

Table 4.1: Sample Characteristics by Life Course Stage of Migration in Percent

	Overall	U.S.-Born	Early-Life Immigrant	Late-Life Immigrant
	(n = 308)	(n = 175)	(n = 89)	(n = 44)
Caregiver				
Age (mean)	55.10	54.38	56.17	55.84
Female	69	69	64	77
Married	52	53	51	50
Household income*				
<$15,000	27	26	26	36
$15,000–$29,999	38	42	42	48
>$30,000	34	33	33	16
Self-rated health				
Poor	5	4	4	11
Fair	35	35	36	36
Good	41	40	44	39
Excellent	19	21	16	14
Care Recipient				
Age (mean)	86.24	85.91	86.42	87.18
Female	67	69	61	75
Education (mean)***	4.90	5.83	4.03	2.93
Married	31	35	23	30
ADL (mean)***	2.14	2.01	1.99	2.93
IADL (mean)*	5.40	5.17	5.11	6.86
MMSE (mean)[a]	19.74	20.27	19.92	17.19
POMA (mean)	4.29	4.38	4.28	3.93
Health insurance coverage***				
Medicare only	24	23	28	20
Medicare and Medicaid	57	51	60	77
Any private insurance	15	23	7	0
Informant did not know	4	3	6	2
Traditional values scale (mean)[b]*	16.03	15.62	15.34	17.02

Notes: HEPESE, wave 7
[a]Based on 293 observations
[b]Asked wave 2
***$p < .001$, **$p < .01$, *$p < .05$

tion and transportation. However, a larger percentage of U.S.-born elderly and early-life immigrants is dependent on themselves, other family members, or multiple caregivers for help than late-life immigrants. Late-life immigrants, on the other hand, are especially reliant on one focal child for

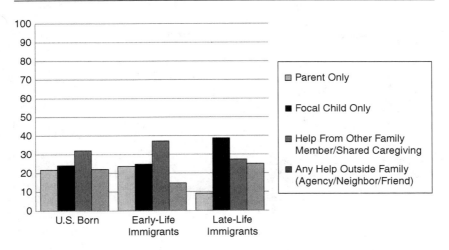

Figure 4.1: Distribution of Household Tasks by Life Course Stage of Migration

Notes: HEPESE, wave 7 (n = 308). χ^2 = 9.49, df = 6, p = 0.15.

help with household tasks, with close to 40 percent relying on one child for help. The general pattern observed here supports the assumption that elderly immigrants rely on family more so than the U.S.-born elderly and that late-life immigrants are especially dependent on one child for help.

We find statistically significant differences in the dispersion of personal care tasks by life course stage of migration in Figure 4.2. In general, more than half of the elderly individuals are responsible for most of their own personal care tasks such as bathing, dressing, and using the toilet. Close to 60 percent of the U.S.-born elderly and early-life immigrants are able to complete most of these tasks themselves compared with 40 percent of late-life immigrants. Similar to results presented for household tasks, a larger percentage of late-life immigrants (25 percent) is dependent on one child for help than the U.S.-born elderly and early-life immigrants (about 10 percent, respectively). Additionally, late-life immigrants are more likely to receive some help outside of the family from agencies, a neighbor, or a friend with personal care tasks (20 percent) than early-life immigrants (3 percent) and the U.S.-born elderly (15 percent).

As shown in Figure 4.3, for financial tasks, the distribution of care tasks is similar for the U.S.-born elderly and early-life immigrants. Less than half take care of their own financial tasks, while 30 percent depend mostly on a focal child for help with paying bills, writing checks, and

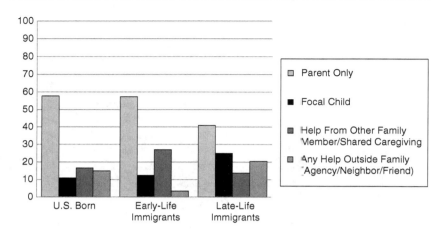

Figure 4.2: Distribution of Personal Care by Life Course Stage of Migration

Notes: HEPESE, wave 7 (n = 308). $\chi^2 = 20.47$, $df = 6$, $p = 0.002$.

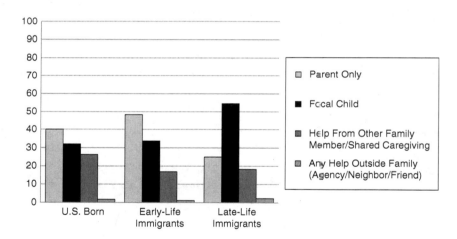

Figure 4.3: Distribution of Financial Tasks by Life Course Stage of Migration

Notes: HEPESE, wave 7 (n = 308). $\chi^2 = 12.14$, $df = 6$, $p = 0.06$.

filing taxes. This is followed by elderly who receive help from other family members and multiple caregivers, with very few receiving help with financial tasks outside of the family. For late-life immigrants, the pattern is somewhat different. Most (55 percent) are dependent on a focal child for help, 25 percent take care of their own financial tasks, less than 20 percent rely on other family members or multiple caregivers, and very few rely on help from outside of the family.

We also examined these differences using multinomial regression analyses controlling for caregiver and care recipient background factors (e.g., age, gender, income, years of education, and marital status). We found one significant difference (results not presented). Late-life immigrants have a lower relative risk of relying on other family members and/or multiple family caregivers than a focal child for help with financial tasks than the U.S. born (RRR = 0.35; 95 percent CI: 0.34-0.89).

DISCUSSION

In this study, we examined the role of the Hispanic family in late-life caregiving. Although longer life is desirable for its own sake, the possibility of an increased number of years characterized by poor health and dependency creates potentially serious economic, social, and political problems related to the care of a large, dependent elderly Hispanic population (Angel, Torres-Gil and Markides 2012). Our analyses of the H-EPESE clearly show that the long-life expectancy observed in the Mexican-origin population portends formidable challenges for family caregivers in the decades ahead. They also point to the way in which Mexican-origin children play a key role in assuming primary responsibility for eldercare at a time when aging parents are fraught with disability, dependency, and vulnerability.

More than half of elderly Mexican Americans report moving in with an adult child in later life, which has been attributed to both cultural and economic factors (Gonzalez 2007). We add to this literature by examining the role of life course stage migration for caregiving structures. The majority of older adults rely on family members for assistance with personal care, household tasks, or financial affairs. The pattern of dispersion of care tasks tended to be similar for the U.S.-born elderly and early-life immigrants. Late-life immigrants, on the other hand, needed more help with care tasks and tended to be more dependent on one focal child for help with care tasks than the U.S.-born elderly or early-life immigrants. Fewer late-life immigrants tended to report calling upon family members outside of the focal child and/or multiple family caregivers for help than the U.S.-born elderly or early-life immigrants, leaving more late-life than early-life immigrants dependent on receiving some type of help from outside of the family.

Overall, the results suggest that the caregiving burden is especially concentrated in poor Mexican-origin families, namely for children of late-life migrants who simply have no choice but to keep their aging parents at home. Given that late-life immigrants tend to report more traditional values and a greater emphasis on familial obligation and reciprocity, having less family sharing and support of care tasks may create an additional burden or strain on both the caregiver and elderly individual.

In conclusion, despite economic disadvantage, the long life expectancy of the Mexican-origin population, the so-called "Hispanic Paradox" presents formidable challenges to families for late-life parental caregiving given that increased frailty and disability now make it difficult for Hispanic families to cope (Angel et al. 2012). Our findings indicate that late-life immigrants are at highest risk of dependency on one child for care tasks. In the absence of increased support, the situation is unsustainable, especially among immigrant families.

These findings also raise new questions on the extent to which home and community-based services are a viable alternative for Latino caregivers. It is clear that the topic merits attention. Future investigations can potentially address this issue in several ways. First, the effect of changes in elderly respondents' physical, mental, and cognitive status on potential caregiver burden and help-seeking outside of the family can be assessed. Another possibility is to identify how changes in living arrangements, including institutionalization, are affected by functional status, immigration, and the availability of family members to provide social support. And, finally, researchers can examine the quality of social support systems for caregivers as needs for assistance change.

REFERENCES

Alzheimer's Association. 2013. "Alzheimer's Disease Facts and Figures." Retrieved from http://www.alz.org/downloads/facts_figures_2013 pdf.

Angel, Jacqueline L., Ronald J. Angel, Judi L. McClellan, and Kyriakos S. Markides. 1996. "Nativity, Declining Health, and Preferences in Living Arrangements among Elderly Mexican Americans: Implications for Long Term Care." *The Gerontologist* 36:464–73.

Angel, Jacqueline L., Fernando Torres-Gil, and Kyriakos S. Markides (eds.). 2012. *Aging, Health and Longevity in the Mexican-Origin Population.* New York: Springer Science.

Angel, Jacqueline L., Sunshine M. Rote, Dustin C. Brown, Ronald J. Angel, and Kyriakos S. Markides. 2014. "Nativity Status and Sources of Care Assistance Among Elderly Mexican-Origin Adults." *Journal of Cross-Cultural Gerontology* 29:243–58.

Angel, Ronald J. and Jacqueline L. Angel. 2009. *Hispanic Families at Risk: The New Economy, Work, and the Welfare State*. New York: Springer Science.

Angel, Ronald J., Jacqueline L. Angel, Carlos Diaz Venegas, and Claude Bonazzo. 2010. "Shorter Stay, Longer Life: Age at Migration and Mortality among the Older Mexican-Origin Population." *Journal of Aging and Health* 22:914–31.

Arias, Elizabeth. 2012. "United States Life Tables, 2008" in *National Vital Statistics Reports*. Hyattsville, MD: National Center for Health Statistics.

Burr, Jeffrey A. and Jan E. Mutchler. 2003. "English Language Skills, Ethnic Concentration, and Household Composition: Older Mexican Immigrants." *The Journals of Gerontology: Social Sciences* 58(2):583–92.

Carpentier, Normand, Paul Bernard, Amanda Grenier, and Nancy Guberman. 2010. "Using the Life Course Perspective to Study the Entry into the Illness Trajectory: The Perspective of Caregivers of People with Alzheimer's disease." *Social Science & Medicine* 70(10):1501–08.

Crist, Janice D., Dianna García-Smith, and Linda R. Phillips. 2006. "Accommodating the Stranger en Casa: How Mexican American Elders and Caregivers Decide to Use Formal Care." *Research and Theory for Nursing Practice: An International Journal* 20(2):109–26.

Dilworth-Anderson, Peggye, Ishan C. Williams, and Brent E. Gibson. 2002. "Issues of Race, Ethnicity, and Culture in Caregiving Research: A Twenty-Year Review (1980–2000)." *The Gerontologist* 42(2):237–72.

Durand, Jorge, Eduardo Telles, and Jennifer Flashman. 2006. "The Demographic Foundations of the Latino Population. Transforming Our Common Destiny: Hispanics in the United States." Washington, DC: National Academy of Sciences.

Evercare. 2007. "Family Caregivers—What They Spend, What They Sacrifice." Bethesda, MD: National Alliance for Caregiving.

— 2008. "Hispanic Family Caregiving in the U.S.: Findings from a National Study." Bethesda, MD: National Alliance for Caregiving.

Flores, Yvette G., Ladson Hinton, Judith C. Barker, Carol E. Franz, and Alexandra Velasquez. 2009. "Beyond Familism: A Case Study of the Ethics of Care of a Latina Caregiver of an Elderly Parent with Dementia." *Health Care for Women International* 30(12):1055–72.

Gonzales, Alicia M. 2007. "Determinants of Parent-Child Coresidence Among Older Mexican Parents: The Salience of Cultural Values." *Sociological Perspectives* 50(4):561–77.

Harrington Meyer, Madonna and Eliza K. Pavalko. 1996. "Family, Work, and Access to Health Insurance Among Mature Women." *Journal of Health and Social Behavior* 37:311–25.

Hazuda, Helen P., Michael P. Stern, and Steven M. Haffner. 1998. "Acculturation and Assimilation among Mexican Americans: Scales and Population-Based Data." *Social Science Quarterly* 69(3): 687–706.

Herrera, Angelica P., Jacqueline L. Angel, Carlos Díaz-Venegas, and Ronald J. Angel. 2012. "Estimating the Demand for Long-Term Care Among Aging Mexican Americans: Cultural Preferences Versus Economic Realities." P. 259-76 in Jacqueline L. Angel, Fernando Torres-Gil, and Kyriakos Markides (eds.) *Aging, Health, and Longevity in the Mexican-Origin Population*. New York: Springer Science.

Herrera, Angelica P., Jerry W. Lee, Guadalupe Palos, and Isabel Torres-Vigil. 2008. "Cultural Influences in the Patterns of Long-Term Care Use among Mexican-American Family Caregivers." *Journal of Applied Gerontology* 27:141-65.

Ho, Alice, Sara R. Collins, Karen Davis, and Michelle M. Doty. 2005. "A Look at Working-Age Caregivers' Roles, Health Concerns, and Need for Support," in *Issue Brief*. New York: The Commonwealth Fund.

Johnson, Richard and Anthony Lo Sasso. 2006. "The Impact of Elder Care on Women's Labor Supply." *Inquiry* 43:195-210.

Kane, Rosalie A., Robert L. Kane, and Richard C. Ladd. 1998. *The Heart of Long-Term Care*. New York: Oxford University Press.

Kelley, Amy S., Kathleen McGarry, Rebecca Gorges, and Jonathan S. Skinner. 2015. "The Burden of Health Care Costs for Patients with Dementia in the Last 5 Years of Life." *Annals of Internal Medicine*. 163(10): 729-736.

Landale, Nancy S., Robert Schoen, and Kimberly Daniels. 2010. "Early Family Formation among White, Black and Mexican American Women." *Journal of Family Issues* 31(4):445-74.

Lee, Ron and Andrew Mason. 2011. "Life Cycles, Support Systems, and Intergenerational Flows: Patterns and Change." P. 79-106 in Ron Lee and Andrew Mason (eds.) *Population Aging and The Generational Economy: A Global Perspective*. North Hampton, MA: Edward Elgar Publishing.

Luppa, Melanie, Tobias Luck, Siegfried Weyerer, Hans-Helmut König, Elmar Brähler, and Steffi G. Riedel-Heller. 2010. "Prediction of Institutionalization in the Elderly. A Systematic Review." *Age Ageing* 39(1):31-8.

Magilvy, Joan K., Joann G. Congdon, Ruby J. Martinez, Renel Davis, and Jennifer Averill. 2000. "Caring for Our Own: Health Care Experiences of Rural Hispanic Elders." *Journal of Aging Studies* 14(2):171-90.

Markides, Kyriakos S. and Kerstin Gerst. 2011. "Immigration, Health and Aging in the United States." P. 103-116 in Richard A. Settersten and Jacqueline L. Angel (eds.) *Handbook of the Sociology of Aging*. New York: Springer Science.

MetLife Mature Market Institute. 2011. "The MetLife Study of Caregiving Costs to Working Caregivers: Double Jeopardy for Baby Boomers Caring for Their Parents." Westport, CT: MetLife Mature Market Institute.

Meyer, Madonna Harrington and Wendy M. Parker. 2011. "The Changing Worlds of Family and Work." P. 263-77 in Richard A. Settersten and Jacqueline L. Angel (eds.) *Handbook of Sociology of Aging*. New York: Springer Science.

Parker, Kim and Eileen Patten. 2013a. "The Sandwich Generation." In *Rising Financial Burdens for Middle-Aged Americans*. Washington, DC: Pew Research Center.

— 2013b. "The Sandwich Generation: Caring for Older Family Members." In *Pew Research Social and Demographic Trends*. Washington, DC: Pew Research Center.

Passel, Jeffrey S., and D'Vera Cohn. 2008. "U.S. Population Projections: 2005–2050." Washington, DC: Pew Research Center.

Pavalko, Eliza K. 2011. *Caregiving and the Life Courses: Connecting the Personal and the Public*. New York: Springer Science.

Pescosolido, Bernice A., Carol Brooks Gardner, and Keri M. Lubell. 1998. "How People Get into Mental Health Services: Stories of Choice, Coercion, and 'Muddling Through' from 'First Timers.'" *Social Science & Medicine* 46(2):275–86.

Rote, Sunshine, Jacqueline L. Angel, and Kyriakos Markides. 2014. "Health of Elderly Mexican American Adults and Family Caregiver Distress." *Research on Aging* 37(3):306–31.

Schulz, Richard and Lynn M. Martire. 2004. "Family Caregiving of Persons with Dementia: Prevalence, Health Effects, and Support Strategies." *The American Journal of Geriatric Psychiatry* 12(3):240–49.

Singley, Catherine. 2008. "The Status of Latinos in the Labor Force." Washington, DC: National Council of La Raza.

Stone, Robyn. 2011. *Long-Term Care for the Elderly*. Washington, DC: Urban Institute Press.

Torres-Gil, Fernando. 2005. "Aging and Policy in Ethnically Diverse Societies." P. 670–81 in M.J. Johnson, V.L. Bengston, P.G. Coleman, & T.L. Kirkwood (eds.). *The Cambridge Handbook of Aging and Aging*. Cambridge: Cambridge University Press.

Van Hook, Jennifer and Jennifer E. Glick. 2007. "Immigration and Living Arrangements: Moving Beyond the Instrumental Needs versus Acculturation 'Dichotomy'." *Demography* 44:225–49.

Witters, Dan. 2011. "The Cost of Caregiving to the U.S. Economy." *Gallup Business Journal*. Retrieved from http://www.gallup.com/businessjournal/151049/cost-caregiving-economy.aspx.

CHAPTER 5

SOCIAL NETWORKS AND SUPPORTS AMONG OLDER GAY AND BISEXUAL MEN

The Impact of HIV

Mark Brennan-Ing, Liz Seidel, Britta Larson, and Stephen E. Karpiak

INTRODUCTION

The number of people aged 50 years and older living with HIV has nearly doubled since 2001 (Centers for Disease Control and Prevention [CDC] 2008) and, as of 2015, half of those with HIV are aged 50 or older (Effros et al. 2008). Gay and bisexual men remain disproportionately affected by HIV; 60 percent of infections among men in this older age group are attributed to male-to-male sexual contact (CDC 2013). The success of antiretroviral therapies (ART) has transformed HIV into a manageable, albeit serious, chronic illness. But this success is not without complications. Older adults with HIV experience high rates of comorbid illnesses, or multimorbidity, two decades earlier than their noninfected peers, having three times as many comorbid conditions as community-dwelling adults 70 years and older (Havlik 2009).

Depression is among the most common comorbidities affecting this population, with five times the rate of depressive symptoms observed in non-HIV samples (Applebaum and Brennan 2009). There is a strong link between depression and specific conditions such as visual impairment as well as overall multimorbidity (Havlik, Brennan, and Karpiak

2011). Depression has significant clinical implications because it is the single most reliable predictor of nonadherence to ART, leading to poor treatment outcomes as well as promoting viral mutation and treatment-resistant strains of the virus. Multimorbidity, along with mental health concerns like depression, suggests that older adults with HIV will need increasing levels of assistance from their informal social networks. The purpose of this chapter is to examine how HIV infection may affect the dynamics and perceptions of informal social support among older gay and bisexual men.

Theoretical Perspectives

Older adults typically turn to family for needed assistance with instrumental tasks such as housekeeping and meal preparation as well as emotional support in coping with the challenges of aging (Cantor and Brennan 2000). But the presence of a social network does not guarantee that caregiving and support will be available in times of need. The more relevant question is the extent of the *functionality* of the network. Namely, are there people who are in regular enough contact that they can reasonably be expected to provide assistance if needed? A functional social support has been defined as someone seen at least monthly or talked to at least weekly by phone (Cantor and Brennan 1993; 2000; Cantor, Brennan, and Shippy 2004).

In addition, many older adults lack family due to geographic separation or other reasons. Social gerontologists have long been interested in how older adults without available family garner needed, informal social support. The dynamics of the informal social network are illustrated by the *Hierarchical Compensatory Theory* of social supports (Cantor and Mayer 1978). According to the theory, older people turn first to close family members, that is, spouses or children. If these individuals are unavailable, they then turn to more distant relatives, followed by friends, neighbors, and, lastly, to formal community-based supports in a hierarchical manner (Cantor and Brennan 2000). The *Hierarchical Compensatory Theory* has received empirical support; older adults using formal services were more likely than their peers to live alone and to not have a partner/spouse, as well as reporting poorer health and fewer economic resources (Cantor and Brennan 1993). Other studies report that older adults lacking informal social supports often turn to community-based institutions such as religious congregations for their needs, viewing them as surrogate families (Sheehan, Wilson, and Marella 1988; Tirrito and Choi 2005). The reliance on more distant social network elements is also evidenced in the social networks of older gay and bisexual men.

Social Networks of Aging Gay Men

In general, older lesbian, gay, bisexual, and transgender (LGBT) adults do not have the informal social resources typical of heterosexuals. Among community-dwelling older adults, 43 percent report a spouse while 77 percent have at least one living child (Cantor and Brennan 1993). However, among older LGBT adults, while approximately 40 percent have a partner/spouse, only 20–25 percent report at least one living child (Cantor et al. 2004; Fredriksen-Goldsen et al. 2011). The social networks of older LGBT adults are characterized by families of choice, comprised of close friends and neighbors, in contrast to the biological family or family of origin that is the foundation for most heterosexuals (Grossman, D'Augelli, and Hershberger 2000; de Vries and Hoctel 2007). This is also true when only the networks of older gay and bisexual men are examined (Shippy, Cantor, and Brennan 2004). However, older LGBT adults without children express concerns about their caregiving needs being met in later life and the willingness of friends to assume the roles of family caregivers (Orel 2014). It is not clear how social support networks of older gay and bisexual men might be affected in the context of a serious, chronic illness such as HIV.

Social Networks of Older Adults with HIV

Shippy and Karpiak (2005a, 2005b) described the social networks of older adults with HIV as being fragile and characterized by a reliance on friends, rather than family, regardless of sexual orientation. Older adults with HIV are most often without spouses/partners. In one recent large-scale study of this population, only 14 percent indicated having a spouse/partner and only 38 percent had functional children, while 70 percent lived alone. Siblings and other relatives were rarely classified as functional, even when present (Cantor, Brennan, and Karpiak 2009). It is not surprising that Nichols and colleagues (2002) found that older

HIV-positive adults did not receive adequate support from their social networks, reported feelings of isolation, and were sometimes unable to cope with the demands of managing their illness, such as adhering to ART. Thus, similar to older LGBT adults, older adults with HIV rely on chosen families, and do so because of the love, acceptance, and support they provide (Grant et al. 2013). However, the dominance of friends who are also infected with HIV in the social network suggests that social supports may be further attenuated if these friends are not healthy due to increased multimorbidity as they age (Poindexter and Shippy 2008).

Support Perceptions and Relation to Mental Health

While the tangible receipt of instrumental and emotional social support is critical to helping older adults face the challenges of aging, perceptions concerning the availability and adequacy of such support are vital to mental well-being. In studies of chronic illness in middle-aged and older adults, such support perceptions have been related to greater levels of psychosocial well-being and adaptation (Brennan 2002; 2004). Regarding older adults with HIV, Chesney and colleagues (2003) observed that when social support was available for older men with HIV, they had lower levels of psychological distress and enhanced well-being. Similarly, among older gay and bisexual men with HIV, perceptions of support have been found to be related to higher levels of health-related quality of life (Emlet, Frederiksen-Goldsen, and Kim 2013).

Purpose and Rationale

Research finds that older gay and bisexual men have friend-centered social networks, as do older adults with HIV, regardless of sexual orientation. The purpose of the present study was to examine how HIV infection might further impact the social support resources of older gay and bisexual men. Given the exploratory nature of this work, we examined the following research questions: First, does HIV status affect the social network configuration and dynamics among older gay and bisexual men? Second, do perceptions of social support availability and adequacy differ based on HIV status after controlling for other factors?

METHODS

Sample and Procedures

Data were obtained in 2010–2011 from a convenience sample of older LGBT adults recruited through the Center on Halsted (COH), a comprehensive LGBT community center in Chicago. Participants were also recruited at AIDS Service Organizations (ASOs), health fairs, and community events. Inclusion criteria were identifying as LGBT, being 50 years of age or older, and sufficiently fluent in English to complete the survey. People with HIV were oversampled in order to have sufficient statistical power to examine the impact of HIV status in the older LGBT community. Two hundred and thirty-three participants were recruited, resulting in 210 usable surveys. Twenty-three surveys were not usable due to incomplete data or were from participants who failed to meet the inclusion criteria, most often for not identifying as LGBT. Informed consent was obtained prior to data collection. The survey instrument was self-administered, taking on average 45–60 minutes to complete. After completion, participants were debriefed, thanked, and given a $25 gift card. Research methods and materials were evaluated and approved by the Copernicus Group Independent Review Board. The current study used a subsample of 146 individuals who identified as male and either gay or bisexual.

MEASURES

Demographic Profile

Single items obtained information on *age, gender identity* (with categories of male, female, male-to-female transgender, female-to-male transgender, or intersex), *sexual identity* (with categories of heterosexual, homosexual, bisexual, queer, or questioning), *race, Hispanic origin, level of education, income adequacy, living arrangement* (with categories of live alone, with spouse/partner, or with others), and *marital/partnership status.*

HIV Status and Morbidity

Single items asked if participants had been tested for HIV and the results of their last test. Participants who indicated a positive HIV test were coded as *HIV positive* while those with a negative result or unknown HIV status were coded as *HIV negative*. Participants were asked if they had experienced any of 27 physical and mental health conditions in the previous year, including HIV-related conditions such as neuropathy, age-related conditions like sensory loss, chronic/terminal illnesses such as diabetes or cancer, and mental or neurological disorders like depression. The number of health comorbidities was calculated by summing the positive responses to these items. Participants self-rated their current health status on a four-point Likert scale from excellent to poor.

Depression

The ten-item version of the Center for Epidemiological Studies Depression Scale was used to assess depressive symptoms (CES-D; Andersen et al. 1994; Radloff 1977). Participants were asked about the frequency of depressive symptoms experienced over the previous week, with responses ranging from none to a little, some or most days. Responses were summed, with higher scores indicating more depressive symptoms. Interitem reliability for the CES-D was high for the total sample (Cronbach's alpha = .84).

Informal Social Network

Detailed information was collected on informal networks based on previous large-scale studies of older adults (Cantor and Brennan 2000). Participants indicated whether they had any living members among five groups which typically compromised informal networks, namely, parents, children, siblings, other relatives, and friends, as well as the number of those network elements present. The overall network size was calculated by summing the number of network elements from each category. Two additional items assessed frequency of contact via in-person visits or telephone conversations. Assessment of contact frequency was necessary to compute the functional status of each network element, based on criteria established by Cantor (Cantor and Brennan 2000), namely, monthly in-person visits or weekly telephone conversations. The proportion of respondents having at least one functional network element in each of the five categories was then calculated. Respondents were also asked the number of neighbors known well and the number of friends who had HIV.

Types and Frequency of Assistance from Family and Friends

Participants indicated the frequency of eight types of instrumental and emotional assistance provided by both family members and friends: shop/run errands, keep house or prepare meals, take or drive you places, help with mail or correspondence, management of money, give advice, talk when you are feeling low, and talk about personal problems. Respondents were also asked about negative support received from both family and friends: reluctant when you need to talk, upset you or hurt your feelings, and refused to help when asked. These responses were summed to create separate indices of family and friend help, and family and friend negative support.

Availability and Adequacy of Social Support

Participants were asked about the availability of both instrumental and emotional support over the previous year, with categories of all/most of the time, some of the time, only occasionally, or not at all. Follow-up questions assessed the adequacy of both instrumental and emotional support with response categories of need a lot more, need some more, need a little more, and got all that was needed. The availability and adequacy items were summed to create two separate indices of instrumental and emotional support sufficiency, with higher scores indicating such support was perceived as available and adequate.

Design and Analysis

For research question one, examining HIV status on the social network configuration and dynamics among older gay and bisexual men, the current study used a preexisting group's design to examine differences between HIV-positive and HIV-negative older gay and bisexual men regarding sociodemographics, physical and mental health, and social support resources. Univariate and descriptive statistics were calculated for all study variables. Bivariate analyses of group differences based on HIV status employed chi-square tests for categorical variables and one-way analysis of variance (ANOVA) for continuous variables. For research question two, pertaining to the impact of HIV on perceptions of the availability and adequacy of social supports, a correlational design was used. Categorical data were dichotomously coded prior to bivariate analyses. Potential covariates included sociodemographic, health, and social support variables that differed significantly based on HIV status. Dependent variables were the two indices of instrumental and emotional support sufficiency. Pearson correlations were computed to examine bivariate relationships between dependent variables, HIV status, and potential covariates prior to multiple regression analyses. Only those covariates that were significantly correlated with the dependent measures at $p < .05$ were retained for multivariate analyses to keep regression models parsimonious. These data are available from the corresponding author upon request. For each dependent measure, hierarchical multiple regression was employed with listwise deletion of missing data, resulting in the loss of ten cases and yielding a listwise N of 136. The first step included HIV status, the second variable block consisted of demographic variables, and the third block contained health covariates, while the fourth block used social support factors. Diagnostics did not find evidence of multicollinearity in the regression models.

RESULTS

Sociodemographic Characteristics

Among the older gay and bisexual men in the current sample, 46 percent reported being HIV-positive with 54 percent reporting negative or unknown status. As shown in Table 5.1, older HIV-positive gay and bisexual men were younger, with an average age of 55.4 years compared with their HIV-negative counterparts, whose mean age was 63.4 years. However, these groups did not differ with regard to sexual identity, with approximately four in five identifying as gay and about one in six identifying as bisexual. However, there were significant group differences regarding race/ethnicity, with nearly two-thirds of the HIV-positive group identifying as black or Hispanic, while in the HIV-negative group, only 13 percent were black and 3 percent were Hispanic. Older gay and bisexual men with HIV also reported significantly lower educational attainment, with 39 percent reporting college/postgraduate education as compared with 71 percent in the HIV-negative group. However, there were no significant between-group differences regarding marital/ partnership or living arrangements. Approximately one-third of each group reported a partner/spouse and two-thirds lived alone. HIV-positive men were significantly more likely to report inadequate incomes, with

Table 5.1: Sociodemographic and Health Characteristics

Variable	HIV-Positive		HIV-Negative	
	M	SD	M	SD
Age*	55.44	6.21	63.41	8.32
Number of Comorbid Conditions (Excluding HIV)**	3.00	2.40	2.05	2.07
CES-D Depressive Symptoms**	9.80	6.66	6.65	5.43
Sexual Identity	N	%	N	%
Gay	51	77.3	63	81.8
Bisexual	12	18.2	11	14.3
Queer	3	4.5	2	2.6
Questioning	0	0.0	1	1.3
Race/Ethnicity*				
Non-Hispanic black	37	55.2	10	12.8
Non-Hispanic white	25	37.3	65	83.3
Hispanic	4	6.0	2	2.6
Asian/Pacific Islander	1	1.5	0	0.0
Other	0	0.0	1	1.3
Education*				
Less than high school	5	7.7	1	1.3
High school graduate	16	24.6	8	10.4
Some college	13	16.9	19	29.2
College graduate/postgraduate	25	38.5	55	71.4
Marital/Partnership Status				
Single/not married	41	64.1	38	48.7
Married	2	3.1	3	3.8
Widowed/partner deceased	1	1.6	6	7.7
Civil union	1	1.6	1	1.3
Registered domestic partner	2	3.1	1	1.3
Life partner	14	21.9	21	26.9
Divorced/separated	3	4.7	8	10.3
Living Arrangements				
Alone	49	73.1	53	67.1
With spouse or partner	12	17.9	13	16.5
With others	6	9.0	13	16.5

Income Adequacy***	N	%	N	%
Not enough for expenses	15	22.7	7	9.1
Just manage to get by	38	57.6	30	39.0
Enough money with a little extra	7	10.6	24	31.2
Money is not a problem	6	9.1	16	20.8
Self-Rated Health				
Excellent	13	19.7	30	38.5
Good	38	57.6	34	43.6
Fair	14	21.2	14	17.9
Poor	1	1.5	0	0.0

Note. N = 146; HIV+ n = 67; HIV(−) n = 79

* $p < .05$, ** $p < .01$, *** $p < .001$

23 percent not having enough for expenses and 58 percent just managing to get by. In the HIV-negative group, these proportions were 9 percent and 39 percent, respectively.

Differences in self-rated health trended toward, but did not reach, statistical significance. Among HIV-negative older men, 39 percent rated their health as excellent and 44 percent reported being in good health. As seen in Table 5.1, in the HIV-positive group, 20 percent considered their health to be excellent and 58 percent said they were in good health. However, not including HIV infection, older HIV-positive gay and bisexual men reported significantly more conditions, on average 3.0, as compared with 2.0 in the HIV-negative group. In addition, the HIV-positive group had higher depressive symptom scores compared with their HIV-negative peers, 9.8 and 6.7 on average, respectively.

Social Network Components

While HIV-positive and -negative older men did not differ significantly in terms of having a living parent or the number of living parents, 37 percent of HIV-positive men reported a functional parent, significantly more than the 20 percent in the HIV-negative group (as shown in Table 5.2). However, older HIV-negative gay and bisexual men were more likely to report having a child, at 31 percent, or a functional child, at 20 percent, compared with HIV-positive men, among whom the proportions were 17 percent and 9 percent, respectively. The HIV-negative group also reported 2.4 children on average, significantly more compared with the 1.5 on average among those

Table 5.2: Social Network Components

Variable	HIV-Positive		HIV-Negative	
	N	%	N	%
Parent	35	53.8	30	38.5
Functional Parent*	25	37.3	16	20.3
Child*	11	16.7	24	30.8
Functional Child*	6	9.0	16	20.3
Grandchild/Great-Grandchild	10	15.4	15	19.5
Functional Grandchild/Great-Grandchild	3	4.5	6	7.6
Sibling	57	87.7	61	78.2
Functional Sibling*	29	43.3	21	26.6
Friend	54	83.1	70	88.6
Functional Friend	51	76.1	60	75.9
	M	**SD**	**M**	**SD**
Number of Parents[a]	1.31	0.68	1.27	0.52
Number of Children[a] *****	1.45	1.13	2.38	1.10
Number of Grandchildren/Great-Grandchildren[a]	3.50	1.84	4.13	3.44
Number of Siblings[a] *****	3.30	2.38	2.20	1.74
Number of Other Relatives in Frequent Contact	1.50	1.91	1.73	3.56
Number of Friends[a]	4.39	5.58	5.74	4.98
Number of Friends with HIV[a] *****	1.61	1.93	0.61	1.67
Number of Neighbors Known Well	1.44	3.14	1.45	2.26
Size of Social Network	10.73	7.68	12.03	8.30

Note. N = 146; HIV+ n = 67; HIV(−) n = 79.
[a] Based on those reporting this social network element.
*$p < .05$, ** $p < .01$, *** $p < .005$

who were HIV-positive. However, less than 20 percent of either group reported a grandchild/great-grandchild, and the likelihood of having a functional grandchild/great-grandchild and the number of grand-children/great-grandchildren did not vary significantly by group. While there were also no group differences in the likelihood of having a sibling, HIV-positive older gay and bisexual men were significantly more likely than the HIV-negative group to report a functional sibling, with proportions of 43 percent and 27 percent, respectively, and reported more siblings, on average 3.3 and 2.2, respectively. There were no significant differences in the number of other relatives in frequent contact; between 1 and 2 on average. Over 80 percent of both groups reported a friend, and 76 percent in both groups reported a functional friend. While the number of friends in the social network

The Impact of HIV

did not differ between the groups, HIV-positive men reported on average 1.6 friends who had HIV, significantly more than the average of 0.6 in the HIV-negative group. The number of neighbors known well was approximately 1.5 in each group. Despite many differences in social network components, the size of the social network did not differ significantly as a function of HIV-status.

Receipt of Assistance and Negative Social Support

With regard to help from family members, as shown in Table 5.3, older gay and bisexual men reported higher levels of emotional support as compared with instrumental help with everyday tasks. Less than 10 percent in either group reported assistance with keeping house/preparing meals or managing money, and only slightly higher proportions received help with shopping or running errands. HIV-positive older men were significantly more likely than HIV-negative men to report receiving help with being taken or driven somewhere they needed to go, with proportions of 21 percent and 9 percent, respectively, as well as help with mail or correspondence, at 8 percent and 0 percent, respectively. HIV-positive men were also more likely to report emotional support in terms of talking to someone when feeling low, at 58 percent, compared with 39 percent of HIV-negative men. But the proportions reporting receiving advice or talking about personal or private matters did not differ significantly by HIV status. On average, HIV-positive older gay and bisexual men received help in more ways from family members: 2.2 tasks on average, compared with 1.3 tasks among the HIV-negative group. In terms of negative social support, less than one-third reported any type of such interactions and there were no significant group differences in the type or index of such interactions, with the most frequent form of negative support reported as someone upsetting the participant or hurting his feelings.

In terms of the type of help received from friends, there were no significant differences based on HIV status for either instrumental tasks or emotional support. Friends were most likely to be involved with taking or driving the participant somewhere, approximately 25 percent, or shopping/running errands at approximately 20 percent. Few friends provided assistance with meal preparation, mail/correspondence, or managing money. Most emotional support was provided in terms of talking when feeling low or talking about personal/private matters, followed by giving

Table 5.3: Receipt of Assistance and Negative Support from Family and Friends

Variable	HIV-Positive		HIV-Negative	
	N	%	N	%
Family Assistance				
Shop or run errands	9	13.8	6	7.6
Keep house or prepare meals	6	9.1	4	5.1
Take or drive you places*	14	21.2	7	8.9
Help with mail or correspondence**	5	7.6	0	0.0
Manage money	6	9.1	2	2.5
Give advice	31	46.3	24	31.2
Talk to you when feeling low*	39	58.2	31	39.2
Talk about personal/private matters	36	53.7	30	38.5
Family Negative Support				
Reluctant when need to talk	13	20.3	13	16.7
Upset you or hurt your feelings	18	27.7	23	29.5
Refused to help when asked	7	10.8	3	3.9
Friend Assistance				
Shop or run errands	14	21.5	14	17.9
Keep house or prepare meals	4	6.2	6	7.8
Take or drive you places	16	24.6	22	28.9
Help with mail or correspondence	4	6.2	3	3.9
Manage money	1	1.5	0	0.0
Give advice	30	46.2	34	44.7
Talk to you when feeling low	35	53.8	39	50.0
Talk about personal/private matters	32	49.2	45	58.4
Friend Negative Support				
Reluctant when need to talk	11	17.2	14	18.2
Upset you or hurt your feelings	15	23.4	18	23.4
Refused to help when asked	4	7.8	5	5.2
	M	SD	M	SD
Number of Ways Family Helps	2.18	2.06	1.32	1.74
Number of Ways Friends Help	2.03	2.11	2.06	1.84
Family Negative Support Index	0.57	0.97	0.49	0.81
Friend Negative Support Index	0.46	0.86	0.46	0.76

Note. N = 146; HIV+ n = 67; HIV(–) n = 79
* $p < .05$, ** $p < .01$

advice. Interestingly, HIV-negative men appeared to receive more emotional support from friends compared with family, while levels of emotional support were nearly equivalent between family and friends in the HIV-positive group. Levels of negative friend support were low, at less than

25 percent, and followed the same pattern as negative family support. The negative friend support index was identical in both groups, on average 0.5.

Perceptions of Social Support Availability and Adequacy

When asked about the availability of instrumental help during the past year, there were no significant differences based on HIV-status with the majority in both groups indicating that this type of support was available at least some of the time, as can be seen in Table 5.4.

Table 5.4: Perceptions of Instrumental and Emotional Support Availability and Adequacy

Variable	HIV-Positive		HIV-Negative	
	N	%	N	%
Instrumental Help Availability				
Not at all	13	19.4	15	19.0
Only occasionally	12	17.9	12	15.2
Some of the time	16	23.9	9	11.4
All/most of the time	26	38.8	43	54.4
Instrumental Help Adequacy				
Need a lot more	5	7.5	1	1.3
Need some more	5	7.5	4	5.2
Need a little more	13	19.4	11	14.3
Received all help needed	44	65.7	61	79.2
Emotional Support Availability**				
Not at all	7	10.4	3	3.8
Only occasionally	13	19.4	13	16.7
Some of the time	18	26.9	9	11.5
All/most of the time	29	43.3	53	67.9
Emotional Support Adequacy*				
Need a lot more	16	23.9	6	7.7
Need some more	10	14.9	11	14.1
Need a little more	13	19.4	20	25.6
Received all help needed	28	41.8	41	52.6
	M	**SD**	**M**	**SD**
Instrumental Support Index*	6.25	1.52	6.74	1.44
Emotional Support Index***	5.82	1.77	6.67	1.55

Note. N = 146; HIV+ n = 67; HIV(–) n = 79

* $p < .05$, ** $p < .01$, *** $p < .005$

However, HIV-negative men had more positive perceptions of support, with over half saying instrumental help was available all/most of the time compared with less than 40 percent of the HIV-positive group. Similarly, while the groups did not differ significantly in ratings of instrumental support adequacy, 80 percent of HIV-negative men reported receiving all the assistance they needed compared with two-thirds of the HIV-positive group. When combining these two items into the index of instrumental support, HIV-negative men reported significantly higher ratings of support on average 6.7, compared with a mean of 6.2 in the HIV-positive group, indicating greater perceptions of sufficiency around instrumental support among HIV-negative men.

However, when assessing emotional support availability and adequacy, significant group differences were apparent at the item level. While over two-thirds of the HIV-negative group indicated that emotional support was available all/most of the time, only 43 percent of the HIV-positive group reported the same level of availability. In the HIV-positive group, nearly one-third indicated that emotional support was never or rarely available compared with about 20 percent of the HIV-negative group. In a similar vein, nearly one-quarter of the HIV-positive group reported needing a lot more support, while 42 percent reported receiving all the support they needed. The proportions in the HIV-negative group were 8 percent and 53 percent, respectively. These group differences were reflected in average emotional support index scores, with HIV-negative participants having significantly higher scores, on average 6.7, compared with an average of 5.8 in the HIV-positive group.

Multivariate Analyses of Instrumental and Emotional Support Sufficiency

In order to examine the impact of HIV status on perceptions of instrumental and emotional support among older gay and bisexual men, the following variables were considered: sociodemographic variables of age, race/ethnicity, income adequacy; physical and mental health variables including the number of comorbid conditions and CES-D scores; and social support variables of having a functional parent, and the number of ways family helps. We selected those variables that both differed as a function of HIV status

THE IMPACT OF HIV

and were significantly correlated with at least one of the support indices for multiple regression analyses. The race/ethnicity variable was dichotomously coded into non-Hispanic black and Hispanic, with non-Hispanic white and all others serving as the reference group. HIV status was dichotomously coded, with HIV-negative status serving as the reference group.

As shown in Table 5.5, for the instrumental support index regression, the first step included HIV status and explained 3 percent of the variance. The second block consisted of sociodemographic variables, and only income adequacy emerged as a significant covariate with those having more adequate incomes perceiving greater sufficiency of instrumental support and explaining 16 percent of the variance in the model. In the third step, with the inclusion of health variables, the CES-D was the only significant covariate with those having greater levels of depressive symptoms having lower perceptions of instrumental support. CES-D scores explained an additional 5 percent of the variance in instrumental support. In the final block of social support variables, both covariates were significant, with having a functional parent being negatively related to instrumental support perceptions while the number of ways family helped was positively

Table 5.5: Multiple Regression on Covariates of Instrumental Support Sufficiency

	Model 1		Model 2		Model 3		Model 4	
	β	SE	β	SE	β	SE	β	SE
HIV Status	−.16	.25	.03	.28	.02	.28	.02	.26
Demographics								
Age			.11	.02	.04	.02	.06	.02
Black			−.07	.31	−.07	.31	−.15	.29
Hispanic			−.02	.60	−.04	.56	−.01	.55
Income Adequacy			.33***	.14	.31***	.15	.32***	.14
Health								
Number of comorbidities					.16	.06	.10	.06
CES-D Depression					−.24**	.02	−.22**	.02
Support								
Functional parent							−.17*	.26
Family assistance							.40***	.06

Note. Listwise N = 136. Model 1 R^2 = .03/F (1, 135) = 3.6, p < .06. Model 2 R^2 = .16/F (5, 131) = 5.2, p < .001. Model 3 R^2 = .21/F (7,129) = 4.8, p < .001. Total R^2 = .35/F (9, 127) = 7.5, p < .001
*p < .05, **p < .01, ***p < .005

associated with this assessment. Social support measures explained an additional 14 percent of the variance in instrumental support.

Results of the multiple regression analysis of the emotional support index were nearly identical to those obtained when assessing instrumental support, as shown in Table 5.6. In the first step HIV status was negatively related to emotional support, explaining 6 percent of the variance. In the second block, HIV status was no longer significant and income adequacy was the only significant sociodemographic covariate, explaining 10 percent of the variance. In the third block, HIV status was not significant as before, with CES-D depressive symptoms having a negative relationship to perceptions of emotional support. However, the CES-D explained almost four times the variance in perceptions of emotional support at 15 percent, compared with 4 percent for instrumental support. In the final block of social support variables, the presence of a functional parent was not related to perceptions of emotional support, while the number of ways family helped was a positive covariate, explaining 6 percent of the variance in emotional support sufficiency. HIV status remained nonsignificant with all the other covariates in the model.

Table 5.6: Multiple Regression on Covariates of Emotional Support Sufficiency

	Model 1		Model 2		Model 3		Model 4	
	β	SE	β	SE	β	SE	β	SE
HIV Status	−.25**	.28	−.15	.32	−.12	.30	−.12	.30
Demographics								
Age			.09	.02	−.01	.02	.02	.02
Black			.08	.34	.07	.31	.01	.31
Hispanic			.05	.68	.03	.63	−.04	.61
Income Adequacy			.32**	.16	.21**	.15	.22**	.15
Health								
Number of comorbidities					.06	.06	.02	.06
CES-D					−.44***	.02	−.43***	.02
Support								
Functional parent							−.10	.29
Family assistance							.27**	.07

Note. Listwise N = 136. Model 1 R^2 = .06/$F(1, 136)$ = 9.1, $p < .01$. Model 2 R^2 = .16/$F(5, 132)$ = 5.1, $p < .001$. Model 3 R^2 = .31/$F(7, 130)$ = 8.2, $p < .001$. Total R^2 = .37/$F(9,128)$ = 8.4, $p < .001$
*$p < .05$, ** $p < .01$, *** $p < .005$

DISCUSSION

Not surprisingly, HIV-positive older gay and bisexual men present with greater needs compared with their noninfected counterparts, as evidenced by inadequate incomes, a higher burden of multimorbidity, and higher levels of depression. These findings suggest that for HIV-positive sexual minority men, needs for social support and caregiving assistance can only be expected to increase as they age.

Our first research question examined how an HIV diagnosis may impact the social supports of older gay and bisexual men. In the current study, those with HIV were more likely to report functional parents compared with those who were HIV-negative. HIV-positive gay and bisexual older men tended to be younger than their peers. Being younger, they are more likely to have a living parent compared with the older men in the HIV-negative group, and hence more likely to have a functional parent. HIV-positive older men were more likely to report functional siblings and greater levels of assistance from their informal network. In contrast, the HIV-negative group was more likely to have children and functional children, in line with past research (Fredriksen-Golden et al. 2011).

The increased functionality of parents and siblings, and greater support received, may be a response to their family member's HIV diagnosis and represent an activation of kin support resources in times of need. However, those with HIV were more likely to be non-Hispanic black compared with HIV-negative gay and bisexual men. Given the well-documented greater functionality of kin and support exchanges in racial/ethnic minority compared with majority adults (Cantor and Brennan, 2000), these observed differences may be more due to cultural factors than HIV *per se*, which should be explored in future research. Interestingly, while both groups received help from family, friends also provided considerable assistance but this did not differ by HIV diagnosis.

With regard to our second research question, current findings suggest that while older gay and bisexual men with HIV receive greater assistance from family, they are also more likely to consider their instrumental and emotional social support to be inadequate and unavailable. This lower perceived support sufficiency among HIV-positive men likely reflects their greater need for support due to inadequate incomes and depression rather than their HIV-status *per se* as supported by multivariate analyses. That the presence of a functional parent was negatively related to positive perceptions of social support sufficiency was an unexpected outcome. However, the concept of functionality, and its putative beneficial effects, was premised on the idea of support flowing from the functional social support to the older person. But given the fact that functional parents are also growing older and likely have needs for assistance from their children functionally in this instance likely reflects the provision of assistance from the older gay and bisexual men to their parents. Indeed, the literature suggests that the provision of caregiving often results in social support insufficiency on the part of the caregiver (Courtin, Jemiai, and Mossiclos 2014; Grapsa et al. 2014; Zeng et al. 2014). In fact, when asked about help reciprocity, approximately two-thirds of the HIV-negative group and one-third of the HIV-positive group reported providing more help to parents than they received in return. The dynamics of parental caregiving in the context of HIV among sexual-minority older men should be explored in more depth in future research.

The prominence of friends in the social networks of older gay and bisexual men, including those with HIV, provides further empirical support for the Hierarchical Compensatory Theory (Cantor and Mayer 1978). However, findings on the levels of family assistance and functionality suggest a more nuanced interpretation may be needed. The linear progression from close family through friends and neighbors and to community-based supports may be interrupted, reversed, or otherwise altered in the context of a serious, chronic illness such as HIV. This may be true in situations where the lack of kin functionality results from factors other than the lack of family members and the ability to communicate with them on a regular basis. In these cases, family resources may be rallied, and perhaps dormant patterns of intrafamily assistance become reactivated due to social and cultural norms concerning helping family members in times of need (Cantor and Brennan 2000). One cannot discount the recent greater acceptance of sexual minorities in developed countries like the United States, which may serve to weaken estrangements among family members due to sexual minority orientation, causing families to reevaluate their stance toward their LGBT members. Future research should examine how an HIV diagnosis alters existing patterns of family and friend support in both older and younger adults.

Program Implications

Given the high unmet needs for emotional support among older gay and bisexual men with HIV in the current study, how might formal community-based programs support this population? Program staff at COH observed that many of the older HIV-positive gay and bisexual men they serve increasingly rely on friends for support. However, these support networks are diminished over the years as a result of HIV and other challenges associated with aging, and many experience HIV stigma. One of the most successful programs offered at COH for older sexual-minority men has been the Men's Sexual and Emotional Health Group. Through a variety of interactive exercises, participants learn about being emotionally and sexually healthy as they age. Topics addressed include communication, conflict resolution, and self-esteem. Additionally, this group serves as a space for discussing difficult topics such as aging, sexuality and HIV, and fear of violence and abuse. The overwhelming success of this group has demonstrated the need for this type of programming which supports the emotional well-being of its participants by increasing social connectedness and reducing isolation. Similar programming to strengthen the emotional wellness of this population could be offered through a variety of community-based services, including ASOs, senior centers, and faith-based organizations.

In terms of limitations, the functionality of network supports was measured by two aspects, namely phone and in-person contact, consistent with Cantor's earlier definition. Because of new modes of communication such as texting and email, the degree of functionality may have been underestimated. Additionally, although limited by the cross-sectional nature of these data and the lack of a population-based sample, findings in this chapter support the observation that the friend-centered social networks of older gay and bisexual men may be influenced in the circumstance of growing older with HIV. The social networks of HIV-positive older gay and bisexual men are responsive to their greater needs for support stemming from greater depression and income inadequacy, yet these men perceive that they do not receive enough assistance from informal sources. Their greater need for emotional support highlights the need to effectively manage depression in this population, which will assuredly result in better life quality and treatment outcomes. The high levels of unmet need for instrumental and emotional support from family and friends supports the conclusion that these men will increasingly turn to formal, community-based sources of support (Shippy and Karpiak 2005a, 2005b). In fact, HIV-positive older adults have been found to use a high volume of government and community services (Brennan-Ing et al. 2014). Thus, it is vital that policies are in place to strengthen the social resources of older gay and bisexual men with HIV. This includes assuring that community-based providers have the competency and resources necessary to serve this population.

ACKNOWLEDGMENTS

Funding for this study was obtained from a grant from the Human Resources Services Administration to the COH, Chicago, Illinois, who commissioned the work with ACRIA. The authors wish to thank Betty Akins, Hope Barrett, Philonise Keithley, and Zach Zimmerman for their assistance in conducting the field effort for the study in Chicago. We also wish to thank Sheila Massinde for her help with data preparation, cleaning, and data entry. Last but not least, we are truly grateful to the over 200 LGBT older adults who took the time to share their lives with us.

REFERENCES

Andersen, Elena M., Judith A. Malmgren, William B. Carter, and Donald L. Patrick. 1994. "Screening for Depression in Well Older Adults: Evaluation of a Short Form of the CES-D (Center for Epidemiologic Studies Depression Scale)." *American Journal of Preventative Medicine* 10:77–84.

Applebaum, Allison and Mark Brennan. 2009. Mental Health and Depression. P. 27–34 in Mark Brennan, Stephen E. Karpiak, R. Andrew Shippy, and Marjorie H. Cantor (eds.) *Older Adults with HIV: An In-Depth Examination of an Emerging Population*, New York: Nova Science Publishers.

Brennan, Mark. 2002. "Spirituality and Psychosocial Development in Middle-Age and Older Adults with Vision Loss." *Journal of Adult Development* 9(1):31–46.

Brennan, Mark. 2004. "Spirituality and Religiousness Predict Adaptation to Vision Loss among Middle-Age and Older Adults." *International Journal for the Psychology of Religion* 14(3):193–214.

Brennan-Ing, Mark, Liz Seidel, Andrew S. London, Sean Cahill, and Stephen E. Karpiak. 2014. "Service Utilization Among Older Adults with HIV: The Joint Association of Sexual Identity and Gender." *Journal of Homosexuality*, 61(1):166–96.

Cantor, Marjorie H. and Mark Brennan. 1993. *Family and Community Support Systems of Older New Yorkers. Growing Older in New York City in the 1990s: A Study of Changing*

Lifestyles, Quality of Life, and Quality of Care, Vol. V. New York: New York Center for Policy on Aging, New York Community Trust.

Cantor, Marjorie H. and Mark Brennan. 2000. *Social Care of the Elderly: The Effects of Ethnicity, Class and Culture.* New York: Springer.

Cantor, Marjorie H., Mark Brennan, and Stephen E. Karpiak. 2009. The social support networks of older people with HIV. P. 61-74 in Mark Brennan, Stephen E. Karpiak, R. Andrew Shippy, and Marjorie. H. Cantor (eds.) *Research on Older Adults with HIV: An In-Depth Examination of an Emerging Population*, New York: Nova Science Publishers.

Cantor, Marjorie H., Mark Brennan, and R. Andrew Shippy. 2004. *Caregiving Among Older Lesbian, Gay, Bisexual and Transgender New Yorkers.* New York: National Gay and Lesbian Task Force Policy Institute.

Cantor, Marjorie H., Mary J. Mayer. 1978. "Factors in Differential Utilization of Services by Urban Elderly." *Journal of Gerontological Social Work* 1(1):47-61.

Centers for Disease Control and Prevention (CDC). 2008. *HIV/AIDS Among Persons 50 and Older.* Retrieved April 15, 2011 from http://www.cdc.gov/hiv/topics/over50/resources/factsheets/pdf/over50.pdf.

Centers for Disease Control and Prevention (CDC). 2013. Diagnoses of HIV Infection Among Adults Aged 50 Years and Older in the United States and Dependent Areas, 2007-2010. *HIV Surveillance Supplemental Report* 18(3).

Chesney, Margaret, Donald B. Chambers, Jonelle M. Taylor, and Lisa M. Johnson. 2003. "Social Support, Distress, and Well-being in Older Men Living with HIV Infection. *Journal of Acquired Immune Deficiency Syndrome* 33:S185-S193.

Courtin, Emilie, Nadia Jemiai, and Elias Mossialos. (2014). "Mapping Support Policies for Informal Carers across the European Union." *Health Policy* 118(1):84-94.

de Vries, Brian and Patrick Hoctel. 2007. Sexual Inequalities and Social Justice. P. 213-32 in Niels Teunis and Gilbert H. Herdt (eds.) *The Family Friends of Older Gay Men and Lesbians*, Berkeley: University of California Press.

Effros Rita B., Courtney V. Fletcher, Kelly Gebo, Jeffrey B. Halter, William R. Hazzard, Frances McFarland Horne, Robin E. Huebner, Edward N. Janoff, Amy C. Justice, Daniel Kuritzkes, Susan G. Nayfield, Susan F. Plaeger, Kenneth E. Schmader, John R. Ashworth, Christine Campanelli, Charles P. Clayton, Beth Rada, Nancy F. Woolard, and Kevin P. High. 2008. "Aging and Infectious Diseases: Workshop on HIV Infection and Aging: What Is Known and Future Research Directions." *Clinical Infectious Diseases: An Official Publication of the Infectious Diseases Society of America* 47(4):542-53.

Emlet, Charles A., Karen I. Fredriksen-Goldsen, and Hyun-Jun Kim. 2013. "Risk and Protective Factors Associated with Health-Related Quality of Life among Older Gay and Bisexual Men Living with HIV Disease." *The Gerontologist* 53(6):963-72.

Fredriksen-Goldsen, Karen I., Hyun-Jun Kim, Charles E. Emlet, Anna Muraco, Elena A. Erosheva, Charles P. Hoy-Ellis, Jayn Goldsen, and Heidi Petry. 2011. *The Aging and Health Report: Disparities and Resilience among Lesbian, Gay, Bisexual, and Transgender Older Adults.* Seattle: Institutional for Multigenerational Health.

Grapsa, Eirini, Kostantinos Pantelias, Edmond Ntenta, Chrysoula Pipili, Eva Kiousi, Maria Samartzi, Stylianos Karagiannis, and Panagiotis Heras. 2014. "Caregivers' Experience in Patients with Chronic Diseases." *Social Work in Health Care* 53(7):670-8.

Grant, Joan S., David E. Vance, Norman L. Keltner, Worawan White, and James L. Raper. 2013. "Reasons Why Persons Living with HIV include Individuals in Their Chosen Families." *Journal of the Association of Nurses in AIDS Care* 24(1): 50–60.

Grossman, Arnold H., Anthony R. D'Augelli, and Scott L. Hershberger. 2000. "Social Support Networks of Lesbian, Gay and Bisexual Adults 60 Years of Age and Older." *Journal of Gerontology: Psychological Sciences* 55B(2):171–9.

Havlik, Richard J. 2009. Health Status, Comorbidities, and Health-Related Quality of Life. P. 13–25 in Mark Brennan, Stephen E. Karpiak, R. Andrew Shippy, and Marjorie H. Cantor (eds.) *Research on Older Adults with HIV: An In-Depth Examination of an Emerging Population*, New York: Nova Science Publishers.

Havlik, Richard, Mark Brennan, and Stephen Karpiak. 2011. "Comorbidities and Depression in Older Adults with HIV." *Sexual Health* 8(4):551–9.

Nichols, Janice E., David C. Speer, Betty J. Watson, Mary Watson, Tiffany L. Vergon, Colette M. Vallee, and Joan M. Meah. 2002. *Aging with HIV: Psychological, Social, and Health Issues*, San Diego, CA: Academic Press.

Orel, Nancy A. 2014. "Investigating the Needs and Concerns of Lesbian, Gay, Bisexual, and Transgender Older Adults: The Use of Qualitative and Quantitative Methodology." *Journal of Homosexuality* 61:53–78.

Poindexter, Cynthia and Andrew R. Shippy. 2008. "Networks of Older New Yorkers with HIV: Fragility, Resilience and Transformation." *AIDS Patient Care and STDs* 22(9):723–33.

Radloff, Lenore S. 1977. "The CES-D Scale: A Self-Report Depression Scale for Research in the General Population." *Applied Psychological Measurement* 1:385–401.

Sheehan, Nancy W., Richard Wilson, and Lisa M. Marella 1988. "The Role of Church in Providing Services for the Aging." *Journal of Applied Gerontology* 7(2):231–41.

Shippy, R. Andrew, Marjorie H. Cantor, and Mark Brennan. 2004. "Social Networks of Aging Gay Men." *Journal of Men's Studies* 13(1):107–20.

Shippy, R. Andrew and Stephen E. Karpiak. 2005a. "The Aging HIV/AIDS Population: Fragile Social Networks." *Aging and Mental Health* 9(3):246–54.

Shippy, R. Andrew and Stephen E. Karpiak. 2005b. "Perceptions of Support among Older Adults with HIV." *Research on Aging* 27(3):290–306.

Tirrito, Terry and Gil Choi. 2005. "Faith Organizations and Ethnically Diverse Elders: A Community-Action Model." *Journal of Religious Gerontology* 16(1/2):123–42.

Zeng, Li, Xiaoping Zhu, Xianmei Meng, Yafen Mao, Qian Wu, Yan Shi, and Lanshu Zhou. 2014. "Responsibility and Burden from the Perspective of Seniors' Family Caregivers: A Qualitative Study in Shanghai, China." *International Journal of Clinical and Experimental Medicine* 7(7):1818–28.

Chapter 6

PREPARATIONS FOR LATER LIFE CARE AMONG LGBT OLDER ADULTS

Brian de Vries

Introduction

Aging is associated with myriad challenges and rewards—many of which are blind to sexual orientation and gender identity. Lesbian, gay, bisexual, and transgender (LGBT) persons, however, experience unique challenges and obstacles that may compromise a healthy later life—and opportunities to prepare effectively for it.

Owing to a history of exclusion from traditional marriage and all that entails, LGBT adults of all ages are much less likely to be married than heterosexual persons of comparable age. In a recent study of LGBT boomers (those persons aged 45-65), one of the very few studies to have drawn samples of LGBT persons as well as those from the general population that allow for national estimates, we found that 61 percent of LGBT boomers were in a partnership of some form compared with 77 percent of boomers in the general population (MetLife 2010). Nine percent of LGBT boomers had never been in a relationship, over four times higher than the general population; these rates were higher among gay men. Among older LGBT adults, the percentage of those not in partnerships is even higher. In a recent San Francisco study (Fredriksen-Goldsen et al. 2013), 51 percent of gay men over the age of 60 were not married, more than twice the national average for men, which was about 25 percent. Among lesbians, bisexual women and men, and transgender persons, the differences were more modest but still exceeded national averages.

At the same time, LGBT persons in the second half of life are also much more likely to live alone. Using data drawn from the California Health Interview studies, Wallace et al. (2011) found that more than half of gay and bisexual men over the age of 50 live alone compared to 13.4 percent of heterosexual men in a similar age range. As above, the differences between heterosexual and lesbian and bisexual women are smaller, but still noteworthy: more than one in four lesbian and bisexual women live alone compared with one in five heterosexual women.

There are dramatic differences when comparing the presence of offspring in the lives of LGBT and heterosexual persons in the second half of life. A recent study of San Francisco LGBT adults over the age of 60 (Fredriksen-Goldsen et al. 2013) found that only 15 percent had children—a proportion that is almost precisely the opposite of the general population. Even more telling, 60 percent of these LGBT adults with children reported that their children were not available to provide support when/should it be needed.

These demographic realities of LGBT lives defy heteronormative customs and expectations of aging persons—they disrupt the patterns apparent in the hierarchical compensatory model of care (Cantor and Mayer 1978). That is, where older adults are expected to first look to their spouses and children for care and then turn to friends and formal organizations, LGBT older adults are much less likely to have access to these traditional caregivers and are consequently more likely to turn first to their friends and others beyond their immediate biological kin. This violation of traditional patterns of care seeking and provision challenges the organizations, policies, and procedures in place to support older adults and imposes additional demands on these nontraditional care seekers and providers. There is the need for greater intentionality and additional effort and actions to be undertaken by LGBT elders to ensure sufficient and affirmative support.

These efforts and this intentionality are the focus of the work reported herein. What follows is a review of the modest research on the fears and concerns, preparations, and plans for later life, with a particular focus on care, among LGBT persons in the second half of life. I draw upon some of my own work as well as that of several colleagues. Inferred but not explicitly addressed in much of this quantitative work are the experiences of LGBT persons in these preparations; the next section of this chapter draws from ongoing qualitative research that explicitly focuses on the affect and thought underlying this intentionality. Together, these areas call for ways to engage LGBT older adults in thoughtful preparations for later life with implications for a more person- and relationship-centered approach that can benefit all, LGBT and heterosexual, in effective end-of-life preparations.

Concerns About and Actions Undertaken in Preparation for Later Life: Survey Findings

North Americans—and perhaps beyond—have, at best, a mixed and complicated relationship with end of life and death, comprising both fascination and denial. The grand presence of death and dying in popular media has been well demonstrated, including the oft-repeated observation that approximately 18,000 murders are witnessed on television by the time an average American individual reaches 16 years of age (Kearl 1995). At the same time, Durbin (2003) refers to the numerous ways in which Americans attempt to deny death, including our use of euphemisms, such as *passed away*, to avoid saying aloud *death*, and adherence to taboos about frank discussions of death and dying. This denial, and these taboos in particular, hamstring individuals contemplating an inevitable future, which could be informed and enhanced by thoughtful preparations and expressions of hopes, fears, and wishes. This applies, of course, to all individuals, but perhaps even more dramatically so to those who eschew heteronormative traditions and could especially benefit from aligning relationships, resources, and directives.

Support for such sentiments may be found in the "Still Out, Still Aging" MetLife study of boomers (2010), which focused on preparations for and concerns about aging and end of life and comprised 1,201 LGBT persons between the ages of 46 and 64 as well as 1,206 from the general population, comprising both LGBT and heterosexual persons, the latter accounting for 94 percent of the sample. A brief survey queried the greatest concerns about aging, revealing substantial comparability and reinforcing the common experience of aging as introduced previously. That is, both LGBT and those from the general population expressed similar aging concerns around self-care, dependence, sickness and disability, income sufficiency, dying alone and in pain, financial care of surviving partners, and parent care (MetLife 2010).

Significant differences were also noted, however. LGBT boomers were *less* likely to fear becoming confused/developing dementia and losing friends and family but were *more* likely to fear being alone. This latter fear of isolation, in particular, is a recurrent theme in the experiences of older LGBT persons, perhaps driven, at least in part, by a lifetime of being shunned and excluded from heterosexual traditions and stigmatized for this failure to adhere. Consistent with such an interpretation, about one in ten LGBT boomers identified discrimination as a concern about aging and at life's end.

The consequences of stigma and discrimination for end-of-life preparation was explored more directly by de Vries et al. (2009). Using data from the earlier MetLife (2006) study of almost 800 LGBT persons between the ages of 40 and 61, two national groups were created: those who lived in states that recognized same-sex relationships (there were eight of those states when these data were analyzed and written) and those who lived in states where such relationships are not recognized. Analyses revealed that those who lived in a state wherein their relationships were not recognized were significantly *more* likely to fear dying in pain and were *more* likely to fear discrimination than those who lived in states wherein such relationships were recognized.

With these same national (2006) data, analyses examined the sorts of preparations boomers have undertaken for their later lives. These preparations included completing a will or living will, durable power of attorney, informal caregiving arrangements, or making funeral arrangements. As described previously, analyses examined the completion of these documents by those LGBT boomers who lived in states where their same-sex relationships were recognized and those who lived in states where those relationships were not recognized. It was found, as before, that those who lived in states where relationships were not recognized were *more* likely to have completed both wills and living wills and to have made informal caregiving arrangements. It is as if the lack of recognition spurs these boomers into action (de Vries 2013). But as seen in the previous analysis along this line, anxiety and fear (of dying in pain, of discrimination) are at the root of such action. The recent U.S. Supreme Court ruling on marriage equality stands to have important and positive health consequences for LGBT persons, reducing stigmatization and discrimination and, hopefully, mitigating the anxiety and fear as reported previously.

The more recent and aforementioned MetLife (2010) study afforded the opportunity to compare the extent to which LGBT and general population boomers differed in the completion of these documents. No significant differences were noted on the completion of a will, which was completed by 37 percent of LGBT boomers and 39 percent of those in the general population; a trust, with comparable respective percentages of 8 and 10; or the purchase of long-term care insurance, completed by 14 percent of LGBT boomers and 11 percent of those in the general population. Importantly, the most frequently completed document, a will, was still only completed by less than 40 percent of either boomer group.

Interestingly, significant differences were noted in the completion of living wills and durable powers of attorney and those documents that may be said to involve others, such as informal caregiving arrangements, partnership agreements, rights of visitation, and funeral arrangements. In all of these cases, LGBT boomers were significantly more likely to have completed these documents, although again, the greatest percentage of completion of any of these was still less than 40 percent (MetLife 2010).

Perhaps the relatively higher rates of document completion and the concomitant need to inform others of wishes and desires for end of life derive from the many caregiving experiences of LGBT persons, particularly in the time and context of HIV/AIDS. For example, during a time when governments of all levels, families, and communities fearfully and shamefully turned their backs on those dying from the mysterious disease that would be later labeled as AIDS, the LGBT community coalesced, organized, and responded by creating numerous groups and community-based organizations that would offer a wide range of health and social services to persons with AIDS.

In this context and from a variety of research studies, LGBT midlife and older adults are significantly more likely to have been caregivers than heterosexual women and men of comparable age. In the MetLife (2010) study, for example, 21 percent of LGBT boomers had provided care in the previous 6 months, which averaged 36 hours per week, compared with 17 percent of the general boomer population, which averaged 29 hours per week. Parents and/or spouses/partners were the most common care recipients; each of these two groups comprised about one-third of care recipients. The most dramatic difference was found outside of traditional family ties: friends comprised just over 20 percent of the care recipients of LGBT boomers but only 6 percent of the care recipients of those in the general population.

Friends were also mentioned more frequently as potential caregivers of LGBT boomers than of boomers in the general population, with respective percentages of 8 and 2. Still, almost 30 percent of LGBT boomers did not know who their caregiver might be, although at 20 percent this was significantly lower for lesbians; among the general population, 24 percent reported that they did know who their caregiver might be.

These experiences and the culture of caregiving that is part of the cohort experiences of LGBT persons in the second half of life may be assumed to be associated with a greater openness to end-of-life issues and discussions of the same. To address this assumption, questions were posed in the MetLife (2010) study about the nature of discussions of end-of-life care and end-of-life treatment that these boomers have had with others in their social environment. These others included spouses or partners, friends, siblings, parents, other relatives, primary care providers, and adult children. It was found, as before, that there are many similarities across sexual orientations and gender identities: overall, 31.4 percent of both samples had *not* had end-of-life discussions with anyone. In response to questions about the participants of such discussions, the single largest category was partners/spouses for 45 percent of the LGBT sample and 48 percent of those in the general population. LGBT boomers were more likely to have had such discussions with their friends—22 percent as compared with 11 percent of the general population—or siblings, with respective percentages of 21 and 14.

Summary

LGBT persons, and especially gay men, are much more likely to live alone, unmarried/unpartnered and without children than are heterosexual persons; these characteristics defy heteronormative patterns of care delivery, mandating additional efforts and attention on the part of LGBT persons across the adult years. This often unspoken awareness may underlie the isolative fears of aging that distinguish LGBT persons in midlife and beyond and prompt the completion of advance directives and related documents in self- and other-protective action. Evidence of this protection may also be seen in the greater experiences of caregiving among

LGBT adults, made more salient and relevant in the historical context of HIV disease. That nontraditional or chosen family members (de Vries and Hoctel 2007; de Vries and Megathlin 2009) distinguish receipt of care and participants in discussions about end-of-life preferences speak once again to the norm-challenging realities of LGBT lives.

Even as evidence suggests that LGBT persons are as likely as are heterosexual persons of comparable age to have prepared advance directive documents and engaged in discussions about end-of-life preferences, these levels of preparation are probably insufficient for both groups but especially for LGBT persons. As noted, it is not only a greater effort demanded of those whose experiences challenge access to the default social structures and practices but it is of a different form. Engaging friends as primary caregivers, for example, requires a type of formalization of an informal association: friends are not always readily accepted in these roles by agency and organization staff or policy (Barker 2002) and may feel unwilling to tread on this family territory or uncertain of what to do (de Vries 2011). The challenges to traditional organizations of care and the uncertainty they create underlie the greater need for explicit preparation. In the qualitative research reported in the next section of this chapter, the experiences of this uncertainty and these preparatory efforts are explored.

Concerns About and Actions Undertaken in Preparation for Later Life: Qualitative Findings

Two ongoing qualitative studies attempt to explore in greater depth the types and sources of concern about later life and issues related to preparations, including discussions about caregiving and care receipt. The first of these, *Paths to Care* (de Vries and Gil 2013), is an interview study of 8 lesbians and 12 gay men between the ages of 50 and 79, 17 of whom identified as Caucasian; approximately 60-minute interviews were transcribed and coded. The second of these, *Planning for Later Life Among Gay Men* (de Vries and Bass 2013), represents two-hour focus groups conducted with gay men ranging in ages from 50 to 82. Two focus groups have been completed with a total of 26 gay men, all but two of whom were Caucasian. These analyses reflect the quantitative findings above, importantly adding texture and dimension and deepening our understanding of these issues.

Participants in the interview study were asked about their concerns and fears for later life. Three broad categories of concerns emerged from the open-ended responses: physical and psychological health, financial well-being, and interpersonal connections. The majority of participants spoke of concerns/fears related to dementia, with specific mention of Alzheimer's and Parkinson's diseases. One man said "Having witnessed my mother in the later stages of Alzheimer's, I realize that my biggest fear is losing mental capacity. A really close second to that is losing physical capacity." Others made reference to declining health more generally: "The fear of physical disabilities that come with age." Many of these concerns were centered on a loss of independence, as noted in the following: "In terms of the future I'm concerned that I might not be as healthy as I want to be when I'm older. I might not be able to take care of myself as much as I want to. I might not be as independent as I want to be. These are probably all questions people ask themselves and fears they have as they get older."

One gay man noted the general concern about finances in his future: "I have some concerns about my future ... mostly money." These thoughts were echoed by others but often framed in terms of the financial health of the country. Another gay man noted, for example: "I'm concerned about Medicare and the state of the country, economically, financially and I don't want to live in social chaos when I'm older." Respondents made clear that financial well-being was more than an individual issue, with anxiety deriving from multiple levels.

The interpersonal concerns addressed being alone, loss of friends through relocation or death, and uncertainty about the ways in which friends may support each other in later life—articulating a concern voiced by many others in the field of LGBT aging health services. This was stated simply and directly: "I don't like to think of myself as alone; that is an unpleasant thought." One woman said that she was concerned about losing contact with her old friends: "I don't think it's smart to move ... to be apart from my family and friends." Another woman noted, "Yeah, the not having—I didn't ever have kids—so thinking about the traditional system of kids pretty much taking care of the parents or manage things or handle things, and the questions about that 'cause I'm aging at the same stage as my friends. So presumably, we're all aging the same, and who knows what's going to happen to who, and stuff and how we can handle taking care of each other." This latter quote, in particular, draws attention to the norm-challenging characteristics of LGBT later lives and uncertainties consequently introduced.

Importantly, permeating these content themes is an overarching concern of being a burden on someone else—noted in a variety of ways. For example, in discussing physical health fears and concerns, many respondents made reference to burden, using this term both explicitly, such as "I worry about being a burden on other people," or implicitly, as in "I don't like the idea of getting old and being cared for." The same was evident in discussions of financial well-being, as noted by one woman: "It's scary to think I'd have to be a financial burden to someone." In comparable fashion, and referring to a broader interpersonal sphere, another man reported that he worries "about being a burden on other people, and about being more conscious of the discomfort of being alive than I am the joy of being alive."

This is an important component overlooked or unavailable in survey data; burden is not just an additional theme—it is a frame within which physical and mental health, financial well-being, and interpersonal concerns are construed, perhaps even driving the experience. It refers to the consequences of independence loss and the experience of relying on someone else. That "someone else" or "other people" are those on whom respondents will have to rely is also worthy of consideration; these ambiguously identified others may well contribute to the experience of burden. That is, not identifying and perhaps not knowing who these "others" might be may well contribute to the concern about future care receipt. In such a way, burden may express both the imposition on someone else and the anxiety of receiving care in a wide number of ways.

In the focus groups, the gay men raised the issue of what it might be like to receive care. Several of the men noted that they had never needed care; one participant reported simply that he "had no experience receiving care," and several others agreed. It is interesting to note the privileged nature of physical care; that is, emotional support/care was not considered, notwithstanding the high likelihood of these men having received such support and care. This raises the evocative issues of the constitution of care and the definition of need.

Most men felt that it was "difficult to call and ask for care," implicitly reinforcing the case of burden, as described previously. In elaborating on this difficulty, a variety of responses were offered: "I don't accept care well; I would rather stay in a corner by myself," one respondent said. Another respondent noted that he felt that "he was not deserving of it. I was feeling like I was using up my wishes," suggesting a finite supply of a somewhat fragile pool of potential care. Others noted that they "had no choice but to receive care;" there was a specific need that had to be addressed. Overall, these comments conform to findings reported by Addis and Mahalik (2003) in a comprehensive review of the literature of men's reluctance to seek help from both informal and formal sources. Gender role socialization such as masculine ideologies and/or gender role conflict has been engaged to account for these robust findings: masculinity continues to play a significant role in the lives of gay men (Sanchez et al. 2009).

Gay men, however, are also members of a group that challenges such traditional norms—explicitly in many instances, as noted in the ACT-UP chant, "we're here, we're queer, get used to it," and implicitly in other instances, as in their presence in nontraditional roles and settings. These challenges to traditional norms were similarly evident in the discussions of care receipt by the gay men in these focus groups. One man noted that a friend came to stay with him after surgery and he accepted this easily and with gratitude: "I make no bones about it." Couples reported that they help each other—"that's just the way it is." Several respondents reported that they were "dumbfounded about the people who came to help ... and those who did not;" their experiences of being assisted afforded them another view of being in relationships/networks—and an unintentional test of the same. Respondents also reported positive experiences in both asking for and receiving care. For example, one man said: "I like getting help. I like that and I don't feel guilty. I feel good about their help." Another man said that he "went to a support group and felt accepted when asking for help." Such is the complex experience of members of sexual minorities—inhabitants of many worlds.

Flowing from these thoughts about the receipt of care, the gay men in the focus groups wondered aloud who might be their caregiver if/ when the need arose. Several men made reference to the history within the LGBT, and especially gay, community of caregiving for those with HIV/AIDS. They spoke, with some pride and adamancy, of how gay men and lesbians rose to the challenges of caregiving, along the lines of that reported earlier: "We have been there during AIDS, we will be there again." Another man said, with some implicit agreement among others in the group, "As gay men, we are used to caring for each other. We would stand tall and do what needs to be done. People show up."

Other group members pointed out, however, that such caregivers do not "magically appear" and commented on the need for greater proactivity. They noted, "in fact, the absence of community in the gay community;" one individual poignantly remarked that, for many gay men, the family they either left behind or lost was not replaced by the gay community and there "remains a hole in that fabric." As above, the modestly veiled notion of isolation, even alienation, is referenced as a concern. A significant number of participants reported that their caregivers would be "hired help." Several others reported that they are not sure who, or if, there would be a designated caregiver. Group members pointed out that the needs of older persons do not mirror the crisis of HIV/AIDS; even as organizations emerge in the LGBT community to address older members, the pace and presence of these organizations lack the immediacy and reach of the dozens of agencies/organizations that emerged in response to crisis of HIV/AIDS.

In both studies, respondents were asked directly if they had had conversations about their end-of-life care with anyone. The animated early discussion in the focus groups and the preliminary responses in the interviews focused on the completion of documents. The majority of those interviewed reported that they had completed advance directives—many expressing so with some pride. Similarly, almost all of the men in the focus groups reported that they had had such discussions and made reference to the completed documents already discussed in the groups; they spoke readily of wanting to be cremated and of how their possessions were to be distributed and that both of these directives were known to many in their social spheres. Many of the men in the focus group treated the question as annoyingly redundant to a previous topic of discussion in the groups explicitly addressing document completion.

When probed further, however, with prompts about receiving care when needed and framed in the period of life "before such documents would come into play," discussion initially subsided then began to reveal the complexity of this issue and the relatively modest thoughts that had been expended in its consideration. The initial quietness in response to the probe was itself dramatic and instructive.

The range of responses to the probes about care conversations is revealed in Table 6.1. Interestingly, participants reported expecting to receive care from friends, family members, or partners, even as the issue was rarely formally addressed; about half of the responses suggested

BRIAN DE VRIES

Table 6.1: Discussions About Receiving Care

Overarching Themes	Codes	Exemplary Quotations
No discussion	No discussion	"Many of us don't have conversations with ourselves let alone with others."
	"About to have … "	" … I think we're just at the point of [having a discussion] …"
	Imagined/ assumed	"These are all assumptions and thoughts I've had based on my familiarity with them … living with them … it doesn't come from any conversations I've had with them … not even with [my partner]."
Ambiguous discussions	Peripheral/ implied Focus on Resources (e.g., Insurance)	"Well, you know, we've touched on it minimally, mostly joking like 'just shoot me if I get that way'" "Have had discussion in the context of financial terms … purchasing long-term care insurance and that sort of thing."
Specific discussions	with Family	" … my brother and sister-in-law … you know … they tell me I could move in with them …"
	explicit	"I've made all of my kids promise me, though, that they will help me get into the kind of care I need and not feel that they have to take me into their homes."

there had been no conversation about potential future needed care, commenting on the fact that end of life is "an unpleasant topic—it's uncomfortable." These absent discussions were in the majority and assumed a variety of forms: from a complete absence with others and with even the self, perhaps attributable to successful socialization in a culture of death denial, to anticipated discussions where respondents were either judging the timing for such discussions or just realizing their need, to the more significantly endorsed response of imagined or presumed understandings: "I just know they'll be there." One woman spoke of her friend, saying: "I've never talked with her about 'would you take care of me?' but I imagine she would." These effectively serve as an absence of discussions without some agreement from both parties on the parameters of care provision.

About one-third of respondents reported discussions of an ambiguous sort, where expectations were either unclear or implied—a tenuous grounding for something so pivotal to well-being in later life. One participant said he had had such a conversation "in a joking manner; it was not written down." Although the importance of such a discussion should not be undermined, it is probably unlikely to be seen as a *roadmap* or plan for future care. One woman noted that her conversations were "more in a theoretical way about politics, women, friends, and community—more about that than 'Shall we take care of one another?'" A gay man reported that: "The closest we've gotten was recently with— we just—I can't say we were kicking it around, but we were toying with wouldn't it be interesting if four or five of us bought a house, but we didn't go further with that ... " It is as if a conversation had begun, but moved no further perhaps because, as one woman noted, "it is too scary; it is too scary." The net result, though, is not that different from the category above—an absent explicit discussion of end-of-life care.

It was the minority of respondents, about one quarter in both focus groups and the interviews, who had had discussions of any explicit sort with others about their future care needs. As above, a range of responses was apparent. One of the couples present in the focus group noted that they had had such a conversation, although "not outside of the couple." They noted, as did another participant, that there was a need "to tell people, more than one person, who might be carrying out the actions" that is ultimately articulated. Another participant reported that he had spoken explicitly with his sister, saying "he wanted no extraordinary procedures." He did not elaborate on this, nor did it sound as though he further elaborated with his sister on this subject. The most focused discussion was reported by an older lesbian whose quote appears in Table 6.1. It is interesting to note that all of these infrequent explicit discussions were with others in more traditional roles: partners/spouses, adult children, and siblings—the presumptive caregivers of older adults in general.

Summary

These qualitative results echo the survey findings reported above, importantly adding further depth and context. The areas of later-life fears and concerns for midlife and older gay men and lesbians include physical and emotional health, financial well-being, and interpersonal connections, comparable to the items noted on the MetLife survey but layered in critical ways and poignantly framed in the terms of burden on a nebulously noted *other*. These latter framing issues—both burden and the poorly defined *other*—are evident in the discussions about the receipt of care of midlife and older gay men. Notwithstanding the higher frequency with which care is provided by LGBT persons, as the reviewed survey findings report, the receipt of care, physically defined, was addressed by gay men in ways consistent with traditional male gender roles, as in difficulty seeking such support and challenging of the same, such as accepted support. This duality highlights the complexity of the issue and of the cultures straddled by gay men—and others.

The source of caregivers was also the subject of discussion, similarly contested; amidst some consideration of a community "rising to the challenge and being there," drawing from the response to HIV/AIDS, the special effort required for such a community response was noted: "Caregivers don't magically appear." Such special effort was directly queried in both of the samples about end-of-life care discussions. It was clear in the process of interviewing and the tenor of the groups that the idea of such discussions was evocative. Most respondents replied by noting, with some pride, their completion of advance directives, again somewhat echoing the survey results; the more particular discussions about the specifics of end-of-life *care*, however, were less forthcoming. Such discussions were the exception, although more likely with traditional family members; most midlife and older gay men and lesbians avoided this "uncomfortable" and "unpleasant"—albeit necessary—topic, presumed others would know, or framed it in indirect ways. In a social and legal environment where such explicit discussions are more necessary, these findings merit greater attention—and action.

Discussion

The quantitative and qualitative findings presented here construct an image of the ambivalence with which end of life is approached, and experienced, by midlife and older LGBT persons, particularly gay men and lesbians. In a demographic context that defies heteronormative customs, practices, and policies, later life—and especially end of life—demands more focused and conscious preparations by LGBT persons.

LGBT persons have responded to these implicit calls to action in varying degrees. Survey data reveal that LGBT boomers have prepared the formal documents and engaged in some discussions articulating end-of-life wishes in greater proportions than comparably aging persons in the general population—even as both groups may be seen as under-prepared in this manner. The fears that accompany and perhaps drive such preparations are also comparable and yet importantly different, as seen in findings of fear of dying in pain and fear of discrimination. The allies in these later-life considerations also replicate in some ways and differ from same-age peers in the general population, with friends figur-ing more prominently in the lives of LGBT older persons.

These differences may be understood in part by the context within which these later-life and end-of-life considerations take place—contex-tual factors included the political (e.g., legal recognition), social/cultural (e.g., legacy of HIV/AIDS), and personal (e.g., aging fears). The personal context was particularly elaborated in the qualitative data, revealing an underlying concern regarding burden on potential caregivers, many of whom are vaguely defined. Interfacing with the social/cultural and gen-der role context, the qualitative data also revealed challenges in the iden-tification of caregivers and discussions with them about later-life and end-of-life care.

These findings provide opportunities for further theoretical, empiri-cal, and practical reflection. Theoretically, for example, these findings echo calls to explore the heteronormativity underlying our understand-ing of the experience of aging—for LGBT *and* heterosexual persons (de Vries and Blando 2004). Cantor and Mayer (1978) have provided a frame-work by which this was compared; an elaboration of such an approach may begin with a more individualized appraisal of networks from which individuals may draw for support. That is, rather than knowing only the categories of relationships from which individuals may choose, it may be of use to understand the specific relationships themselves, as in social network theories and analyses such as the convoy model of social sup-port (Antonucci, Ajrouch, and Birditt 2013). This could similarly serve as a forum for empirical and practical applications.

Empirically, for example, identifying the network members and their roles and socio-emotional placement could serve to contextualize the data and perhaps provide direct predictors of support and prepared-ness and indirect predictors of stress and anxiety about aging and end

91

of life, perhaps through mediators such as burden and alienation. The qualitative data also reveal the need to examine more specific, and personal, concepts in the research on LGBT aging and later-life preparations. That is, survey questions about document preparation or even whether conversations have taken place provide solid evidence of frequency but gloss over what it means to those responding to have completed such documents or engaged in such conversations—both of which are important factors that ultimately qualify frequency responses.

The practical implications of these data emerge most clearly from the respondents themselves. For example, several of the gay men in the focus groups addressed the need of gay men and LGBT persons in general to be more proactive about their own aging, caring, and end of life: "We can help each other develop the language of caregiving," as one gay man noted, recognizing that "the consideration of the care we will need is new, foreign and/uncharted territory for many of us." Several of the men spoke of the need to have venues and persons with whom to have discussions about these issues, given that "such discussions don't happen naturally—particularly for gay men," as at least one person noted. In a quote already shared (Table 6.1), one gay man noted that "many do not have the conversations with ourselves," let alone with others. "We need a venue for such dialog and to initiate such thinking and groups like this [the focus group] provides this space."

An idea was proposed, and endorsed enthusiastically by many in one of the groups, of a type of *Gay Care Co-Op*: a group of persons who would volunteer to provide care in a variety of forms, such as groceries to more personal care, and be called into action when needed. That is, the gay men in the group offered that a list could be created of persons willing to help out when/if needed and who also could call for help when/if needed so that the work of caregiving falls on many shoulders, burdening fewer or no one and contributing to a sense of community. Someone could volunteer to coordinate the efforts, when needed, including the person for whom care was to be provided, if he was able to do so. Most of the men in the group reported that this was a manageable and accessible way of thinking about care. The example of CaringBridge was offered as a type of format for this exchange.

In fact, following the group meeting, as the men socialized prior to parting ways, it was further proposed that a group, such as the one meeting on that day, could become a support group for individuals. Several gay men pointed out that the active seeking of support is "not typical in our culture, particularly in male culture." Group members noted the need to change the paradigm and the attitudes—and they reported that they could do so. One member took a piece of paper and asked that others write their names and email addresses on it if they were interested in and willing to participate in the Care Co-Op; all of the men in the group did so!

CONCLUSION

The study of later-life issues in general and preparations for end of life in particular among LGBT persons in the second half of life shines a light on the many challenges of aging, particularly among a stigmatized minority. The challenges derive largely within a context of heteronormativity, a restrictive set of parameters characterizing progressively fewer individuals. That is, many of the hallmarks of LGBT aging—without partners or children, relying on non-kin sources of support—certainly apply to non-LGBT persons. Understanding ways to engage LGBT older adults in thoughtful preparations for later life has implications for a more person- and relationship-centered approach that can benefit all, LGBT and heterosexual, in effective end-of-life preparations. Hospice and palliative care already espouse such principles, framing services around individual circumstances, wishes, fears, and desires; those who accompany the older adult through life and life's end are best identified by the individual without presumption and without judgment. This holistic approach is optimally suited to support well-being throughout life through its location in the lived experiences and worlds of individuals, whenever possible drawing upon resources of their own creation and supplementing in meaningful and approachable ways.

REFERENCES

Addis, James R. and Michael E. Mahalik. 2003. "Men, Masculinity and the Contexts of Help Seeking." *American Psychologist* 58(1):5-14.

Antonucci, Toni C., Kristine J. Ajrouch, and Kira S. Birditt. 2013. "The Convoy Model: Explaining Social Relations from a Multidisciplinary Perspective." *The Gerontologist* 53(6).

Barker, Judith. 2002. "Neighbors, Friends, and Other Nonkin Caregivers of Community Living Dependent Elders." *Journal of Gerontology* 57(3):158-64.

Cantor, Majorie H. and M. Mayer. 1978. "Factors in Differential Utilization of Services by Urban Elderly." *Journal of Gerontological Social Work* 1(1):47–61.

de Vries, Brian. 2013. "LG(BT) Persons in the Second Half of Life: The Intersectional Influences of Stigma and Cohort." *LGBT Health* 1(1):16–21.

de Vries, Brian. 2011. The Value and Meaning of Friendship in the Second Half of Life. P. 141–62 in Thomas Cole, Ruth Kastenbaum, and Robert Ray (eds.) *Guide to Humanistic Studies in Aging: What Does it Mean to Grow Old?* Baltimore, MD: Johns Hopkins Press.

de Vries, Brian and Richard Bass. 2013. "Planning for Later Life among Gay Men." Data analysis in progress.

de Vries, Brian and John A. Blando. 2004. The Study of Gay and Lesbian Aging: Lessons for Social Gerontology. P. 3–28 in Gilbert Herdt and Brian de Vries (eds.) *Gay and Lesbian Aging: Research and Future Directions.* New York: Springer.

de Vries, Brian and Francisco-Jose Gil. 2013. "Paths to Care." Data analysis in progress.

de Vries, Brian and Patrick Hoctel. 2007. The Family Friends of Older Gay Men and Lesbians. P. 213–32 in Niels Teunis and Gilbert Herdt (eds.) *Sexual Inequalities and Social Justice.* Berkeley, CA: University of California Press

de Vries, Brian, Anne Mason, Jean Quam, and Kim Acquaviva. 2009. "State Recognition of Same-Sex Relationships and Preparations for End of Life among Lesbian and Gay Boomers." *Sexuality Research and Social Policy* 6(1):90–101.

de Vries, Brian and David Megathlin. 2009. "The Meaning of Friends for Gay Men and Lesbians in the Second Half of Life." *Journal of GLBT Family Studies* 5:82–98.

Durbin, Keith. 2003. Death, Dying and the Dead in Popular Culture. P. 43–9 in *Handbook of Death and Dying.* New York: Sage.

Fredriksen-Goldsen, Karen I, Hyun-Jun Kim, Charles P. Hoy-Ellis, Jayn Goldsen, Diana Jensen, Marcy Adelman, Michael Costa, and Brian de Vries. 2013. "LGBT Older Adults in San Francisco: Recommendations for the Future." Report prepared for the LGBT Aging Policy Task Force. Institute for Multigenerational Health: University of Washington, Seattle.

Kearl, Michael C. (1995). Death in Popular Culture. P. 23–30 in John B. Williamson and Edwin Schneidman (eds.) *Death: Current Perspectives* (4th ed), Mountain View, CA: Mayfield.

MetLife Mature Market Institute. 2010. "Still Out, Still Aging." Westport, CT: MetLife Mature Market Institute.

MetLife Mature Market Institute. 2006. "Out and Aging." Westport, CT: MetLife Mature Market Institute.

Sánchez, Francisco, J. S. Greenberg, William Liu, and Eric Vilian. 2009. "Reported Effects of Masculine Ideals on Gay Men." *Psychology of Men & Masculinity* 10:73–87.

Wallace, Steven P., Susan D. Cochran, E. M. Durazo, and Chandra L. Ford. 2011. *The Health of Aging Lesbian, Gay and Bisexual Adults in California.* Los Angeles, CA: UCLA Center for Health Policy Research.

CHAPTER 7

LGBT OLDER ADULTS EMERGING FROM THE SHADOWS

Health Disparities, Risk & Resilience

Karen I. Fredriksen-Goldsen and Charles P. Hoy-Ellis

INTRODUCTION

Lesbian, gay, bisexual, and transgender (LGBT) older adults have largely been an invisible population, although they are now emerging from the shadows. Along with shifting demographics and profound graying of the global population, the older adult population is becoming increasingly diverse. Estimates indicate that more than 100 million Americans are aged 50 and older (U.S. Census Bureau 2013b). By 2030, it is estimated that nearly 133 million Americans will be aged 50 and older with the 50–64 age group shrinking slightly, and those 65 and older nearly doubling (U.S. Census Bureau 2013a).

Given population aging and the increasing diversity of the older adult population, the number of LGBT older adults is steadily increasing. Recent population-based data suggest that 2.4 percent of Americans aged 50 and older, which represents more than 2.7 million adults, self-identity as LGBT when adjusting for nonresponse and noncoverage rates (Fredriksen-Goldsen and Kim 2017). Due to the projection that the numbers of older adults in the United States will more than double by 2060, LGBT adults aged 50 and older will number more than 5 million within the next few decades (Fredriksen-Goldsen and Kim 2017). When expanding beyond self-identification and taking into consideration intimate and romantic relationships and sexual behavior, the number of LGBT adults aged 50 and older is estimated to more than double. Despite the increasing number of LGBT older adults, they are rarely considered in health or aging research (Institute of Medicine 2011). Both the Institute of Medicine (2011) and the Centers for Disease Control and Prevention (CDC 2011) identify the lack of attention to sexual orientation and age as critical gaps in our understanding to reduce health disparities.

To date, most studies of LGBT aging have relied on those in midlife with limited attention to those over the age of 65. Yet, there are three cohorts of midlife and older adults living today (Novak 2013). Both age and cohort differences are important to consider among LGBT older adults, given the shifting social context as it relates to sexuality and the social and legal standing of LGBT people (see Table 7.1). LGBT older adults of both the Greatest and the Silent Generations came of age prior to the modern gay rights movement and during a time when same-sex behaviors, typically characterized as sodomy, were criminal acts in all 50 U.S. states (Carpenter 2012) and homosexuality was considered a sociopathic personality disorder by the American Psychiatric Association (Silverstein 2009). The Greatest Generation (b. 1901–24) came of age during the Great Depression and fought during World War II—a period wherein LGBT identities were largely absent from the public discourse. The Silent Generation (b. 1925–45) experienced the postwar boom and their coming of age occurred during the backdrop of the McCarthy era "lavender scare." With the widespread television broadcasts of the McCarthy trials, sexual and gender-minority identities not only entered into the popular public discourse but were cast as a threat to the very security of the nation (Canaday 2009; Johnson 2004).

Public discourse took a decidedly different turn during the period when the baby boomers (b. 1946–64) were coming of age and forming their sexual and gender identities. As a result of the Stonewall riots and other social movements of the time, LGBT people became visible to each other and to American society in an unprecedented way, marking the beginning of the modern gay rights movement. During this era, we also witnessed the beginning of the decriminalization of same-sex sexuality in 1962 and the removal of homosexuality as a sociopathic personality disorder from the revised second edition of the *Diagnostic and Statistical Manual*

Table 7.1: LGBT Midlife and Older Adults and
Historic Events by Cohort

Historical Event	Year of Event	Cohorts		
		Greatest Generation (born 1901–24)	Silent Generation (born 1925–45)	Baby Boom Generation (born 1946–64)
		Cohort ages in years when experienced		
Emergence of medical discourse of "sexual inversion" as illness[1]	~1860s			
First known use of term "homosexual" in English language[2]	1892			
First of Greatest Generation cohort born (1901–24)	1901	0		
First of Silent Generation cohort born (1925–45)	1925	1–24	0	
Great Depression begins	1929	5–28	0–4	
World War II begins	1939	15–38	0–14	
World War II ends	1945	21–44	0–20	
First of Baby Boom Generation cohort born (1946–64)	1946	22–45	1–21	0
The Lavender Scare, a witch-hunt against homosexuals begins[3]	1950	26–49	5–25	0–4
Homosexuality designated as a mental illness in *DSM-I*[3]	1952	28–51	7–27	0–6
Mandated firing of federal and civilian homosexual employees[4]	1953	29–52	8–28	0–7
McCarthy hearings broadcast on television	1954	30–53	9–29	0–8
Illinois becomes first state to decriminalize sodomy[5]	1962	38–61	17–37	0–16
Civil Rights Act	1964	40–63	19–39	0–18
Stonewall riots[5]	1969	45–68	24–44	5–23
Homosexuality as a pathology removed from *DSM-II-R*[1]	1973	49–72	28–48	9–27
Gender identity differentiated from homosexuality in *DSM-III*[1]	1980	56–79	35–55	16–34
159 cases reported of what would come to be known as HIV/AIDS[6]	1981	57–80	36–56	17–35

(continued)

Table 7.1: Continued

Historical Event	Year of Event	Cohorts		
		Greatest Generation (born 1901–24)	*Silent Generation (born 1925–45)*	*Baby Boom Generation (born 1946–64)*
		Cohort ages in years when experienced		
Total U.S. AIDS cases reported: 733,374; died: 429,825[6]	1989	65–88	44–64	25–43
"Don't Ask, Don't Tell" military policy enacted[5]	1994	70–93	49–69	30–48
First protease inhibitors approved; HIV/AIDS soon becomes chronic[6]	1995	71–94	50–70	31–49
Defense of Marriage Act (DOMA) enacted[5]	1996	72–95	51–71	32–50
US Supreme Court rules sodomy laws unconstitutional[5]	2003	79–102	58–78	39–57
First baby boomers turn 65 years old "Don't Ask, Don't Tell" military policy ends[5]	2011	87–110	66–86	47–65
Supreme Court strikes down Section III of DOMA[7] Gender Identity Disorder becomes Gender Dysphoria in *DSM–5*[8]	2013	89–112	68–88	49–67
Supreme Court rules bans on same-sex marriage unconstitutional; full marriage equality state and federal[9]	2015	91–114	70–90	51–69

[1]Institute of Medicine 2011.
[2]Penhallurick 2010.
[3]Canaday 2009.
[4]Johnson 2004.
[5]Carpenter 2012.
[6]AVERT 2015.
[7]Liptak 2013.
[8]American Psychiatric Association 2013.
[9]*Obergefell v. Hodges* 2015.

of Mental Disorders (DSM-II-R) in 1973 (Silverstein 2009). The youngest of the Baby Boom generation also came of age during the early years of the AIDS pandemic in the United States, as LGBT communities organized to care for one another. According to findings from a Gallup poll (Gates and Newport 2012), approximately 1.9 percent of the surviving 30 million members of the Greatest and Silent Generations and 2.6 percent of the 76.5 million members of the Baby Boom generation identify as LGBT.

In order to investigate the complexity in the relationships between risk and protective factors and physical and mental health of LGBT older adults across age groups, we utilize the Health Equity Promotion Model (Fredriksen-Goldsen et al. 2014). The Health Equity Promotion Model recognizes disparities in health and highlights the need to promote the full health potential of LGBT older adults. This model illustrates how social positions and structural and societal risks, such as discrimination and victimization, intersect with adverse and health-promoting mechanisms to influence health outcomes in LGBT communities. The Health Equity Promotion Model expands upon earlier conceptualizations by taking into consideration how intersectionality of social positions, age group differences, and historical and cultural contexts over the life course influence both positive and negative health outcomes. LGBT older adults share some similar risk and protective factors with older adults in the general population, while they also experience unique strengths and challenges due to the marginalization of their sexual and gender identities. The Health Equity Promotion Model accounts for LGBT-specific factors that span individual, community, and societal levels, such as the disclosure of sexual and/or gender identity, internalized stigma, victimization, discrimination, diverse social networks, and social integration into the LGBT community, which have been documented to influence health and well-being in the LGBT population (Fredriksen-Goldsen et al. 2013a; 2013b). This model is a logical progression in LGBT health research; it provides an actionable framework that moves beyond documenting factors associated with LGBT health disparities by highlighting key leverage points for intervention and prevention efforts.

Based on a health equity perspective, in this chapter we draw from the extant literature and findings from *Caring and Aging with Pride* (Fredriksen-Goldsen et al. 2011; 2013a; 2013b; 2013c; 2014; 2015) to examine health disparities among LGBT older adults and explore how structural and environmental risks intersect with personal and social resources and health behaviors. We also highlight the importance of understanding age group differences as they relate to the risks and opportunities experienced by LGBT older adults. In conclusion, the next steps for policy, services, and research are outlined to address the growing needs of LGBT older adults and their families. By examining the health and well-being and the risks and resilience of LGBT older adults, this chapter addresses the increasing heterogeneity in our growing, older adult population.

HEALTH DISPARITIES

Healthy People 2020 aims to reduce population health disparities and improve quality of life and, for the first time, LGBT people have been recognized as an at-risk population in national health initiatives. The critical need to expand health disparities research related to sexual orientation and gender identity has been identified in order to make informed decisions about health-related practices and policies (Institute of Medicine 2011; U.S. Department of Health and Human Services 2011). Health disparities are defined as preventable differences in population health that are attributable to environmental, economic, and social disadvantage associated with characteristics such as socioeconomic status, race/ethnicity, gender, sexual orientation, and gender identity (American Public Health Association 2008).

Most early LGBT-related health research focused on mental health outcomes (Fredriksen-Goldsen and Muraco 2010). This is understandable because LGBT people have a long history of being pathologized; it was only four decades ago that homosexuality was declassified by the American Psychiatric Association from being a "sociopathic personality disorder" (Silverstein 2009). Even today, gender variance continues to be stigmatized in the *DSM-5* (American Psychiatric Association 2013), with gender identity disorder reformulated as *gender dysphoria*, which is diagnosed as a psychological disorder only if its presence causes clinically significant distress.

Caring and Aging with Pride is the first federally funded project investigating LGBT aging, health, and well-being. In the first phase of the project, data from the 2003–10 Washington State Behavioral Risk Factor Surveillance System (WA-BRFSS) were analyzed (n = 96,992) to examine health disparities among lesbian, gay, and bisexual adults aged 50 and older. Next, to understand distinct risks and protective factors associated with LGBT older adult health, we distributed questionnaires via 11 community-based agencies' mailing lists from June to November of 2010. To be eligible to participate in the study, potential respondents had to be 50 years of age or older and identify as LGBT. A demographically diverse sample of LGBT adults 50–95 years old, with a majority over the age of 60, was obtained (2,560 completed questionnaires that met study criteria were returned, with a response rate of 63 percent of mailed surveys).

The results of the study are yielding important insights into the lives of LGBT older adults and improving our understanding of the full range of health outcomes, as well as health disparities related to sexual orientation and gender identity. For example, lesbian, gay, and bisexual adults aged 50 and older, when compared with heterosexuals of a similar age, have an elevated risk of functional limitations and mental distress and some adverse health behaviors, even when controlling for age, income, and education (Fredriksen-Goldsen et al. 2013c).

While the term LGBT is often used in research, we found distinct variations and unique needs among these subgroups. Older lesbian and bisexual women have higher rates of disability and an elevated risk of obesity and cardiovascular disease compared with older heterosexual women; gay and bisexual older men are at higher risk of poor health and living alone than older heterosexual men (Fredriksen-Goldsen et al. 2013c). Using pooled data from the 2003, 2005, and 2007 California Health Interview Survey (CHIS) of adults 50–70 years old, Wallace and colleagues (2011) also found that lesbian and bisexual women and gay and bisexual men were more likely to live alone compared with heterosexuals and had a greater risk for disability, poor general health, and psychological distress; gay and bisexual older men were also at higher risk for hypertension and diabetes than older heterosexual men. In addition, transgender older adult participants had elevated rates of poor physical health, disability, and depression compared with nontransgender LGB older adult participants in *Caring and Aging with Pride* (Fredriksen-Goldsen et al. 2013a).

Different cohorts experience different historical eras and events, and have differential risks and access to resources. In our *Caring and Aging with Pride* study, we cannot disentangle age, cohort, and period effects because of the cross-sectional design, and although longitudinal designs are not able to fully distinguish between age, cohort, and period effects (Glenn 2005), we can nonetheless begin to examine age group differences among midlife and older LGBT adults as a starting point. Health outcomes among LGBT older adults vary by distinct age groups and these health-related patterns by age are similar to those found in the general adult population (Blanchflower and Oswald 2008; Blanchflower and Oswald 2009). In general, LGBT older adults aged 80 and older report poorer physical health-related quality of life than younger age groups, including those aged 50-64 and 65-79, and those aged 65-79 report better mental health-related quality of life than those aged 50-64 and those 80 and older (Fredriksen-Goldsen et al. 2015). However, we find a different configuration of resources and risks by distinct age groups (Fredriksen-Goldsen et al. 2011).

RESILIENCE AND RESOURCES

Despite a long history of discrimination and marginalization, most LGBT older adults experience good health. In *Caring and Aging with Pride*, we found that approximately three-fourths of LGBT older adult participants report good or excellent health. The personal and social resources available to LGBT older adults, such as disclosure, marriage, partnership, and social support, likely offset some of the challenges older LGBT adults face. Resources are important because, as protective factors, they may buffer against adversity and risk and can be found at individual, family, and community levels.

Disclosure of sexual orientation and gender identity is generally associated with both psychological (Meyer 2003) and social well-being (Kertzner et al. 2009), in part through providing access to social support from other LGBT people and a potential sense of "belongingness." At the individual level, disclosure of sexual orientation or gender identity can buffer the effects of internalized stigma and foster psychological well-being (Meyer 2003). Disclosure to one's primary care physicians also supports good health, as it allows for important discussion about sexual health (American Medical Association 2013). Disclosure may also have a more direct effect on health through modulating important processes of immune system functioning (Kemeny and Schedlowski 2007; Meyer 2003).

Partners and spouses provide a broad range of physical, emotional, and economic benefits to older adults in the general population. Evidence suggests that these benefits generally extend to same-sex couples (Wienke and Hill 2009), especially when such relationships are supported by important others, like family members (Blair and Holmberg 2008). Based on data in *Caring and Aging with Pride*, having a same-sex partner was associated with better general health and less depressive symptomology as compared with being single, after controlling for gender, age, education, income, sexuality, and relationship duration (Williams and Fredriksen-Goldsen 2014). Interestingly, length of time of the relationship did not significantly influence the association between relationship status and health among LGBT older adult participants. However, the specific nature of same-sex relationships may be important. For example, legal marriage but not domestic partnership has a protective effect on midlife and older gay men's health (Wight et al. 2012).

Social networks and social support, reflecting both the structure and function of social relationships, have also been found to attenuate the risk of depression, disability, and poor physical health among LGBT older adults (Fredriksen-Goldsen et al. 2013a; 2013b). The LGBT older adult participants in our study report, on average, a large social network with moderate levels of social support; lesbians and bisexual women report higher levels of social support compared with gay and bisexual men (Kim, Fredriksen-Goldsen, and Hoy-Ellis 2011). In addition to social network size and support, being connected to LGBT communities may provide important resources (Meyer 2003). At the individual level, LGBT people may be able to more positively reappraise their stigmatized identities by making meaningful comparisons with "like" others rather than negative comparisons with heterosexuals. Identification with other LGBT people is also important in the development of a positive group identity. Being able to connect with other LGBT people also provides other important social resources such as having supportive others to turn to when one experiences discrimination (Meyer 2003). In addition to conferring a sense of belonging, which in and of itself has protective effects on mental health (Hagerty et al. 1992), older lesbians, gays, and bisexuals who regularly engage with other lesbians, gays, and bisexuals are less likely to experience loneliness than those who are not (Fokkema and Kuyper 2009).

Like older adults in the general population, the LGBT older age groups in our study, 65–79, and 80 and older, had levels of social support comparable to those aged 50–64 but had smaller social network sizes and lower levels of community connectedness (Fredriksen-Goldsen et al. 2015). Interestingly, in our study, those aged 80 and older are understandably more likely to be receiving informal care than their younger counterparts in the 50–64 and 65–79 age groups, yet they were equally likely to be providing informal care to others. This is important because, in some contexts, providing social support may actually be more beneficial to well-being than receiving it (Thomas 2010).

ADVERSITY AND RISKS

Compared with older adults in general, LGBT older adults experience some unique risk factors that are associated with their mental and physical health. Experiences of discrimination and victimization based on sexual orientation and gender identity have consistently been linked to poor physical and mental health (Fredriksen-Goldsen et al. 2013a; 2013b). Experiences of discrimination and the larger structural context can lead to the "social patterning of stress," which not only can result in less availability of resources that buffer stress but can result in greater levels of stress itself (Meyer, Schwartz, and Frost 2008). Stressors can be acute and objective, such as actual experiences of discrimination and victimization; they can also be chronic and more subjective, such as the lived experience of heterosexism by LGBT individuals (Hendricks and Testa 2012; Meyer 2003).

Stigma, a constellation of experiences that include stereotyping, social exclusion, labeling, discrimination, and loss of status that directly result from marginalization due to minority status are considered by some as a "fundamental cause" of population health disparities (Hatzenbuehler, Phelan, and Link 2013). Such risk factors are associated with multiple health outcomes, resulting in limited access to social, economic, and environmental resources that either circumvent risks or attenuate poor health outcomes (Hatzenbuehler et al. 2013). "Inequities in health systematically put groups of people who are already socially disadvantaged ... at further disadvantage with respect to their health; health is essential to ... overcoming other effects of social disadvantage" (Braveman and Gruskin 2003: 254).

This is particularly relevant to LGBT older adults as they are already socially disadvantaged in a heterosexist society (Meyer 2003), and the health disparities that they experience make it more challenging to address their social disadvantage. In addition to its external manifestations (e.g., discrimination and victimization), stigma can also be internalized with additional negative consequences for health. In our study, we found that internalized stigma is linked to poor physical and mental health outcomes among LGBT older adults (Fredriksen-Goldsen et al. 2013a; 2013b). Because of the recursive nature of the relationship between stigma and expressions of societal heterosexism, for example, victimization and discrimination, with the presence of one increasing the risk for the other (Wolkowitz, Reus, and Mellon 2011), it likely increases the risk of both physical and mental health disparities.

LGBT older adults, as a result of their sexual orientation and/or gender identity, are also often excluded from full participation in society. According to the World Health Organization (WHO), adverse structural contexts can also result in social exclusion, which in turn increases the risk for disease, especially cardiovascular disease (CVD), disability, substance abuse, and social isolation (Wilkinson and Marmot 2003). Social isolation itself has consistently been linked with increased risk of CVD and consequent death, especially among the most isolated (Arthur 2006). Although living alone does not necessarily mean one is socially isolated, it does significantly increase the risk (Cacioppo and Hawkley 2003). Older gay and bisexual men are at particular risk of living alone, which may place them at higher risk of social isolation (Fredriksen-Goldsen et al. 2013c; Wallace et al. 2011). In addition, we have found that gay and bisexual men are at elevated risk of loneliness (Fredriksen-Goldsen et al. 2011).

When examining such risks by age group among LGBT older adults, the degree of internalized stigma is higher for the oldest age groups, those 80 and older, yet lifetime discrimination and degree of identity disclosure is lower than in the 50–64 and 65–79 groups. Since the older age groups are less likely to disclose their sexual orientation, it may be protective in the sense that it resulted in fewer discriminatory experiences in an earlier, more hostile society. Interestingly, the 50–64-year-old age group reports significantly higher levels of loneliness than both the 65–79 and 80 and older age groups, which increases their risk for social isolation and its consequent risks.

Health Behaviors

Health behaviors can adversely affect or promote health. Many chronic conditions are linked to the lack of regular physical activity, excessive drinking, tobacco use, and poor nutrition (CDC and National Center for Chronic Disease Prevention and Health Promotion 2010). In our study, we found that most LGBT older adult participants engage in regular physical activity (Fredriksen-Goldsen et al. 2011) at rates similar to older adults in the general population (Fredriksen-Goldsen et al. 2013c). Similar to older adults in the general population, the lack of physical activity has been found to be an independent predictor of depression, disability, and poor general health among older lesbian, gay, and bisexual adult participants (Fredriksen-Goldsen et al. 2013b), and is significantly associated with better physical and mental health outcomes among older transgender adults (Fredriksen-Goldsen et al. 2013a).

Tobacco use and excessive drinking are leading causes of preventable morbidity and mortality in the United States (CDC 2010). Lesbian, gay, and bisexual older adults have higher rates of both smoking and excessive drinking than heterosexual older adults (Fredriksen-Goldsen et al. 2013c). Substance abuse refers to both the use of illicit substances and the use of legal substances in a manner not prescribed by a physician. Because of age-related physiological changes, substance abuse may have an even stronger effect on the health and functioning of older adults (Substance Abuse and Mental Health Services Administration 2010). A similar trend has been observed among lesbian, gay, and bisexual midlife adults who appear to have more serious problems with substance abuse compared with previous generations (Jessup and Dibble 2012). Approximately 5 percent of older adults in the general population reported past-year illicit substance use (Substance Abuse and Mental Health Services Administration and Office of Applied Studies 2009). In our study, 12 percent of the LGBT older adult participants reported using nonprescribed drugs within the previous 12 months, and another 9 percent took prescription drugs in a manner other than prescribed by their physician, including both over and under use (Fredriksen-Goldsen et al. 2011).

LGBT midlife and older adults also experience some unique barriers to health care. Eight percent fear accessing health care inside the LGBT community and nearly twice as many (15 percent) fear accessing health care in the general community. In fact, 13 percent reported they received inferior health care or were denied health care as a result of their sexual orientation or gender identity. In addition, 7 percent of participants have been unable to see a doctor or obtain needed medications because of cost. Although older lesbian and bisexual women are less likely than older heterosexual women to have had a mammogram during the preceding year, they are more likely to have been tested for HIV; older gay and bisexual men are also more likely to have been tested for HIV and vaccinated for influenza compared with older heterosexual men (Fredriksen-Goldsen et al. 2013c).

When examining differences in health behaviors among LGBT older adults by age group, we see trends similar to the general population. Among LGBT adults, the older age groups, those aged 65–79 and 80 and older, are less likely to engage in substance use and more likely to receive a routine health check-up compared with the 50–64 age group. While these older age groups are also less likely to engage in vigorous physical activities, they continue to engage in wellness activities at the same rate as the younger age groups.

BACKGROUND CHARACTERISTICS

The sociodemographic profile of LGBT older adults, including gender, race/ethnicity, income, and education, are associated with physical and mental health similar to older adults in the general population. For a full description of the original *Caring and Aging with Pride* sample; extensive tables showing risk, protective, and other factors; and significance-testing by sexual orientation, gender, gender identity, age group, and race/ethnicity, see Fredriksen-Goldsen et al. (2011). In the study, women had poorer physical and mental health and higher rates of disability than men (Fredriksen-Goldsen et al. 2011). On the other hand, they also evidence some additional resources, including higher levels of disclosure and social support combined with lower levels of discrimination and victimization. Compared with men, women in this study also report lower levels of stigma, are more connected to their communities, and are more likely to participate in spiritual or religious activities. In comparisons by gender identity, transgender older adult participants have poorer physical and mental health than their nontransgender counterparts, even after controlling for age, income, and education (Fredriksen-Goldsen et al. 2011). They also experience higher levels of discrimination, victimization, and stigma, and have lower levels of disclosure, social support, and community connectedness. Yet, they are more likely to participate in spiritual or religious activities, which may be linked to race and ethnicity, since a significant proportion of the transgender participants in the study are Hispanic (Fredriksen-Goldsen et al. 2011).

When examining differences by race and ethnicity, we also found that, compared with non-Hispanic white LGBT older adults, both LGBT Hispanic and Native American older adults are at elevated risk of poor physical and mental health outcomes, combined with higher levels of disability, victimization, discrimination, and stigma as well as less access to resources such as income and other types of support.

Several recent studies have documented that sexual minorities have higher levels of education, but equivalent or lower levels of income. Despite significantly higher levels of education and higher rates of employment, older lesbian and bisexual women's incomes are similar to those of older heterosexual women (Fredriksen-Goldsen et al. 2013c). However, older gay and bisexual men have significantly higher levels of education and similar rates of employment to older heterosexual men, but their incomes do not differ (Fredriksen-Goldsen et al. 2013c). A meta-analysis by The Williams Institute indicated that equally qualified gay and bisexual men have incomes that are 10 percent to 32 percent less than heterosexual men (Badgett et al. 2007), which will have important repercussions for retirement and aging.

Moving Forward: Implications for Services, Policy, and Research

LGBT older adults are a health disparate population. It is imperative to identify and establish mechanisms of risk and protection that may influence their health trajectories in ways that may differ from the general older adult population, and to recognize that their risk profiles may differ by age and cohort as well as other sociodemographic characteristics, such as gender. Because structural and societal risks and individual health behaviors interact through a variety of mechanisms, a variety of approaches are necessary to promote health equity for LGBT older adults.

Both upstream and downstream interventions are needed. Since smoking, excessive drinking, poor nutrition, and lack of physical activity significantly increase the risk for developing chronic health conditions and poor health (CDC and National Center for Chronic Disease Prevention and Health Promotion 2010), they are undoubtedly important points for intervention and prevention efforts. Yet, it is also necessary to understand how structural barriers may thwart such efforts. For example, LGBT adults often use tobacco, alcohol, and other substances to alleviate stress (Jessup and Dibble 2012). Supportive social networks can also be instrumental in making positive behavioral changes (Wilkinson and Marmot 2003), such as smoking cessation and substance use reduction. Targeted efforts to bolster the social networks of LGBT adults aged 50-64 years old may be particularly germane, as they smoke, drink, and engage in illicit substance use at higher rates; report more loneliness; and have higher levels of suicidal ideation than their LGBT peers aged 65 and older. In addition to individual interventions, community-level interventions to address social exclusion are needed (Wilkinson and Marmot 2003). At the very time in their lives when LGBT older adults are likely to experience an increased need for community-based supports, they may be less likely to access them out of fear of discrimination and victimization. Aging and health services need to address prejudice and bias among both staff and clientele. The U.S. Department of Health and Human Services has issued directives clarifying that the Affordable Care Act (ACA) prohibits any agency, service, or program that receives federal funding from discriminating on the basis of sexual orientation or gender identity under the "sex" and "sex stereotyping" prohibitions of Title VII of the 1964 Civil Rights Act (Bradford and Mayer 2014).

LGBT organizations should also engage in targeted educational outreach efforts to ensure that LGBT older adults are aware of their rights and mechanisms for redress under the ACA. Actively soliciting LGBT older adults to serve on community advisory boards and as consumers can also be an effective step toward addressing the need to create culturally responsive aging and health services. In addition, in-depth and systematic reviews of agency policies and procedures can help identify those that exclude and marginalize LGBT older adults. It is essential that intake forms and all other materials be reviewed and modified as necessary to include questions regarding sexual orientation and gender identity as part of gathering sociodemographic information.

Just as mainstream aging agencies need to recognize and adapt to the reality that they may be excluding *LGBT* older adults, services and programs in LGBT communities must recognize and address the fact that they may not be creating a welcoming environment for LGBT *older adults* and their families. For example, mainstream aging agencies should assess whether the images in their printed materials (e.g., fliers, newsletters) and in their lobbies, waiting areas, and offices (e.g., magazines, artwork) depict LGBT couples and individuals and/or symbols that are easily recognizable and meaningful to LGBT people (e.g., the rainbow flag). Such visual signs and symbols are visual cues that LGBT older adults are recognized and will be affirmed. Services and programs in LGBT communities should not only examine whether older LGBT adults are depicted in their materials but also how their services and programs could be successfully expanded or revised to specifically address the needs of LGBT adults. Programs that foster social networks and physical activities among LGBT older adults are needed in mainstream aging agencies and in LGBT communities. In addition to providing direct mental and physical health benefits, these practices also represent upstream interventions in that they are steps toward interrupting the stigma of heterosexism and ageism, both of which contribute to health disparities.

Because LGBT older adults generally provide informal care to and receive informal care from one another (Muraco and Fredriksen-Goldsen 2011), services and programs must be tailored to support the full range of caregiving relationships, which may be particularly challenging as these relationships may not be legal or biological in nature, in contrast to those of the general older adult population. This not only places additional burdens on LGBT older adult caregivers and care recipients in terms of ability to make legal decisions regarding care, but may also deny important direct and ancillary benefits that other caregivers and those receiving care enjoy. Furthermore, LGBT adults aged 80 and older are just as likely as their younger peers to be providing informal care, and are more likely to be receiving care. Hence, care planning for LGBT older adults, especially those aged 80 and older, should assess any need for respite care when simultaneously assessing other types of care needed. The LGBT community has a rich history of advocating for and supporting some of its most vulnerable and disenfranchised members, as was evident during the height of the U.S. AIDS pandemic. If similarly applied, such political activism and community organizing would directly benefit the older members of the LGBT community and could also provide a model of caring that would benefit the general population, especially in light of the projected rapid expansion in both size and diversity of the older adult population in the coming decades.

Socially integrated relationships appear to play a role in better health for LGB midlife and older adults (Williams and Fredriksen-Goldsen 2014). Yet, not all LGBT older adults are able to participate fully in society. On June 26, 2015 in *Obergefell v. Hodges* (2015), the Supreme Court of the United States ruled that same-sex couples have the constitutional right to full legal marriage and that all states must recognize those marriages as such. However, legal marriage in and of itself does not bestow full protection under the law. Explicit and comprehensive protections for LGBT people in employment and public accommodations are still lacking in 31 states (Human Rights Campaign 2015). There are no definitive, blanket federal protections against discrimination in public accommodations based on sexual orientation or gender identity. Federal employees and contractors are barred from discriminating based on sexual orientation or gender identity, yet many federal entities, such as the Department of Housing and Urban Development and the Equal Employment Opportunity Commission, are interpreting sexual orientation and gender identity as protected classes under the "sex" and "sex stereotypes" prohibitions in Title VII of the 1964 Civil Rights Act. The Equality Act, H.R. 3185 that would amend the Civil Rights Act to include sexual orientation and gender identity was introduced in 2015, but currently stands almost no chance of being passed. There is a growing backlash against LGBT people in the wake of marriage equality. Increasingly, legislation is being proposed and passed across the country that would exempt individuals and groups in both the public and private sectors from laws and statutes that do protect LGBT people under the guise of religious freedom. Currently, 25 states have pending or enacted bills that allow legal discrimination against LGBT people based on religious beliefs, including refusing to recognize or perform same-sex marriages, provide health-care services, or allow LGBT people to adopt or provide foster care to children (American Civil Liberties Union 2015). Due to a long history of institutionalized discrimination and the ongoing discourse around religious freedom, it will be some time before LGBT Americans have the same legal rights as heterosexuals.

Although health disparities have been documented among LGBT people, large gaps remain in our knowledge about LGBT health and well-being. To date, there are limited data available to monitor health in these communities. In fact, most health surveys do not include sexual orientation or gender identity questions. One important step has been made with the inclusion of a sexual orientation question recently added to the National Health Interview Survey. Other national surveys such as the Health and Retirement Study (HRS), the American Community Survey (ACS), and the Behavioral Risk Factor Surveillance Surveys (BRFSS) should routinely include questions related to both sexual orientation and gender identity for all participants. What little is known about transgender health comes primarily from large community-based surveys (Fredriksen-Goldsen et al. 2013a; Grant et al. 2011), which means that findings are not generalizable. Routinely gathering sexual orientation and gender identity data in medical records will also significantly enhance our knowledge of LGBT health (Institute of Medicine 2011). In particular, research is needed that better differentiates the unique experiences and needs of older compared with younger transgender adults.

There is every indication that LGBT older adults are just as heterogeneous as their heterosexual counterparts and research should reflect this. Rather than treating age solely as a confounder, researchers should consider it as an independent variable. Studies are needed to further elaborate similarities and differences *within* LGBT older adult cohorts (e.g., 50–64, 65–79, 80 and older) and *between* their respective younger LGBT and midlife and older LGBT cohorts (e.g., younger than 50 vs. 50 and older), and their heterosexual peers of similar age. We also need longitudinal studies that follow LGBT people from adolescence through old age, as today's younger LGBT people are tomorrow's midlife and older LGBT adults.

Although resilient, LGBT older adults are an at-risk population, evidencing significant health disparities. Additional research and community-based interventions are needed to promote health equity and the full health potential of LGBT midlife and older adults. While *Caring and Aging with Pride* provides important new information about the health, aging, and well-being of LGBT midlife and older adults, it is cross-sectional and the findings are not generalizable. Although longitudinal studies cannot completely disentangle age, period, and cohort effects, they are needed in order to work toward clarifying the temporal order between risk and protective factors and to better understand the full range of health outcomes and health trajectories in these communities. Such studies will be vital in disentangling age, period, and cohort effects. Most studies to date have relied heavily on self-reported measures, with no functional or biological measures. The next wave of LGBT health and aging studies must more comprehensively address the diversity and subgroups within these communities as well as identify underlying mechanisms of risk to design and test the effectiveness of culturally appropriate interventions. Such efforts will affirm LGBT older adults, and enhance our understanding of diversity in our aging world.

REFERENCES

American Civil Liberties Union. 2015. Anti-LGBT Religious Refusals Legislation across the Country, Washington, DC. Retrieved October 30, 2015 (https://www.aclu.org/anti-lgbt-religious-refusals-legislation-across-country).

American Medical Association. 2013. AMA Policies on GLBT Issues: H-65.973 Health Care Disparities in Same-Sex Partner Households. Washington, DC: American Medical Association. Retrieved November 1, 2013 (http://www.ama-assn.org//ama/pub/about-ama/our-people/member-groups-sections/glbt-advisory-committee/ama-policy-regarding-sexual-orientation.page).

American Psychiatric Association. 2013. *Diagnostic and Statistical Manual of Mental Disorders: DSM-5*. Arlington, VA: American Psychiatric Publishing.

American Public Health Association. 2008. Health Disparities: The Basics. Washington, DC: American Public Health Association. Retrieved June 20, 2013 (http://www.apha.org/NR/rdonlyres/54C4CC4D-E86D-479A-BABB-5D42B3FDC8BD/0/HlthDisparty_Primer_FINAL.pdf).

Arthur, Heather M. 2006. "Depression, Isolation, Social Support, and Cardiovascular Disease in Older Adults." *Journal of Cardiovascular Nursing* 21(5 Suppl 1):S2-7.

AVERT. 2015. "History of HIV & AIDS Overview" *Global Information and Advice on AIDS*, Brighton, UK. Retrieved October 30, 2015 (http://www.avert.org/professionals/history-hiv-aids/overview).

Badgett, M. V. Lee, Holning Lau, Brad Sears, and Deborah Ho. 2007. *Bias in the Workplace: Consistent Evidence of Sexual Orientation and Gender Identity Discrimination*. Los Angeles: The Williams Institute.

Blair, Karen L. and Dianne Holmberg. 2008. "Perceived Social Network Support and Well-Being in Same-Sex Versus Mixed-Sex Romantic Relationships." *Journal of Social and Personal Relationships* 25(5):769-91.

Blanchflower, David G. and Andrew J. Oswald. 2008. "Is Well-Being U-Shaped over the Life Cycle?" *Social Science & Medicine* 66(8):1733-49.

Blanchflower, David G. and Andrew J. Oswald. 2009. "The U-Shape without Controls: A Response to Glenn." *Social Science and Medicine* 69(4):486-88.

Bradford, Judith and Kenneth Mayer. 2014. "Public Comment on Notice of Proposed Rule Making RIN 0991-AB92, the Voluntary 2015 Edition Electronic Health Record Certification Criteria; Interoperability Updates and Regulatory Improvements, Including 2017 Certified EHR Technology (CEHRT) Proposals," edited by National Coordinator for Health Information Technology. Boston, MA: The Fenway Institute.

Braveman, Paula and Sofia Gruskin. 2003. "Theory and Methods: Defining Equity in Health." *Journal of Epidemiology and Community Health* 57:254-58.

Cacioppo, John T. and Louise C. Hawkley. 2003. "Social Isolation and Health, with an Emphasis on Underlying Mechanisms." *Perspectives in Biology and Medicine* 46(3 Suppl):S39–52.

Canaday, Margot. 2009. *The Straight State: Sexuality and Citizenship in Twentieth-Century America*. Princeton, NJ: Princeton University Press.

Carpenter, Dale. 2012. *Flagrant Conduct: The Story of Lawrence V. Texas*. New York: W.W. Norton.

Centers for Disease Control and Prevention. 2010. "*Tobacco Use: Smoking & Second-Hand Smoke.*" *Vital Signs*. Atlanta, GA: Centers for Disease Control and Prevention. Retrieved December 12, 2013 (http://www.cdc.gov/vitalsigns/tobaccouse/smoking/).

Centers for Disease Control and Prevention and National Center for Chronic Disease Prevention and Health Promotion. 2010. "*Chronic Diseases and Health Promotion.*" Atlanta, GA: Centers for Disease Control and Prevention and National Center for Chronic Disease Prevention and Health Promotion. Retrieved December 13, 2011 (http://www.cdc.gov/chronicdisease/overview/index.htm).

Centers for Disease Control and Prevention. 2011. "CDC Health Disparities and Inequalities Report—United States, 2011." *MMWR 2011* 60(Suppl):1–116.

Fokkema, Tineke and Lisette Kuyper. 2009. "The Relation between Social Embeddedness and Loneliness among Older Lesbian, Gay, and Bisexual Adults in the Netherlands." *Archives of Sexual Behavior* 38:264–75.

Fredriksen-Goldsen, Karen I. and Anna Muraco. 2010. "Aging and Sexual Orientation: A 25-Year Review of the Literature." *Research on Aging* 32(3):372–413.

Fredriksen-Goldsen, Karen I., Hyun-Jun Kim, Charles A. Emlet, Anna Muraco, Elena A. Erosheva, Charles P. Hoy-Ellis, Jayn Goldsen, and Heidi Petry. 2011. *The Aging and Health Report: Disparities and Resilience among Lesbian, Gay, Bisexual, and Transgender Older Adults*. Seattle, WA: Institute for Multigenerational Health.

Fredriksen-Goldsen, Karen I., Loree Cook-Daniels, Hyun-Jun Kim, Elena A. Erosheva, Charles A. Emlet, Charles P. Hoy-Ellis, Jayn Goldsen, and Anna Muraco. 2013a. "Physical and Mental Health of Transgender Older Adults: An At-Risk and Underserved Population." *The Gerontologist* 54(3):488–500.

Fredriksen-Goldsen, Karen I., Charles A. Emlet, Hyun-Jun Kim, Anna Muraco, Elena A. Erosheva, Jayn Goldsen, and Charles P. Hoy-Ellis. 2013b. "The Physical and Mental Health of Lesbian, Gay Male, and Bisexual (LGB) Older Adults: The Role of Key Health Indicators and Risk and Protective Factors." *The Gerontologist* 53(4):664–75.

Fredriksen-Goldsen, Karen I., Hyun-Jun Kim, Susan E. Barkan, Anna Muraco, and Charles P. Hoy-Ellis. 2013c. "Health Disparities among Lesbian, Gay Male and Bisexual Older Adults: Results from a Population-Based Study." *American Journal of Public Health* 103(10):1802–9.

Fredriksen-Goldsen, Karen I., Jane M. Simoni, Karina L. Walters, Hyun-Jun Kim, Keren Lehavot, Joyce Yang, Charles P. Hoy-Ellis, and Anna M. Muraco. 2014. "The Health Equity Promotion Model: Reconceptualization of Lesbian, Gay, Bisexual and Transgender (LGBT) Health Disparities." *American Journal of Orthopsychiatry* 84(6):653–63.

Fredriksen-Goldsen, Karen I., Hyun-Jun Kim, Cheng-Shi Shiu, Jayn Goldsen, and Charles E. Emlet. 2015. "Successful Aging among LGBT Older Adults: Physical and Mental Health-Related Quality of Life by Age Group." *The Gerontologist* 55(1):154–68.

Fredriksen-Goldsen, Karen I., and Kim, Hyun-Jun. 2017. "The science of conducting research with LGBT older adults—An introduction to Aging with Pride: National Health, Aging and Sexuality/Gender Study (NHAS)." *The Gerontologist* 57(S1): S1–S14.

Gates, Gary J. and Frank Newport. 2012. Special Report: 3.4% of U.S. Adults Identify as LGBT. Inaugural Gallup Findings Based on More Than 120,000 Interviews. Princeton, NJ: Gallup Polls. Retrieved October 23, 2012 (http://www.gallup.com/poll/158066/special-report-adults-identify-lgbt.aspx).

Glenn, Norval D. 2005. *Cohort Analysis.* Thousand Oaks, CA: Sage Publications.

Grant, Jaime M., Lisa A. Mottet, Justin Tanis, Jack Harrison, Jody L. Herman, and Mara Keisling. 2011. "Injustice at Every Turn: A Report of the National Transgender Discrimination Survey." Washington, DC: National Center for Transgender Equality and National Gay and Lesbian Task Force.

Hagerty, Bonnie M. K., Judith Lynch-Sauer, Kathleen L. Patusky, Maria Bouwsema, and Peggy Collier. 1992. "Sense of Belonging: A Vital Mental Health Concept." *Archives of Psychiatric Nursing* 6(3):172–77.

Hatzenbuehler, Mark L., Jo C. Phelan, and Bruce G. Link. 2013. "Stigma as a Fundamental Cause of Population Health Inequalities." *American Journal of Public Health* 103(5):813–21.

Hendricks, Michael L. and Rylan J. Testa. 2012. "A Conceptual Framework for Clinical Work with Transgender and Gender Noncomforming Clients: An Adaptation of the Minority Stress Model." *Professional Psychology: Research and Practice* 43(5):460–67.

Human Rights Campaign. 2015. "*Why The Equality Act?*" *Resource*, Washington, DC: Human Rights Campaign. Retrieved October 29, 2015 (http://www.hrc.org//resources/entry/why-the-equality-act).

Institute of Medicine. 2011. *The Health of Lesbian, Gay, Bisexual, and Transgender People: Building a Foundation for Better Understanding.* Washington, DC: The National Academies Press.

Jessup, Martha A. and Suzanne L. Dibble. 2012. "Unmet Mental Health and Substance Abuse Treatment Needs of Sexual Minority Elders." *Journal of Homosexuality* 59(5):656–74.

Johnson, David K. 2004. *The Lavender Scare: The Cold War Persecution of Gays and Lesbians in the Federal Government.* Chicago: University of Chicago Press.

Kemeny, Margaret E. and Manfred Schedlowski. 2007. "Understanding the Interaction between Psychosocial Stress and Immune-Related Diseases: A Stepwise Progression." *Brain, Behavior & Immunity* 21(8):1009–18.

Kertzner, Robert. M., Ilan H. Meyer, David M. Frost, and Michael J. Stirratt. 2009. "Social and Psychological Well-Being in Lesbians, Gay Men, and Bisexuals: The Effects of Race, Gender, Age, and Sexual Identity." *American Journal of Orthopsychiatry* 79(4):500–10.

Kim, Hyun-Jun, Karen I. Fredriksen-Goldsen, and Charles P. Hoy-Ellis. 2011. "Living Arrangement and Relationship Status as Predictors of Health among Older LGBT Adults: The Impact of Social Support." in *The Gerontological Society of America's 64th Annual Scientific Meeting*, Boston, MA.

Liptak, A. 2013, June 26, "Supreme Court Bolsters Gay Marriage with Two Major Rulings." *The New York Times.*, New York. Retrieved July 8, 2013 (http://www.nytimes.com/2013/06/27/us/politics/supreme-court-gay-marriage.html?pagewanted=all&_r=0).

Meyer, Ilan. H. 2003. "Prejudice, Social Stress, and Mental Health in Lesbian, Gay, and Bisexual Populations: Conceptual Issues and Research Evidence." *Psychological Bulletin* 129(5):674-97.

Meyer, Ilan H., Sharon Schwartz and David M. Frost. 2008. "Social Patterning of Stress and Coping: Does Disadvantaged Social Statuses Confer More Stress and Fewer Coping Resources?" *Social Science and Medicine* 67(3):368-79.

Muraco, Anna and Karen I. Fredriksen-Goldsen. 2011. "'That's What Friends Do': Informal Caregiving for Chronically Ill Lesbian, Gay, and Bisexual Elders." *Journal of Social and Personal Relationships* 28(8):1073-92.

Novak, Jill. 2013. "The Six Living Generations in America." Chichester, UK: Marketing Teacher Ltd. Retrieved February 2, 2014 (http://www.marketingteacher.com/lesson-store/lesson-six-living-generations.html).

Obergefell v Hodges. 2015. Supreme Court of the United States 14-556 Washington, DC.

Penhallurick, Robert J. 2010. *Studying the English Language*. New York: Palgrave Macmillan.

Silverstein, Charles. 2009. "The Implications of Removing Homosexuality from the DSM as a Mental Disorder." *Archives of Sexual Behavior* 38(2):161-63.

Substance Abuse and Mental Health Services Administration. 2010. "Increasing Substance Abuse Levels among Older Adults Likely to Create Sharp Rise in Need for Treatment Services in Next Decade." Retrieved June 17, 2011 (http://www.samhsa.gov/newsroom/advisories/1001073150.aspx).

Substance Abuse and Mental Health Services Administration and Office of Applied Studies. 2009. "The NSDUH Report: Illicit Drug Use among Older Adults." Rockville, MD: Substance Abuse and Mental Health Services Administration & Office of Applied Studies.

Thomas, Patricia A. 2010. "Is It Better to Give or to Receive? Social Support and the Well-Being of Older Adults." *Journals of Gerontology: Series B: Psychological Sciences & Social Sciences* 65B(3):351-57.

U.S. Census Bureau. 2013a. "2012 National Population Projections: Summary Tables. Table 12. Projections of the Population by Age and Sex for the United States: 2015 to 2060." U.S. Census Bureau. Retrieved December 5, 2013 (http://www.census.gov/population/projections/data/national/2012/summarytables.html).

U.S. Census Bureau. 2013b. "Annual Estimates of the Resident Population for Selected Age Groups by Sex for the United States, States, Counties, and Puerto Rico Commonwealth and Municipos: April 1, 2010 to July 1, 2012." Washington, DC: U.S. Department of Commerce. Retrieved June 21, 2013 (http://www.census.gov/popest/data/national/asrh/2013/index.html).

U.S. Department of Health and Human Services. 2011. "*Healthy People 2020 Objectives: Lesbian, Gay, Bisexual, and Transgender Health*." Retrieved October 26, 2011 (http://www.healthypeople.gov/2020/topicsobjectives2020/overview.aspx?topicid=25).

Wallace, Steven P., Susan D. Cochran, Eva M. Durazo, and Chandra L. Ford. 2011. "The Health of Aging Lesbian, Gay and Bisexual Adults in California." Los Angeles, CA: UCLA Center for Health Policy Research.

Wienke, Chris and Gretchen J. Hill. 2009. "Does The 'Marriage Benefit' Extend to Partners in Gay and Lesbian Relationships?: Evidence from a Random Sample of Sexually Active Adults." *Journal of Family Issues* 30(2):259–89.

Wight, Richard G., Allen J. LeBlanc, Brian de Vries, and Roger Detels. 2012. "Stress and Mental Health among Midlife and Older Gay-Identified Men." *American Journal of Public Health* 102(3):503–10.

Wilkinson, Richard G. and Michael G. Marmot. 2003. "Social Determinants of Health: The Solid Facts." Copenhagen, Denmark: World Health Organization.

Williams, Mark and Karen I. Fredriksen-Goldsen. 2014. "Same-Sex Partnerships and the Health of Older Adults." *Journal of Community Psychology* 42(5):558–70.

Wolkowitz, Owen M., Victor I. Reus, and Synthia H. Mellon. 2011. "Of Sound Mind and Body: Depression, Disease, and Accelerated Aging." *Dialogues in Clinical Neuroscience* 13(1):25–39.

CHAPTER 8

CAREGIVING IN LATER LIFE

Challenges and Policies

Carole Cox

> There are only four kinds of people in the world. Those who have been caregivers, those who are currently caregivers, those who will be caregivers, and those who will need caregivers.
>
> *Rosalynn Carter*

INTRODUCTION

Estimates on caregiving in the United States show that roughly 14.3 percent of all American adults act as a caregiver to an adult aged 50 years or older (National Alliance for Caregiving [NAC] and AARP 2015). These caregivers have a median age of 49 years and are predominantly women (60 percent) caring for women (62 percent). Nearly half are caring for a parent or parent-in-law while 10 percent care for a spouse.

Another significant group of caregivers is grandparents who are raising their grandchildren. It is estimated that 2.7 million grandparents are responsible for the basic needs of one or more grandchildren living in their households (U.S. Census 2015). As with other caregivers, this group is predominantly women, between the ages of 45–69. However, they are frequently disabled themselves (Pew Research Center 2013).

As these data on caregivers indicate, caregiving is predominantly a woman's role and concern. Gender norms continue to socialize women into caregiving and the normative expectation is that throughout life they will meet their associated role obligations. However, for many, these obligations become challenges.

118

The 53rd Commission on the Status of Women of the United Nations (2009) underscored the inequality and toll that caretaking can have on the lives of women and the need for greater attention to their unpaid care work. Among its many recommendations are ensuring that care work is recognized, measured, and valued, promoting the sharing of care work by men and women, and adopting gender-sensitive policies to improve the rights and protections of unpaid care workers.

This chapter explores the challenges encountered by these two groups of caregivers, those caring for a frail relative and those raising a grandchild. Both groups confront a myriad of issues that necessitate sensitive policies and services to support them and enable their caregiving abilities.

BACKGROUND

Caregiving is primarily a family affair in that it is the family who continues to provide most of the assistance required by family members. In 2013, about 43.5 million family caregivers assisted an adult with limitations in physical activities and 61.6 million provided some care during the year (NAC and AARP 2015). These caregivers spent an average of 24.4 hours per week providing assistance, with approximately one-quarter providing more than 41 hours per week (NAC and AARP 2015).

The care that grandparents provide is equally demanding, as they are often without any support or assistance. Dealing with the developmental stages and needs of grandchildren can be taxing and stressful. Moreover, such stress is often exacerbated by the children themselves who frequently come to the grandparents with emotional and behavioral problems and histories of neglect and abuse (Smith and Palmieri 2007).

REASONS FOR CAREGIVING

Reciprocity is often given as a reason for caregiving. People feel obligated to assist those who have cared for them, perceiving it as a normative responsibility. An estimated 83 percent of Americans say they would feel very obligated to provide assistance to a parent in a time of need (Pew Research Center 2010). Moreover, such obligations can even extend to more distant kin as persons feel bound to reciprocate for earlier assistance. Feelings of commitment and affection are strong motivations for providing care (Litwak 1985).

In many instances, persons assume the caregiving role out of default, because no one else is available to provide care (Radina 2007) or because there is a vacuum within the social network as ties have become weakened (Pope, Kolemer, and Glass 2012). However, when caregivers feel they have little choice in the decision to become a caregiver, the role is more likely to be experienced as stressful (NAC and AARP 2005).

Cultural norms and values are often influential in caregiving as they dictate the importance of the family in providing assistance. Filial piety and obligations can be important motivators in the care of older persons. Familism, the value and belief that families should provide care for relatives, underlies the motivations and roles of many caregivers. At the same time, fulfilling the role can itself be stressful as it may prevent caregivers from seeking additional support or contribute to dysfunctional perceptions of their own abilities (Losada et al. 2010; Scharlach et al. 2006).

The caregiving relationship has both rewards and costs. Feelings of reciprocity, affection, and the fulfilling of expected roles can buffer the stress that the role may demand (Savundranayagam 2013). Persons who perceive caregiving as a means to spiritual growth (Quinn, Clare, and Woods 2012) and who see themselves as effective and competent in the role experience less stress and are more likely to perceive it as a positive experience (Romero-Moreno et al. 2012). Conversely, to the extent that persons feel overwhelmed by caregiving demands, have a lack of supports, and doubt their own self-efficacy as caregivers, they are likely to experience greater stress and feelings of burden.

Factors Conducive to Caregiver Well-Being

As with all roles, caregiving stress can be reduced through interventions that enable persons to feel more positive about their situations and to cope with them (McLennon, Habermann, and Rice 2011). Foremost among these are interventions that build feelings of self-efficacy and esteem and strengthen resilience. Successful coping has been related to better reported physical and mental well-being with decreased feelings of burden and stress. In addition, feelings of mastery, the belief that one can effectively deal with the challenges incumbent in the caregiving role, is an important buffer to the stresses that the person encounters (Pioli 2010). Being able to perceive the positive aspects of the situation is critical to ameliorating negative responses that are conducive to stress.

Equally important are support systems that provide both tangible and emotional support to caregivers (Chappell and Funk 2011).

CAREGIVERS OF OLDER RELATIVES AND GRANDPARENT CAREGIVERS

Both caregivers of older relatives and grandparent caregivers confront challenges and demands that engender a need for support, policies, and services that recognize these needs. Common to each group is an overpowering sense of family responsibility for meeting the demands of their dependent relatives. These caregivers also share a need for information; education that can strengthen their caregiving roles and skills; support that offers both emotional and tangible assistance, such as respite from caregiving; and, in many instances, financial assistance that can help to ameliorate many of the strains encumbered in the caregiving role.

POLICIES TO SUPPORT FAMILY CAREGIVERS

Given the immensity of the caregiving role and the demands that it entails, it becomes increasingly difficult for family to provide continued assistance without some support. However, support for these caregivers remains limited through policies that have not been commensurate with their needs or the challenges that they face.

The National Family Caregiver Support Program (NFCSP)

The NFSCP was enacted in 2000 to provide grants to states to help them in the support of family caregivers. The program recognizes the major role that families play in providing care and the stresses that they commonly encounter. The range of services provided includes information about services, assistance to caregivers in gaining access to services, individual counseling, organization of support groups and caregiver training, respite care, and limited supplemental services. The goal of the program is to reduce caregiver depression, anxiety, and stress so that caregivers can continue to provide care and thus delay the need for institutionalization. Those eligible for the program are informal caregivers providing care to persons over the age of 60, caregivers to persons with Alzheimer's disease or another dementia, and grandparents caring for children under 18 years or those caring for adults with disabilities.

Data on the program from 2010 show that access assistance was the primary service provided, with over 1 million contacts; counseling and training were provided to 125,000 caregivers and respite was offered to 64,000 (Administration on Aging 2012). Those receiving the services reported that they were very satisfied and that the assistance enabled them to provide care for a longer period of time. Approximately 12 percent of the family caregivers receiving some type of support were grandparents caring for a grandchild.

Currently, the NFCSP is being evaluated to determine its effectiveness in achieving client outcomes. The evaluation is assessing the impact of the program on the family and the persons for whom they provide care. Three specific areas are being studied: the access that it provides to caregivers and the systems that are needed for such access; the outcomes on caregivers and care receivers; and whether the program has contributed to the efficiency of the long-term care system, including cost savings, by helping families to delay institutionalization (Administration on Aging 2012).

In comparison, the latest appropriations for the Act (FY2013) were $143.6 million, which has changed very little since 2001 (Napili and Colello 2013). With approximately 65.7 million caregivers in the United States, each caregiver is entitled to approximately $233 per year through the program. Given the nature, length of time, and extent of the tasks associated with caregiving, the ability of the program to really impact the lives of these caregivers is questionable.

States with a history of providing caregiver support services are more likely to provide services under the National Family Caregiving Support Act (Giunta 2010). States that have experience in identifying and serving caregiver needs may be better prepared to implement programs and provide training and emotional support (Giunta 2010). Other barriers to the implementation of the Act are its limited funding, which severely restricts services, lack of public knowledge of the Act, cultural or linguistic barriers, and a lack of uniform assessment tools (Buhler-Wilkerson 2007; Scharlach et al. 2006).

Lifespan Respite Care Act

One of the most pressing needs for caregivers is respite, temporary relief from caregiving. It is usually provided at home but can also be provided in a nursing home where persons leave their relatives for a short time. As part of a long-term care system, it can provide support to family caregivers, which can enable them to continue caregiving for longer periods of time.

The Lifespan Respite Care Act was passed in 2006 as part of the Public Health Service Act. With its "lifespan" approach, it is not limited to one age group but serves caregivers of both children and adults with disabilities. It provides funds to state agencies to develop or improve respite activities; improve the dissemination of information about respite care; improve coordination; and provide, supplement, or improve access to and quality of services. Between 2007 and 2011, grants were awarded to 30 states with a total appropriation of $289 million. In 2011, the Lifespan Respite Care Program was funded at just under $2.5 million and funding has not changed since then (Napili and Colello 2013).

A primary concern with respite care is that even when available it may not be used. Early research (Cox 1997) found that even after qualifying for respite benefits, many caregivers did not use them. A common response was that they were waiting "until they really needed it." The same findings were replicated in a more recent study (Robinson, Buckwalter, and Reed 2013), which found that 79 percent of caregivers applying for the program failed to use it. In comparison with program users, nonusers were older, more depressed, and had less social support. They were also caring for persons less impaired than the users. Both studies indicate that respite appears to be used more as a remedial program after a crisis or when caregiving has become most difficult rather than as a preventive measure that could further enable and support the caregivers.

The Family and Medical Leave Act (FMLA)

The Family and Medical Leave Act of 1993 (FMLA) is the only law that deals specifically with employed caregivers. It enables family members caring for a parent, child, or spouse to take time off of up to 12 weeks of leave per year to provide care. The leave is unpaid and it is restricted to those working for companies with 50 or more employees and who have worked for the employer for at least 12 months for a minimum of 1,250 hours in that period. Upon their return, employees are not guaranteed the same position although they are guaranteed an equivalent salary and benefits.

The restrictions of the Act make it difficult for low-income employees to use as they potentially forfeit their salary and benefits. Those working less than full time are not eligible and the Act also does not attend to the caregiving needs of others such as those caring for partners or grandparents caring for children. Expanding the Act to cover these groups would help to assure their ability to continue as employed caregivers by assisting them in balancing the demands of caregiving and employment.

Fourteen states have expanded the provisions of the FMLA so that it meets the needs of more workers. Among the changes that states have made are covering workers in businesses with fewer than 50 employees; expanding the definition of family member so that it includes domestic partners, grandparents, parents-in-law or siblings; and expanding the use of the FMLA so that it can be used for taking people to medical appointments. Thus, at the state level, the Act may be more supportive of these employed caregivers.

Employed Caregivers

Employed caregivers encounter particular stresses as they attempt to balance their work role with that of caregiver. This is most challenging for those caring for a person with Alzheimer's disease or a related dementia (ADRD) as the demands placed upon them continue to escalate. Leaving early from work, taking time off for caregiving activities, taking leaves of absence, and even reducing hours or giving up employment are among the common responses that caregivers have had to make (NAC and AARP 2009). The outcomes of such responses can further impact caregivers, as their own benefits and pensions may be reduced.

A recent study of 103 employers and their responses to dementia and its impact on the workplace found that the most common problems were caregivers leaving work early and missing work (Cox and Pardasani 2013). Over half, 52 percent, had requested changes to their work schedules to accommodate their caregiving.

However, few employers, less than one-third (29 percent), had any specific policies to assist caregivers. Most relied on the Family Medical Leave Act and only one employer reported permitting telecommuting and efforts to be flexible to meet the employee's needs. At the same time, almost all of the employers thought that caregiving and dementia were important issues for the workplace and that more information on the illness would assist them in dealing with its human, legal, and ethical ramifications. As stated by one employer, "It is very disturbing for staff to watch a long-time colleague decline. Unfortunately, this sometimes leads to inappropriate decisions about keeping them long beyond their ability to work effectively warrants it."

Family caregivers continue to struggle to meet their role obligations and demands. Policies appear to recognize their needs but still do little to actually support them. Services such as respite care that can actually relieve and assist them are sorely inadequate or inaccessible. Consequently, many are faced with inordinate stress as they attempt to balance their own needs with those of their relatives. In many instances, employed caregivers, forced to alter their own work schedules to provide care, may actually jeopardize their own future security.

GRANDPARENTS AS CAREGIVERS

Since the 2000 Census, there has been a 12 percent increase in the number of children being raised by a grandparent in a household without any parent present (Livingston 2013). These children are more likely to be living in households below the poverty line and with lower median incomes than children not being raised by grandparents (Livingston 2013). The majority of these grandparent caregivers have been raising the grandchildren for more than 3 years, are grandmothers, and are likely to have some type of disability (Pew Research Center 2013). Through my empowerment program, which has served over 200 grandparent caregivers, I have become familiar with many of the issues that they face (Cox 2009).

Grandparents assume the parenting role for a myriad of reasons, with the prevailing being that no one else is available to provide care. Few grandparents anticipated raising their grandchildren and thus they are unprepared for the new situation. Among the negative consequences that may evolve are poor psychological health and distress (Musil et al. 2011), poor physical health (Hughes et al. 2007), and financial strain (Baker and Mutchler 2010).

The functioning of the grandparents is often challenged by the grandchildren themselves. As noted, the situations that precede the move to the grandparent's home often include parental substance abuse, neglect, parental conflicts, and even abuse which can place these children at risk of psychological problems (Pinson-Milburn et al. 1996). Consequently, raising these children can be extremely trying as it demands immense patience and skill.

Raising children requires resources and these families often find that such resources are unavailable. Policy has failed to keep abreast of the economic needs of grandparents, offering only minimal benefits within a very fragmented system to those motivated to find them. In fact, a major barrier to assistance is a lack of information of what is available on the part of the grandparents and agency staff who are uninformed about potential benefits (New York City Kincare Taskforce 2009).

Finding suitable housing is another challenge faced by many grandparent caregivers. Data from the 2000 Census show that more than a quarter of grandparent-headed families were living in overcrowded conditions and that almost half of these families were spending 30 percent or more of their income on rent. Equally troubling is that 60 percent of those below the poverty line did not receive any government housing subsidy (Simmons and Dye 2003).

Health is another critical factor that can impact the effectiveness and well-being of grandparent caregivers. In comparison with noncaregivers, grandparents raising grandchildren have significantly more health problems, including depression, coronary heart disease physical disabilities, and chronic health conditions such as asthma and diabetes (Baker and Silverstein 2008). Transitioning into the caregiver role increases obesity rates and also contributes to poorer self-rated health and health status (Hughes et al. 2007).

Concomitantly, grandparent caregivers have a low propensity to use preventive care or undergo health screenings. Long waits at clinics, often accompanied by young children, can deter many from using services. Moreover, some may be reluctant to seek care out of fear that a condition or diagnosis could force them to relinquish the children. As one grandmother in my empowerment group reported, she did not want to go to the doctor as he might find that she was not healthy enough to care for her granddaughter. With no one else to assume responsibility, grandparents may overlook their own health issues as they focus on the children (Cox 2008). Moreover, their own self-care is also jeopardized: many have stated that they cannot stay in bed if they do not feel well, since this can cause the grandchildren to become extremely anxious and worried.

Given the many stresses and conflicts faced by these families, there is a strong need for mental health services and supports. However, barriers such as their own health, responsibilities, previous experiences, income, insurance, childcare, and transportation tend to minimize their use of mental health programs (Smithgall et al. 2006). Even when available, grandparents often find the service itself ineffective or the therapists themselves insensitive. As noted by one grandmother in my program, her granddaughter resisted going to therapy because the therapists continued to change, causing her even more distress. The insensitivity of untrained staff is underscored by an intake worker who said, "If you had done a better job with your own children, you wouldn't be here in the first place." Thus, finding accessible professionals who are skilled in dealing with the issues faced by these families can in itself be a challenge.

Loss

A particularly intense feeling that tends to pervade these grandparent relationships is that of "loss" (Cox 2007). Grandparents are coping with the loss of their own child or their child's incapacity to raise their own children. While attempting to deal with their own feelings and grief, they are also confronted with the demands incumbent in the parenting role. Taking on the new responsibilities frequently means giving up both activities and plans and, in some instances, even employment. Consequently, their own futures can be jeopardized as they assume the parenting role and subsequent losses. One grandmother in my group summed up this situation by telling me, "My life is finished."

The feelings of loss experienced by grandparents are frequently amplified by those of their grandchildren, who, for whatever reason, have lost their parent. Yet, as children, they frequently are unwilling to express their feelings, sometimes out of fear of further upsetting their grandparents. Consequently, the feelings may be displaced into behavioral problems at school or at home. Parents who make unfulfilled promises to children such as planning visits that do not happen or dropping by for only a minute tend to exacerbate these feelings, often causing children to feel abandoned and unloved. In some instances, children respond through rage and anger toward the grandparent, making the grandparent's role even more difficult. As grandparents do not understand the impact that loss can have on children or the ways in which they respond to grief, they may doubt their own ability to parent.

However, as with other caregiving, the new role can also encumber rewards and benefits. Among these are knowing that they are helping the child (Cox 2003), a sense of being needed and improving the child's life, and pleasure in watching the child grow and develop (Conway and Consedine 2013). By keeping the child out of the "system," grandparents often feel satisfaction in knowing that they are keeping the family together. At the same time, the realization that their own children are absent may cause concern over who is going to care for them when they need assistance.

POLICIES TO SUPPORT GRANDPARENT CAREGIVERS

The Fostering Connections to Success and Increasing Adoptions Act

The 2008 Fostering Connections to Success and Increasing Adoptions Act recognized the important role of kinship care in providing for children through its provision of federal resources to support kinship care families. The Act instructs states to ensure that relatives are identified and involved when children are removed from the parent's home. The Act also includes a Navigator program that helps to link caregivers with services and supports, provides funds for guardianship assistance that can help children to leave foster care, and permits states to ease some licensing standards so that more kinship caregivers can become part of the foster care system.

However, as the majority of grandparent caregivers are caring for their grandchildren informally without any formalized relationship (Raphel 2008; Sakai, Lin and Flores 2011), they are not able to access many of the benefits and services of the Act. Reasons for not wanting to formalize their relationships include prior negative experiences with child welfare, family members with criminal records, inadequate housing, and negative attitudes of workers (Lorkovich et al. 2004). Grandparents are also reluctant to formalize their relationships as it may lead to conflict with the child's parents and even impede the parent's ability to eventually resume responsibility for the child.

Foster Care Payments

Grandparents are entitled to foster care payments if they become licensed by their state through the child welfare system. Nevertheless, only one-fourth of children in foster care are living with a relative (U.S. Department of Health and Human Services 2014). Barriers that deter grandparents from the foster care system are its rules and regulations, concern that the child could be removed and placed for adoption, and worries that the relationship could strain ties with the child's parents. Taking a child into the home without notifying child welfare may also make a grandparent ineligible to become a foster parent.

Subsidized Guardianships

The 2008 Fostering Connections Act also permitted states to finance subsidized guardianships for grandparents and other kinship caregivers that would enable children in the foster care system to exit the system into the legal care of their relatives. Eligibility is restricted to children who have been in foster care with the relative for at least 6 months and for whom reunification with the parent and permanent adoption are not possible. The subsidy that the state pays cannot exceed the foster-care payment of the state. As well as giving subsidies to the grandparent, the programs also reduce administrative costs to the state as the role of foster care agencies in managing and supervising families is relinquished.

Temporary Assistance to Needy Families (TANF)

Children raised by grandparents may be entitled to TANF payments under the child-only cases. These are grants made to the children with no adult included in the benefits. Children living with nonparental caregivers, usually grandparents, make up 41 percent of these grants (Golden and Hawkins 2012). The grant amount varies by state but is typically small. In 2011, the average grant was about $8.00 per day per child (U.S. GAO 2011). Generally, these cases are not restricted to the TANF income limits as only the child's income is considered. Most states also provide links to the families to other services such as Medicaid and nutrition programs, although even with such links, these children receive few services (Golden and Hawkins 2012).

A major issue impacting the receipt of these grants is a lack of information among the providers themselves. Often, grandparents seeking assistance are told that these grants do not exist, that they are not eligible, or that there is a waiting period to receive the grants (New York State

Kincare Coalition 2011). Consequently, many families who could benefit from the grants become frustrated during the application process and, although entitled to them, never receive them.

LEGACY (Living Equitably, Grandparents Aiding Children and Youth)

Finding appropriate housing can be a major challenge for grandparent caregivers. With limited resources, suitable housing with sufficient space is often difficult to find. In 2003, Congress enacted legislation as a program to help ease the housing crisis for grandparents (Public Law 108–186). The Act authorized the development of demonstration programs through the U.S. Department of Housing and Urban Development (HUD) Section 202 program for grandparent-headed families.

LEGACY also called for the training of all HUD personnel so that grandparent-headed families could be adequately served by existing housing programs as well as research to determine the number of intergenerational families and their housing needs. According to HUD (2008), 265,000 grandparent-headed households qualified for assistance under the LEGACY Act. Unfortunately, the Act terminated in 2008.

Intergenerational housing meets many of the needs of these families. One of the first buildings, opened in 2005, designed specifically for grandparent-headed families is the PSS/WSF Family Apartments in the South Bronx. The building has 50 units, including both two- and three-bedroom apartments. Among the services that it provides are after-school programs, support groups, mentoring, and counseling. Eligibility is restricted to grandparents 62 and older with legal custody of their grandchildren and for those with incomes below the area median. Residents are required to pay 30 percent of their adjusted income in rent. The development offers a model of housing that can meet the needs of both grandparents and grandchildren. Similar housing is being planned or developed in other parts of the country although subsidies for such projects remain precarious, as both federal and state assistance is limited.

DISCUSSION

As discussed in this paper, two very large groups of caregivers, the majority of whom are women, are providing care without any substantial policies to support them. At the same time, the contribution of their work both to their families and to society is immense. The latest estimate of the value of the care and services that family caregivers provide is $450 billion annually (Feinberg et al. 2011). Grandparents raising grandchildren save taxpayers more than $6.5 billion annually by keeping children out of the formal foster care system (Generations United 2013).

Underlying both groups of caregivers are values and commitments that stress the role of the family in providing care to their dependent relatives. Even those assuming the caregiving role out of default rather than choice attest to the importance that is placed on family care and their responsibilities. At the same time, both groups experience costs and rewards as a result of their caregiving. Fulfilling caregiving demands, whether for an older person with dementia or a rebellious adolescent, is frequently stressful and challenging. An absence of assistance and lack of resources can exacerbate this challenge, severely taxing the well-being of both groups of caregivers.

Among the common needs shared by these caregivers are those for programs and services that offer skill building and information. Knowing what to expect and how to deal with problems and issues is important for strengthening coping abilities and confidence. Information about relevant resources and services is fundamental to further enabling caregivers' ability and effectiveness. Concomitantly, respite programs that provide relief from caregiving and can thus help to reduce stress are sorely needed resources for each. All of these programs can contribute to a feeling of mastery, the sense that one is effectively dealing with the tasks of caregiving, which is tantamount to caregivers' well-being.

Policies are enacted to solve social problems and thus, as long as caregiving is not perceived as a problem but as a normative and expected duty, fulfilled primarily by women, policies to support caregivers will remain restrictive and caregivers remain vulnerable. As noted by Kittay (2013), the social arrangements and advances that moved women out of the singular role as caregiver are falling apart as the means to meet the most basic caregiving needs are often lacking. Caregiving must be perceived as a shared responsibility with the ethic of care brought into the public domain. When this occurs, the rights and needs of all caregivers may finally be addressed.

Until then, caregivers, whether caring for frail relatives or raising grandchildren, will have to contend with sparse economic assistance, fragmented services, and eligibility criteria that do not reflect their needs. Particularly troubling is that even when such needs have been recognized through policies such as the National Family Caregiver Support Program or the Lifetime Respite Program, the policies remain severely underfunded, offering further evidence that caregiver support is not an urgent legislative priority.

Social policies reflect social values and American values, including both those of the family and the importance of work. Unfortunately, family appears to have less public support than work, suggesting that until caregivers' unpaid labor is recognized as work, they will continue to struggle for resources (Abramowitz 1988). The restrictive policy for employed caregivers, with its absence of paid leave and its eligibility requirements, does little to decrease the burden experienced by many as they attempt to juggle caregiving responsibilities with those of employment. The economic assistance for grandparent caregivers remains sparse, with many eligibility criteria and barriers. Consequently, providing for grandchildren on limited financial resources remains an overriding challenge.

With the aging of our population, increasing numbers of persons will find themselves acting as caregivers. While maintaining relationships and relieving society of actual services costs, they are frequently jeopardizing their own health, resources, and futures. Policies that assist and support these caregivers and provide them with options are urgently needed so that they can fulfill their critical roles with dignity and security.

References

Abramowitz, Mimi. 1988. *Regulating the Lives of Women: Social Welfare Policy from Colonial Times to the Present*. Boston: South End Press.

Administration on Aging. 2012. Retrieved from http://www.aoa.gov/AoARoot/AoA_Programs/HCLTC/Caregiver/index.aspx.

Baker, Lindsey and Jan Mutchler. 2010. "Poverty and Material Hardship in Grandparent-Headed Households." *Journal of Marriage and Family* 72:947–62.

Baker, Lindsey and Merril Silverstein. 2008. "Preventive Health Behaviors among Grandmothers Raising Grandchildren." *The Journals of Gerontology Series B, Psychological Science and Social Sciences* 63: S304–11.

Buhler-Wilkerson, Karen. 2007. "Care of the Chronically Ill at Home: An Unresolved Dilemma in Health Policy for the United States." *The Milbank Quarterly* 85:611–39.

Chappell, Neena and Laura Funk. 2011. "Social Support, Caregiving, and Aging." *Canadian Journal of Aging* 30:335-70.

Conway, Francine and Nathan Consedine. 2013. Orienting to the Positive: A Practice Framework for Grandparent Caregiving. In Bert Hayslip and Gregory Smith (eds.) *Resilient Grandparent Caregivers: A Strengths-Based Perspective*, New York: Routledge.

Cox, Carole 1997. "Findings from a Statewide Program of Respite Care: A Comparison of Service Users, Stoppers, and Non-Users." *The Gerontologist* 37:511-7.

Cox, Carole 2003. "Designing Interventions for Grandparent Caregivers: The Need for an Ecological Perspective." *Families in Society* 24:127-34.

Cox, Carole 2007. "Grandparent-Headed Families: Needs and Implications for Social Work Interventions and Advocacy." *Families in Society* 88:561-6.

Cox, Carole. 2008. "Empowerment as an Intervention with Grandparent Caregivers." *Journal of Intergenerational Relationship* 6:465-77.

Cox, Carole 2009. "Custodial Grandparents: Policies Affecting Care." *Journal of Intergenerational Relationships* 7:177-90.

Cox, Carole and Manoj, Pardasani. 2013. "Alzheimer's in the Workplace: A Challenge for Social Workers." *Journal of Gerontological Social Work* 56:643-56.

Family and Medical Leave Act of 1993. Pub.L. 103-3; 29 U.S.C. sec. 2601; 29 CFR 825.

Feinberg, Lynn, Susan Reinhard, Ari Houser, and Rita Choula. 2011. *Valuing the Invaluable: 2011 Update. The Growing Contributions and Costs of Family Caregiving.* Washington, DC: AARP Public Policy Institute.

Generations United. 2013. *Grandfamilies Statistics.* Washington, DC: Author.

Giunta, Nancy 2010. "The National Family Caregiver Support Program: A Multivariate Examination of State-Level Implementation." *Journal of Aging and Social Policy* 22:249-66.

Golden, Olivia and Amelia Hawkins. 2012. *TANF Child-Only Cases.* Issue Brief 03, Washington, DC: Urban Institute.

Hughes, Mary Elizabeth, Linda Waite, Tracey LaPierre, and Ye Luo. 2007. "All in the Family: The Impact of Caring for Grandchildren on Grandparents' Health." *Journal of Gerontology, B, Psychol Sci Soc Sciences* 62:S108-19.

Kittay, Eva. 2013. "Caring for the Long Haul: Long Term Care Needs and the (Moral) Failure to Acknowledge Them." *International Journal of Feminist Approaches to Bioethics* 6:66-88.

Litwak, Eugene. 1985. *Helping the Elderly.* New York: Guildford Press.

Livingston, Gretchen. 2013. *To Grandmother's House We Stay,* Washington, DC, Pew Research Center.

Lorkovich, Tami, Trista Piccola, Victor Groza, Merri Brindo, and Jonnie Marks. 2004. "Kinship Care and Permanence: Guiding Principles for Policy and Practice." *Families in Society* 85(2):157-62.

Losada, Andrés, María Marque-Gonzalez, Bob Knight, Javier Yahguas, Philip Sayegh, and Rosa Romero-Moreno. 2010. "Psychosocial Factors and Caregivers' Distress: Effects of Familism and Dysfunctional Thoughts." *Aging and Mental Health* 13:193-202.

McLennon, Susan, Barbera Habermann, and Marti Rice. 2011. "Finding Meaning as a Mediator of Burden on the Health of Caregivers of Spouses with Dementia." *Aging and Mental Health* 15:522-30.

Musil, Carol, Nahida Gordon, Camille Warner, Jaclene Zauszniewski, Theresa Standing, and May Wykle. 2011. "Grandmothers and Caregiving to Grandchildren: Continuity, Change, and Outcomes over 24 Months." *Gerontologist* 51:86–100.

Napili, Angela and Kirsten Colello. 2013. *Funding for the Older Americans Act and other Aging Services Programs.* Washington, DC: Congressional Research Service.

National Alliance for Caregiving and AARP. 2015. *Caregiving in the U.S.,* Washington, DC: Author. Retrieved from http://www.aarp.org/ppi.

National Alliance for Caregiving and AARP. 2009. *Caregiving in the United States.* Washington, DC: Author.

New York City Kincare Task Force. 2009. *Removing Barriers to Successful Kin Caregiving.* New York: Author.

New York State Kincare Coalition. 2011. *Kinship Care in New York: Keeping Families Together.* New York: Author.

Pew Research Center. 2010. *Social and Demographic Trends: The Decline of Marriage and Rise of New Families.* Washington, DC: Author.

Pew Research Center. 2013. *To Grandmothers House We Stay.* Washington, DC: Author.

Pinson-Milburn, Nancy M., Ellen S. Fabian, Nancy K. Schlossberg, and Marjorie Pyle. 1996. "Grandparents Raising Grandchildren." *Journal of Counseling and Development* 74:548–54.

Pioli, Mark. 2010. "Global and Caregiving Mastery as Moderators in the Caregiving Stress Process." *Aging and Mental Health* 14:603–12.

Pope, Nathalie, Stacey Kolomer, and Anne Glass. 2012. "How Women in Late Midlife become Caregivers for their Aging Parents." *Journal of Women and Aging* 24:242–61.

Robinson, Karen, Kathleen Buckwalter, and David Reed. 2013. "Differences between Dementia Caregivers Who Are Users and Nonusers of Community Services." *Public Health Nursing* 6:501–10.

Quinn, Catherine, Linda Clare, and Robert Woods. 2012. "What Predicts Whether Caregivers of Persons with Dementia Find Meaning in Their Role?" *International Journal of Geriatric Psychiatry* 27:1195–202.

Radina, M. Elise. 2007. "Mexican American Siblings Caring for Aging Parents: Processes of Caregiver Selection Designation." *Journal of Comparative Family Studies* 38:143–63.

Raphel, Sally. 2008. "Kinship Care and the Situation for Grandparents." *Journal of Child and Adolescent Psychiatric Nursing* 21(2):118–20.

Romero-Moreno, R., M. Marquex-Gonzale, B. Mausbah, and A. Losada. 2012. "Variables Modulating Depression in Dementia Caregivers: A Longitudinal Study." *International Psychogeriatrics* 24:1316.

Sakai, Christina, Hua Lin, and Glenn Flores. 2011. "Health Outcomes and Family Services in Kinship Care: Analysis of a National Sample of Children in the Child Welfare System." *Archives of Pediatric & Adolescent Medicine* 165(2):159–65.

Savundranayagam, Marie. 2013. "Receiving While Giving: The Differential Roles of Receiving Help and Satisfaction with Help on Caregiver Rewards among Spouses and Adult Children." *International Journal of Geriatric Psychiatry* 29:41–8.

Scharlack, Andrew, Terersa Dal Santo, Amanda Lehning, Kristen Gustavson, Suzanne Lee, Erica Auh, Patrick Fox, and Julian Chow. 2006. *Caregiving in California: Final*

Report of the University of California Family Caregiver Support Project. Berkeley, CA: Center for the Advanced Study of Aging Service.

Simmons, Tavia and Jane Lawler Dye. 2003. *Grandparents Living with Grandchildren: 2000.* Census 2000 Brief, U.S. Department of the Census, Washington, DC: Author.

Smith, Gregory and Patrick Palmieri. 2007. "Risk of Psychological Difficulties among Children Raised by Custodial Grandparents." *Psychiatric Services* 58:1303–10.

Smithgall, Cheryl, Sally Mason, Lisa Michels, Christina LiCalsi, and Robert George. 2006. *Caring for their Children's Children,* http://www.chapinhall.org/research/report/caring-their-childrens-children.

United Nations. 2009. 53rd Commission on the Status of Women, Final Report. New York: United Nations.

U.S. Census 2015. *FFF: National Grandparents Day 2015: Sept 13.* Retrieved from https://www.census.gov/newsroom/facts-for-features/2015/cb15-ff15.html.

U.S. Department of Health and Human Services. 2014. *The AFCARS Report 21, Preliminary FY 2013 Estimates as of July 2014.* Washington, DC: U.S. Government Printing Office.

U.S. Department of Housing and Urban Development, Office of Policy Development and Research. 2008. *Intergenerational Housing Needs and HUD Program Options: Report to Congress 6.*

U.S. Government Accountability Office (GAO). 2011. *TANF and Child Welfare Programs: Increased Data Sharing Could Improve Access to Benefits and Services* (Washington, DC: GAO, October 2011). Retrieved from www.gao.gov/products/GAO-.

CHAPTER 9

LONG-DISTANCE CAREGIVING

Unique Challenges and Service Needs

Amy Horowitz and Kathrin Boerner

INTRODUCTION

Family caregiving to frail and disabled elderly relatives has been a topic of extensive research over the past five decades. Starting with the pioneering work of Ethel Shanas, Elaine Brody, and Marjorie Cantor, we have developed a rich knowledge base on the processes and consequences of caregiving, as well as on a range of evidence-based interventions to reduce the stresses on caregivers and improve care for elders. Yet, it is clear that almost all of the research conducted to date has focused on the geographically proximate, primary caregiver. As follows, the vast majority of evidence-based interventions have targeted caregivers with direct, hands-on care responsibilities for the elder.

However, in our increasingly mobile society, long-distance caregiving is a growing phenomenon. Families move away from their home of origin for educational, career, and relationship purposes, and elders may move away from their family home for health and/or social reasons in later life. While the relative ease of travel and communication systems can overcome geographic barriers and maintain family ties under normal circumstances, with increasing frailty and need for care, distance now poses unique challenges for elders, families, and health-care professionals.

Although far from a rare occurrence, long-distance caregiving remains a relatively unstudied phenomenon (Benefield and Beck 2007; Bevan and Sparks 2011). We know very little about what it means to be a long-distance caregiver, and especially the types of supports that they need to fulfill their caregiving role (Benefield and Beck 2007; Bledsoe, Moore, and Collins 2010). This is not only a function of the relatively limited number of studies but also of the types of studies that have been conducted to date. Two primary types of studies are predominant: large-sample, descriptive online or telephone surveys; and small-sample qualitative studies. Among the former is the *Miles Away: The MetLife Study of Long-Distance Caregiving* study conducted by the National Alliance for Caregiving and the American Association of Retired Persons (NAC 2004), which is one of the most cited studies of long-distance caregiving, drawing upon 1,130 long-distance caregivers nationwide; another major national survey conducted by National Council on Aging is *Caring Across the Miles: Findings of a Survey of Long-Distance Caregivers* (NCOA 1997). These studies provide important descriptive data on the demographics of long-distance caregivers and an overview of the types of care they provide and the impact on their lives, especially on employment. However, like most national large-sample studies, these data can only skim the surface of the long-distance caregiving phenomenon, with no in-depth exploration of what this experience truly entails in terms of the complexity of negotiating care arrangements with other family members and formal care providers, information that is critical for identifying specific unmet needs of these family caregivers. Furthermore, the Metlife study was an online survey, which resulted in a sample that was primarily white, educated, and affluent. The experience of long-distance caregiving among other socioeconomic and ethnic/racial groups remains unknown. The second type of study has tended to take a qualitative approach with very small samples to explore individual experiences of long-distance caregivers. These provide some depth to complement the breadth of the national surveys, resulting in interesting case illustrations, but allow limited analyses and generalizations to other types of caregivers. Thus, although we are cognizant of their limitations, these studies provide the foundation for our current understanding of long-distance caregiving.

In this chapter, we provide an overview of our current knowledge regarding the prevalence, characteristics, and challenges of long-distance caregiving, as well as identify where the literature suggests similarities and differences with the experience of proximate caregiving. Attention will also be given to service needs identified in the literature as well as potential service models relevant to long-distance caregivers. Results of a pilot study of long-distance caregivers to elders in residential long-term care conducted by the authors (n=20; primary or coprimary caregivers, living at least two hours' travel distance away) will be discussed where relevant to illustrate the main themes emerging from the literature. Data for the pilot were collected via telephone interviews, taking approximately 20–30 minutes. Sixty-five percent of the sample was female and the mean age was 65 years. Forty percent were caring for a parent, 30 percent for an aunt/uncle, 15 percent for a sibling, 10 percent for a friend, and 5 percent for a grandparent.

Finally, we conclude the chapter with a discussion of the major research gaps and priorities for a research agenda on long-distance caregiving.

HOW FAR IS FAR? DEFINITIONS AND PREVALENCE OF LONG-DISTANCE CAREGIVING

One major challenge in integrating and interpreting findings from the long-distance caregiving literature is the diversity in how both "distance" and "caregiver" are defined (Bevan and Sparks 2011). The most recent data from the 2015 *Caregiving in the U.S.* survey and its companion report, *Caregivers of Older Adults: A Focused Look at Those Caring for Someone Age 50+*, indicate that 12 percent of the more than 34 million family caregivers in the United States who care for an adult aged 50 and older live an hour or more away, and at least 7 percent live more than two hours' travel distance away (NAC and AARP 2015a; 2015b). Interestingly, this estimate is slightly lower than the 15 percent and 11 percent, respectively, that were reported in the 2009 survey (NAC and AARP, 2009), but may be more a function of variation in sampling and data collection methodology than a substantive decline. Estimates of those caring for older adults with dementia indicate that approximately 9 percent live more than two hours from the care receiver (Alzheimer's Association 2013). Estimates based on a Canadian national representative sample of caregivers aged 45 and older are even higher, with 22 percent of all caregivers found to live more than one hour away while 7 percent had more than a half day's travel to reach their elder's residence (Vezina and Turcotte 2010). Average one-way travel time reported by long-distance caregivers has ranged from 4 to 7 hours (NAC 2004; NAC and AARP 2009; Wagner 1997).

While studies of long-distance caregivers may differ on definitions of distance, most are inclusive of all caregivers regardless of their role as primary or secondary caregivers. However, it would be incorrect to assume that long-distance caregivers primarily provide supportive roles to geographically proximate caregivers. In fact, findings from the Metlife study (NAC 2004) suggest that almost half of all long-distance caregiving situations do not involve a primary caregiver on-site. In fact, 5 percent of participants in this study were the only caregiver, 18 percent were the primary caregiver, and 23 percent shared caregiving responsibilities equally with another caregiver (who might also be providing care from afar). Similarly, the 1997 National Council on Aging (NCOA 1997) study of 200 long-distance caregivers found that 21 percent were primary caregivers and 31 percent shared caregiving with another. A higher estimate comes from the 2009 *Caregiving in the U.S.* survey, with 35 percent of all long-distance caregivers who live at least one hour away self-reporting as primary caregivers (NAC and AARP 2009). Thus, we can estimate that as many as half of all long-distance caregivers are sole, primary, or coprimary caregivers. Further, long-distance caregiving is not limited to elders with only physical and functional impairments; approximately 30 percent of long-distance caregivers report that they are caring for an older adult with dementia (NAC and AARP 2009).

WHO ARE LONG-DISTANCE CAREGIVERS AND WHAT DO THEY DO?

Studies of long-distance caregivers indicate that there are both differences and similarities in characteristics when compared with proximate caregivers. Similar to proximate caregivers, with the exception of spouses, most report caring for parents, parents-in-law, and step-parents (Cagle and Munn 2012). Yet, our pilot data indicate that long-distance caregivers also serve a primary role for grandparents, uncles/aunts, and siblings, suggesting that they take on this role, even at a distance, when more closely related kin are not available. Koerin and Harrigan (2003) report that long-distance caregivers have been providing care for an average of 4.5 years, suggesting that this is not a short-term, transitional care arrangement for many.

Interestingly, data from national studies point to a more equal gender distribution among long-distance caregivers, with men representing a larger percent than they do among proximate caregivers (Cagle and Munn 2012; Koerin and Harrigan 2003). However, because most national surveys have not made the distinction between primary and secondary long-distance caregivers, it is not clear whether the higher percentage of males is, in part, due to the greater likelihood of daughters in sibling networks to remain geographically closer to parents, leaving geographically distant sons more likely to serve in a supportive rather than primary role.

Overall, data available to date indicate that long-distance caregivers are more likely to be employed (NAC and AARP 2004) and tend to be primarily Caucasian, well-educated, and relatively more affluent than those in more traditional caregiving studies (Alzheimer's Association 2013; NAC 2004; NAC and AARP 2004, 2009; Vezina and Turcotte 2010; Wagner 1997). We hypothesize that this is not only related to the association between geographic mobility and upward social mobility but is also a consequence of the methodologies used to study long-distance caregiving which have relied on telephone and online surveys and thus tend to underrepresent less educated and non-English-speaking caregivers. Other studies have documented that greater geographic distance between adult children and their elder relatives is more likely among caregivers with more children of their own, living in western United States, and with a history of geographic mobility, as well as among elders living in rural areas (Alzheimer's Association 2013).

Although long-distance caregivers have less face-to-face contact than proximate caregivers, one-third do report visiting their care recipient at least once a week and more than half visit at least several times a month (NAC 2004), with women traveling farther and more frequently to visit (Joseph and Hallman 1998). Furthermore, phone and e-mail contact is frequent (Roff et al. 2007; Joseph and Hallman 1998). Although greater distance is related to less frequent visiting (Joseph and Hallman 1998), the ability to share closeness as well as to provide comfort and gifts remains (Dewitt, Wister, and Burch 1988). Income has an inverse relationship with visiting, with low-income, long-distance caregivers visiting three times more frequently than those with higher income (NAC and AARP 2009). It is also important to note that long-distance caregivers are more likely to engage in long-term visits (Bevan and Sparks 2011), that is, engaging in an extended stay over several days or weeks to provide respite to a primary or coprimary caregiver, if there is one, and/or accomplish as many caregiving tasks as may have somewhat flexible time frames (e.g., doctor visits, haircuts, household repairs, visits to other family and friends) to make best use of face-to-face time.

Although living at a distance from their older relative, the available data do suggest that long-distance caregivers remain very much involved in direct caregiving activities, with the range of tasks similar to that documented for more proximate caregivers. Long-distance caregivers report helping with personal care, transportation, financial management, household assistance, assistance with medications, decision-making, and monitoring and arranging care with formal providers and/or near relatives and neighbors (Baldock 2000; Koerin and Harrigan 2003; NAC 2004; Vezina and Turcotte 2010). For example, data from the Metlife study of long-distance caregivers found that 72 percent helped the elder with IADLs, devoting an average of 22 hours per month, while 40 percent did so with ADLs, devoting an average of 12 hours per month (NAC 2004). Using data from the 1997 NAC/AARP Family Caregiver Survey, Chou et al. (2001) found that long-distance caregivers provided an average of 19.6 hours of care per week, less than the 46.8 hours provided by caregivers sharing a household with the older relative but, interestingly, a greater amount than that provided by those living less than an hour's travel distance away, perhaps reflecting the greater time spent in travel. A somewhat lower, but still substantial, estimate of time spent in care tasks of 22 hours and 41 hours per month, respectively, is reported in the NAC (2004) and NCOA (1997) studies. At the same time, however, a cross-national study of five countries (England, Germany, Spain, Norway, and Israel) found that elder parents having at least one child living less than an hour away received more support than those who did not have a geographically close child (Lowenstein, Katz, and Gur-Yaish 2008). We did not find data comparing the disability levels of elders with proximate caregivers compared with those with distance caregivers only, but it is possible that the latter have fewer care needs than the former and that when needs increase, distance caregivers and their elder relatives may need to make relocation decisions. This is an important issue addressed later in this chapter and remains on our future research agenda.

Although there is a more equal gender distribution among long-distance caregivers, gender differences similar to those among proximate caregivers are still found. For example, women reported more time spent in caregiving than men, regardless of distance, and that while male involvement declines with increasing travel time, women's involvement does not. Thus, women are more willing to travel farther to provide assistance at any given frequency than are men (Joseph and Hallman 1998).

Probably the most distinguishing characteristic of long-distance caregiving is the effort that goes into care management. Although it has been reported that both groups used many of the same services (Watari et al. 2006), long-distance caregivers who served as primary caregivers were most likely to involve formal care for the family member (NAC 2004), highlighting the importance of managing and monitoring a network of providers from afar. In fact, the most recent data show that 41 percent of long-distance caregivers report the use of paid help (NAC and AARP 2015a).

These activities have been found to be time intensive, in that long-distance caregivers spent 3.4 hours per week on average arranging services and another 4 hours per week checking on the person or monitoring care (NAC 2004). Further, care management does not have to only involve formal providers; long-distance caregivers often talk about making arrangements with informal providers as well such as arranging for neighbors, friends, and more distant relatives to check up on and provide companionship for the elder.

The question of whether long-distance caregivers provide these services to an elder relative due to an extraordinary commitment to the older relative that is even greater than that of proximate caregivers and/or a strong adherence to the norm of familial obligation or simply because they have no alternatives is still open to question. Silverstein, Conroy, and Gans (2008) studied sibling networks and the allocation of care to older mothers, examining how both distance and the strength of commitment to filial responsibility norms influenced frequency of support. While they found that more distance children did generally provide less frequent support than those proximate, the amount of support provided by proximate children was positively associated with the strength of their filial norms; however, for those children over 100 miles' distance, the amount of support provided was independent of their sense of filial obligation, thus suggesting that distance was a barrier that could not be breached even by a strong sense of filial responsibility. However, other analyses of these same data looked at intrafamily patterns and took into consideration the amount of support provided and values held by other siblings, contrasting underproviders (those at closer proximity but providing less than 25 percent of the average family provision of services) and overproviders (those at greater geographic distance but providing more than 25 percent of average family provision). Findings from these analyses did indicate that, compared with their siblings, overproviders had a stronger sense of filial responsibility than the proximate underproviders who evidenced a relatively weaker sense of responsibility. Thus, a more complex pattern emerged in which one's own sense of filial responsibility interacts with that of others in the helping network to determine the extent to which distance does or does not serve as a barrier to the amount of care provided.

However, it is important to note that this study, by its very purpose, examined families with multiple siblings in order to shed light on the allocation of care within sibling networks. Yet, we would hypothesize that the adult child living at a distance who takes on the *primary* responsibility for caregiving to an older parent when more proximate siblings are available is not the norm, either among sibling networks or among long-distance caregivers in general. While evidence is extremely limited, some prior qualitative studies as well as our own pilot study suggest that long-distance caregivers take on this role by default, primarily because there are no proximate alternatives available. Long-distance caregivers are often only children or another relative (e.g., niece, nephew, grandchild, sibling) of an elder with no spouse or living children. Thus, the circumstance of the long-distance primary caregiver may be likened to that which was found in early caregiving research on adult sons who took on the role of primary caregiver; that is, they were there by default, being only children, having a male-only sibling network, or having a geographically distant sister (Horowitz 1985). This remains a question, however, for future research.

Unique Challenges of Long-Distance Caregiving

While sharing many common characteristics with proximate caregivers, there are several specific challenges associated with long-distance caregiving that have emerged in the literature. These will be discussed in this section and include sources of stress, assessing and responding to need, the "Moving Closer" decision, and communication with both family and formal health-care providers.

143

Sources of Stress

Interestingly, long-distance caregivers report equal or even greater levels of emotional stress compared with those living with or closer to the older relative (Chou et al. 2001; NAC 2004; NAC and AARP 2004; Thompsell and Lovestone 2002), and tend to report more emotional stress than physical strain (Koerin and Harrigan 2003). Three sources of stress are especially relevant to long-distance caregivers. First, the stress associated with caregiving is often directly attributed to dealing with the distance that separates them from the elder relative and the barrier it places on face-to-face contact (Bledsoe et al. 2010; Koerin and Harrigan 2003). To illustrate, drawing from our pilot study, typical responses when we asked participants what the most challenging aspects of long-distance caregiving were, included:

> ... hard being so far away. [female caregiver, age 63, friend]
> ... not being able to visit more frequently. [male caregiver, age 70, nephew]
> ... the distance—I would visit more often if I was closer. [female caregiver, age 75, niece]
> ... I'm frustrated I can't be there more often. [female caregiver, age 66, daughter]
> ... caregiving is very emotional. I wish I could be there more often, but I can't because of my job. The commute is also stressful and expensive. [male caregiver, age 55, son]

These responses speak to the distress, frustration, and often guilt experienced by long-distance caregivers because the distance limits the nature and frequency of contact that they can have with the elder relative and their capacity to provide care (Cagle and Munn 2012), with evidence that this distress and guilt is more prevalent among female compared with male distance caregivers (Schoonover et al. 1988).

Second, the financial implications of long-distance caregiving can be greater than those of proximate caregiving and thus represent an additional source of stress (Alzheimer's Association 2013; Chou et al. 2001; Vezina and Turcotte 2010). For example, while 30 percent of those living with a care recipient aged 50 and older report high financial strain, this is true of 21 percent of those living one or more hours away compared with only 14 percent of other non-coresidents (NAC & AARP 2015b). Further, long-distance caregivers to people aged 50 and older spent $8,728 per year compared with \$5,531 and \$5,885 for coresident and proximate caregivers, respectively (NAC and Evercare 2007). Although the specific numbers vary, there is evidence that greater distance is associated with greater cost, even among long-distance caregivers. That is, caregivers living between one and three hours away average approximately \$400 per month, while those more than three hours away spend an average of about \$700 per month (NAC 2004). While travel expenses account for much of the extra financial burden, there are also expenses involved with hiring services that may be needed to supplement the long-distance caregivers' efforts or provide the help that distance prevents them from providing directly.

Third, the impact of long-distance caregiving on employment seems to be especially severe, with physical distance being significantly associated with work strain (Bledsoe et al. 2010; Chou et al. 2001; Parker, Church, and Toseland 2006; Watari et al. 2006). For example, more than two-thirds of long-distance caregivers in one study reported negative impacts on employment (Koerin and Harrigan 2003). While proximate caregivers are able to drop by for brief visits before and/or after work, or can take a few hours off during the day if needed, this is not typically possible for the long-distance caregiver. As noted earlier, distance often requires caregivers to make extended visits with their older relatives, and this often means that holidays and vacations have to be sacrificed and substantial amounts of money have to be spent to cover travel costs. At the same time, long-distance caregivers also report greater disruptions to their paid employment compared with proximate caregivers (Bledsoe et al. 2010; NAC 2004; Watari et al. 2006). Long-distance caregivers are more likely to rearrange work schedules (NAC 2004), miss full days at work (NAC 2004; Vezina and Turcotte 2010), and take sick leave (Joseph and Hallman 1998). It is significant that as many as one-fourth to one-third of long-distance caregivers report having taken a leave of absence from work, a proportion significantly higher compared with coresident or proximate caregivers (Chou et al. 2001; Koerin and Harrigan 2003). In terms of gender differences, female, as compared with male, long-distance caregivers are also more likely to move from full- to part-time employment (NAC 2004).

Assessing and Responding to Need

The adage that "a picture is worth a thousand words" is nowhere more true than in the context of long-distance caregiving. Distance creates problems in assessment and thus the long-distance caregiver often has difficulty determining when on-site help is needed (Koerin and Harrigan 2003; Mazanec et al. 2011). This can be made more difficult when older relatives do not want their relatives to worry about them. They will withhold information and/or downplay the extent of their needs (Bevan, Jupin, and Sparks 2011; Mazanec et al. 2011) and take advantage of what has been termed "geographic privacy"—protecting the caregiver from upsetting news (Hooyman and Lustbader 1986). Further, when cognitive or hearing impairments are involved, even telephone communication may be impossible and/or of limited value. Thus, distant caregivers may not be as aware of mental and/or physical deterioration and, as a result, their involvement is often more crisis oriented than crisis preventative (Joseph and Hallman 1998).

Participants of our pilot study talked specifically about this challenge, describing themselves as feeling "frustrated" and 'helpless," for example:

> ... it is difficult for me every day because of the distance ... I can't see my mother and what she looks like on a day to day basis ... Moving away was one of the most difficult things I've had to do. [female caregiver, age 48, daughter]

The "Moving Closer" Decision

As the elder's care needs intensify, the distant caregiving strategies that once worked may become strained. One of the questions that both caregivers and elders need to address is whether, and if so, when, a move closer together is necessary. But this is not an easy decision for either party. And, often, this can result in conflict if the elder dismisses the caregiver's suggestion that they move (Bevan et al. 2012). As many of the participants in our pilot study noted, moving is not on the elder's agenda and only 10 percent thought it was a viable option, primarily because the older relative did not want to move away from familiar surroundings and/or social networks. For example:

... my mother refused to move ... she has friends in the city and has lived there for many years ... but not all of her friends are healthy enough to visit ... " [female caregiver, age 48, daughter]

... I brought up the topic, but she is a New Yorker and so is her husband, they do not want to leave [female caregiver, age 62, daughter]

... my mother has friends nearby and she is happy here ... [male caregiver, age 58, son]

Communication with Both Family and Formal Health-Care Providers

Long-distance caregiving also has implications for extended family relationships, especially when the caregiver is an adult child of the elder and has to negotiate care arrangements as a primary or shared caregiver with other siblings. Schoonover et al. (1988) found evidence of tension and communication difficulty between near and distant siblings, and Roff et al. (2007), in a study of 22 distant caregivers, found many had negative feelings about their siblings' capacity to provide care and decisions about the division of labor. Overall, long-distance caregivers report higher rates of family disagreement around care decisions and distribution of responsibilities (Watari et al. 2006). These experiences of family conflict among long-distance caregivers are not only emotionally distressing but have been found to be associated with more negative health outcomes for the caregiver (Bevan et al. 2012).

As a function of having to manage care from afar and the greater likelihood of sharing care responsibilities with formal providers (Vezina and Turcotte 2010), one of the major challenges that long-distance caregivers face is communication with health and other formal care providers. Whether the elder enters an acute care setting, in-patient rehabilitation hospital, assisted living, or long-term care facility or remains in the home with supportive services, the caregiver is faced not only with the task of finding and arranging for these services, but with monitoring services and maintaining communication with providers. This is clearly one of the most prevalent and stressful aspects of distance caregiving. Not surprisingly, long-distance caregivers consistently report more difficulty in locating and securing local services compared with proximate caregivers (Koerin and Harrigan 2003), as well as more difficulty in coordinating the variety of services that may be involved (Watari et al. 2006).

Not knowing who to talk to (doctor, nurse, and/or social worker) or what questions are appropriate and necessary to ask and problems getting information in a timely manner are all commonly reported frustrations. Studies have shown that long-distance caregivers report the need for better communication and information from health-care providers (Mazanec et al. 2011) and are much less satisfied with the health information they received compared with proximate caregivers (Thompsell and Lovestone 2002). At the same time, for doctors, nurses, and social workers, who continue to have more patients to care for and less time to do so, the physical absence of a responsible family member may be interpreted as the absence of *interested* family members, making it that much harder for long-distance caregivers to establish their role in the care team.

Over 70 percent of the participants in our pilot study, all of whom were caregivers for elders living in residential long-term care facilities, reported at least some difficulty communicating with health-care providers. They reported dissatisfaction at not being able to coordinate phone calls with staff or meet with the team rather than speaking to individuals, and frustration at not getting regular updates on their relative's condition or status. For example:

> ... *it is a nightmare ... Very difficult for me to follow up with staff. [female caregiver, age 48, daughter]*
> ... *I wish I could get more information more often. [male caregiver, age 58, son]*
> ... *I feel like I am bothering the staff when I call. The staff is not receptive to getting any inquiry. Sometimes they also sound patronizing.... "Of course your mother is fine." This is not very helpful or reassuring. [female caregiver, age 62, daughter]*
> ... *Staff changes and I am not informed of who does what ... If I lived in New York I would be "raising hell" at the care and communication (problems)... but I don't*
> ... *so I just gave up. [male caregiver, age 80, brother]*

When both family members and health-care staff used e-mail for regular communication, however, satisfaction increased since the flow of information and the flexibility in time of communication was evaluated positively. Unfortunately, in our litigious society, formal care providers are becoming much less likely to convey important health information in written e-mails and the opportunity for this type of communication may decrease dramatically over the coming years.

SERVICE NEEDS AND SERVICE/TECHNOLOGICAL OPTIONS

At the current time, very few service models exist that have been developed specifically for long-distance caregivers, and almost none have been rigorously evaluated. While on-site private care managers can be enlisted, and can be very helpful to the long-distance caregiver, this is an option available only to the relatively affluent. Video-visiting programs have been implemented primarily within long-term care facilities, where a webcam or videophone is made available to both resident and family members (Demiris et al. 2008; Mickus and Luz 2002; Savenstedt, Brulin, and Sandman 2003; Hensel, Parker-Oliver, and Demiris 2006). The largest of these studies, however, was conducted in only ten dyads and all primarily rely on testimonial data. The latter do suggest, however, that for some families, video-visiting does have a great deal of potential in terms of giving the families a greater sense of involvement, supporting more effective communications, and reducing worry by providing visual information to help assess the elder's physical and emotional well-being. They also have the potential for facilitating communication with long-term care staff (Savenstedt et al. 2003). One community-based model was developed by a local Alzheimer's Association provider (Watari et al. 2006) and included working with a professional consultant who acted as liaison between the long-distance caregiver and the care recipient, a community resource guide, a website to help get information on local services, a telephone consultation regarding state financial support programs, and the Safe Return Program (a system of returning older adults with dementia home when they wander). Consumer feedback was very positive, but, again, this program represents one of few isolated attempts to tailor interventions for long-distance caregivers. Other research, including our pilot study, indicates that long-distance caregivers are looking for support groups but want them to be comprised of other long-distance caregivers since they feel that their issues are sufficiently different from those of on-site caregivers (Mazanec et al. 2011).

Innovations in technology have great potential for providing support to all caregivers, and are especially relevant for long-distance caregivers to help bridge communication barriers. As noted, videophones and Skype can facilitate communication with the elderly and allow caregivers to visually assess their relatives' status as well as to engage in communication with in-home formal providers. Using video-conferencing systems with health-care providers also can allow family members to participate in team meetings within health-care facilities. Several of the participants in our pilot study noted that they had regularly attended team meetings with the rehabilitation or long-term care staff when they were geographically close but it stopped when they moved, which contributed to their frustration when seeking information from staff. Sponsoring organizations can also host Internet-based and/or telephone support groups specifically for long-distance caregivers. Long-distance caregivers represent an untapped market for a range of technological interventions currently available and/or being developed. In fact, a 2011 survey of 1,000 caregivers conducted by the National Council on Aging to assess their knowledge and openness to technologies that would support them and help them meet the challenges of caregiving found that long-distance caregivers were more likely than on-site caregivers to think that technology could make them feel more effective as caregivers (National Alliance for Caregiving 2011).

FUTURE DIRECTIONS

While we have attempted to highlight the existing evidence about long-distance caregiving in this chapter, it is important to emphasize that we are only at the very beginning of developing the empirical knowledge base needed to understand the full breadth and depth of the long-distance caregiving experience. Only recently has long-distance caregiving been recognized as a unique phenomenon and the multidimensional nature of long-distance caregiving remains largely unexplored.

At the most basic level, the variability in definitions of distance and caregiver type across studies complicates our ability to develop an integrated and interpretable knowledge base. We would argue that setting the lower limit of distance to one hour can obscure the true constraints associated with long-distance caregiving. We propose that a minimum of two hours' travel defines long-distance caregiving, as this would include caregivers for whom a one-day, round-trip may be possible if needed but would be a hardship on an ongoing basis, and thus more accurately reflects the constraints on providing care from afar. Furthermore, most studies are inclusive of both primary and secondary caregivers when discussing long-distance caregivers. However, we believe strongly that it is important to distinguish between these two groups and focus future research on long-distance caregivers who are primary or sole caregivers, or who share caregiving equally with another family member who may also be providing care from afar. Doing so recognizes that those who have sole or coresponsibility have unique stressors and unique needs not shared by those who play a supportive role to a geographically proximate caregiver.

Not surprisingly, information on racial/ethnic and socioeconomic differences among long-distance caregivers is practically nonexistent. Except for a publication reporting a case study of one African American long-distance caregiver (Collins et al. 2003), we have not found any studies that address racial/ethnic differences in long-distance caregiving. As mentioned previously, the large-sample national surveys have recruited primarily white, educated, and affluent long-distance caregivers. The extent to which culture and financial and other resources influence the long-distance caregiving experience remains to be explored.

As follows, we need a fuller description of long-distance caregiving activities, and how such activities may differ across age, gender, ethnic, and socioeconomic subgroups, as well as by the physical and cognitive status of the elder. We need a better understanding of the unique stressors that long-distance caregivers experience, and the factors that promote or hinder distance caregiving and influence caregiver well-being. Communication and coordination challenges with formal service providers as well as with family and friends must be better understood in order to identify specific "trigger" points for intervention.

We also know little about how the specific care needs and functional impairments of the care receiver influence distance caregiving and decision-making about alternatives. We noted earlier that many distance caregivers may confront a decision at some point, when the needs of the elder increase, whether to move closer to the elder, have the elder move closer to them, or to use more comprehensive services (e.g., residential long-term care) in the elder's community. At which point long-distance caregivers need to confront this decision undoubtedly varies widely among families based on a number of factors including, but not limited to, financial resources, other family resources, local policies funding aging services, elder's functional needs, elder's cognitive status, and feelings of familial obligation, to name just a few. We do hypothesize that, except for those older adults who have minimum care needs, most long-distance caregivers inevitably need to involve and work with local formal services while the long-distance caregiver who can do it all will be the exception to the norm. But, again, this is open to empirical study, as is the question of when and what types of services are engaged over time.

The limited body of research in long-distance caregiving also means that we lack an evidence base for the development and evaluation of supportive interventions and technologies that specifically address the needs of long-distance caregivers. Structurally, it would make sense for health-care agencies to build in a support mechanism for long-distance caregivers. However, such support mechanisms are not typically in place, and evidence is needed to identify how existing programs for proximate caregivers can be adapted to guide the design of new models and to foster an evidence-based policy response to the needs of this growing group of caregivers to frail elders.

REFERENCES

Alzheimer's Association. 2013. "Alzheimer's Disease Facts and Figures." *Alzheimer's & Dementia: The Journal of the Alzheimer's Association* 9(2):208.

Baldock, Cora Vellekoop. 2000. "Migrants and their Parents: Caregiving from a Distance." *Journal of Family Issues* 21(2):205–24.

Benefield, Lazelle E. and Cornelia Beck. 2007. "Reducing the Distance in Distance-Caregiving by Technology Innovation." *Clinical Interventions in Aging* 2(2):267–72.

Bevan, Jennifer L., Ashley M. Jupin, and Lisa Sparks. 2011. "Information Quality, Uncertainty, and Quality of Care in Long-Distance Caregiving." *Communication Research Reports* 28(2):190–5.

Bevan, Jennifer L. and Lisa Sparks. 2011. "Communication in the Context of Long-Distance Family Caregiving." *Patient Education and Counseling* 85(1):26–30.

Bevan, Jennifer L., Sean K. Vreeburg, Sherri Verdugo, and Lisa Sparks. 2012. "Interpersonal Conflict and Health Perceptions in Long-Distance Caregiving Relationships." *Journal of Health Communication* 17(7):747–61.

Bledsoe Linda K., Sharon E. Moore, and Wanda Lott Collins. 2010. "Long Distance Caregiving: An Evaluative Review of the Literature." *Ageing International* 35(4):293–310.

Cagle, John G. and Jean C. Munn. 2012. "Long-Distance Caregiving: A Systematic Review of the Literature." *Journal of Gerontological Social Work* 55(8):682–707.

Chou, Kee-Lee, Sum Yeung, and Iris Chi. 2001. "Does Physical Distance Make a Difference in Caregiving?" *Journal of Gerontological Social Work* 35(1):21–37.

Collins, Wanda Lott, Tangerine A. Holt, Sharon E. Moore, and Linda K. Bledsoe. 2003. "Long-Distance Caregiving: A Case Study of an African-American Family." *American Journal of Alzheimer's Disease and Other Dementias* 22(2):120–8.

Demiris, George, Debra Oliver, Brian Hensel, Geraldine Dickey, Marilyn Rantz, and Marjorie Skubic. 2008. "Use of Videophones for Distant Caregiving: An Enriching

Experience for Families and Residents in Long-Term Care." *Journal of Gerontological Nursing* 34(7):50-5.

DeWitt, David J., Andrew V. Wister, and Thomas K. Burch. 1988. "Physical Distance and Social Contact Between Elders and Their Adult Children." *Research on Aging* 10(1):56-80.

Hensel, Brian K., Debra Parker-Oliver, and George Demiris. 2006. "Videophone Communication between Residents and Family: A Case Study." *Journal of American Medical Directors Association* 8(2):123-7.

Hooyman, Nancy R. and Wendy Lustbader. 1986. *Taking Care: Supporting Older People and their Families*. New York: Free Press.

Horowitz, A. 1985. Family Caregiving to the Frail Elderly. P. 194-246 in M. Powell Lawton and George Maddox (eds.) *Annual Review of Geriatrics and Gerontology*. New York: Springer Publishing Co.

Joseph, Alun E. and Bonnie C. Hallman. 1998. "Over the Hill and Far Away: Distance as a Barrier to the Provision of Assistance to Elderly Relatives." *Social Science & Medicine* 46(6):631-9.

Koerin, Beverly B. and Monica P. Harrigan. 2003. "P.S. I Love You: Long-Distance Caregiving." *Journal of Gerontological Social Work* 40(1-2):63-81.

Lowenstein, Ariela, Ruth Katz, and Nurit Gur-Yaish. 2008. Cross-National Variations in Elder Care: Antecedents and Outcomes. P. 93-112 in Maximiliane E. Szinavacz and Adam Davy (eds.) *Caregiving Contexts: Cultural, Familial and Societal Implications*. New York: Springer Publishing Company.

Mazanec, Polly, Barbara J. Daly, Betty Rolling Ferrell, and Maryjo Prince-Paul. 2011. "Lack of Communication and Control: Experiences of Distance Caregivers of Parents with Advanced Cancer." *Oncology Nursing Forum* 38(3):307-13.

Mickus, Maureen A. and Clare C. Luz. 2002. "Televisits: Sustaining Long Distance Family Relationships among Institutionalized Elders through Technology." *Aging and Mental Health* 6(4):387-96.

NAC & AARP. 2004. Caregiving in the US. Retrieved from http://caregiving.org/data/04finalreport.pdf.

NAC & AARP. 2009. *Caregiving in the US: A Focused Look at Those Caring for the 50+*. Washington, DC: National Alliance for Caregiving.

NAC & AARP. 2015a. *Caregiving in the U.S. 2015*. Washington, DC: NAC and AARP Public Policy Institute.

NAC & AARP. 2015b. *Caregivers of Older Adults: A Focused Look at Those Caring for Someone Age 50+*. Washington, DC: NAC and AARP Public Policy Institute.

National Alliance for Caregiving. 2004. *Miles Away: The Metlife Study of Long-Distance Caregiving*. Retrieved from http://www.caregiving.org/data/milesaway.pdf.

National Alliance for Caregiving. 2011. *e-Connected Family Caregiver: Bringing Caregiving into the 21st Century*. Washington, DC: National Alliance for Caregiving.

National Alliance for Caregiving & Evercare. 2007. *Family Caregivers – What They Spend, What They Sacrifice: The Personal Financial toll of Caring for a Loved One*. Retrieved from http://www.caregiving.org/data/Evercare_NAC_CaregiverCostStudyFINAL 20111907.pdf.

National Council on the Aging. 1997. *Caring Across the Miles: Findings of a Survey of Long-Distance Caregivers.* Washington, DC: National Council on Aging.

Parker, Michael, Wesley Church, and Ronald Toseland. 2006. "Caregiving at a distance." P. 391–406 in Barbara Berkman, and Sarah D'Ambruoso (eds.) *Handbook of Social Work in Health and Aging,* New York: Oxford University Press.

Roff, Lucinda L., Shadi S. Martin, Lisa. K. Jennings, Michael W. Parker, and Dana K. Harmon. 2007. "Long Distance Parental Caregivers' Experiences with Siblings: A Qualitative Study." *Qualitative Social Work: Research and Practice* 6(3):315–34.

Sävenstedt, Stefan, Christine Brulin, and Per-Olof Sandman. 2003. "Family Members' Narrated Experiences of Communicating via Video-Phone with Patients with Dementia Staying at a Nursing Home." *Journal of Telemedicine & Telecare* 9(4):216–20.

Schoonover, Claire B., Elaine M. Brody, Christine Hoffman, and Morton H. Kleban. 1988. "Parent Care and Geographically Distant Children." *Research on Aging* 10(4):472–492.

Silverstein, Merril, Stephen J. Conroy, and Daphna Gans 2008. Commitment to Caring: Filial Responsibility and the Allocation of Support by Adult Children to Older Mothers. P. 71–91 in Maximiliane E. Szinavacz and Adam Davy (eds.) *Caregiving Contexts: Cultural, Familial and Societal Implications.* New York: Springer Publishing Company.

Thompsell, Amanda and Simon Lovestone. 2002. "Out of Sight, Out of Mind? Support and Information given to Distant and Near Relatives of Those with Dementia." *International Journal of Geriatric Psychiatry* 17(9):804–7.

Vezina, Mireille and Martin Turcotte. 2010. "Caring for a Parent Who Lives Far Away: The Consequences." *Canadian Social Trends, Statistics Canada* 11(8):3–13.

Wagner, Donna L. 1997. "Long-Distance Caregiving for Older Adults." *Innovations in Aging* 26(2):6–9.

Watari, Kecia, Julie Loebach Wetherell, Margaret Gatz, Judith Delancey, Catgt Ladd, and Debra Cherry. 2006. "Long-Distance Caregivers: Characteristics, Service Needs, and Use of a Long-Distance Caregiver Program." *Clinical Gerontologist* 29(4):61–77.

CHAPTER 10

IMPROVING ACCESS TO GERIATRICS CARE FOR RURAL VETERANS

A Successful Partnership Between Urban Medical Centers and Rural Clinics

Judith L. Howe, Jennifer L. Griffith, William W. Hung, and B. Josea Kramer

INTRODUCTION

Training of the U.S. health-care workforce has not kept pace with the growing population of aging Americans. The Institute of Medicine (IOM) (2008) has called for innovative approaches to address the lack of geriatrics specialists in all clinical fields of practice. The aging of the U.S. population is well documented, with an estimated 88.5 million Americans aged 65 and older projected for 2050, more than doubling the 2010 number of 40 million (U.S. Census Bureau 2010). Forty-three percent of U.S. veterans are aged 65 or older, with an average age of 58 (Department of Veterans Affairs 2011).

In 2012, there were 7,429 geriatricians nationwide, which falls far short of the 17,000 currently needed (AGS 2014). In the Veterans Health Administration (VHA), the ratio of geriatricians to the older veteran population is even lower than for the overall U.S. population. While 2.5 million older veterans receive health care in the system, only 60,000 older veterans receive specialty care in geriatrics (K. Shay, personal communication, March 29, 2013). Similarly, there is a shortage of psychologists who are trained in treating the mental health needs of older adults; it is estimated that the United States has only 5 percent of the needed workforce (Pachana et al. 2010). Nurse practitioners are more likely to work with underserved populations who are uninsured and receiving Medicaid and Medicare, making them a greater presence in the rural primary care workforce (Paradise, Dark, and Bitler 2011). However, the majority of nurse practitioner programs do not include education and training in geriatrics (IOM 2008). While the social work profession is growing in the United States (NASW 2012), there is a shortage of social workers trained to work with older adults, with just one-third of the number needed by 2020 (IOM 2008; Maiden, Horowitz, and Howe 2010). There are similar shortfalls in projected needs for trained geriatrics specialists in other associated health professions such as pharmacy and occupational and physical therapy.

For older people living in rural areas, the lack of geriatrics specialists has particularly serious implications. The Census Bureau does not actually define "rural." "Rural" encompasses all population, housing, and territory not included within an urban area (which is defined as 50,000 or more people). In general, rural aged are more likely to have higher rates of chronic illness, disability, and mortality when compared with their urban counterparts, more difficulties with activities of daily living, lower incomes, less education, and a higher dependence on Social Security, Medicare, and Medicaid for income security (IOM 2008). Additionally, rural older adults have less access to family caregivers since many younger adults move from rural areas (Gamm and Hutchison 2004). The rural workforce is also aging at a faster rate than the urban workforce, resulting in increasing gaps in care for older adults (National Advisory Committee on Rural Health and Human Services 2010). While 23 percent of North Americans reside in rural areas, 10 percent of rural counties do not have a primary care physician (Affordable Health Care for America 2010; Gamm and Hutchison 2004).

Responding to this need, the VHA began to focus 5 years ago on delivering primary care to rural veterans because of the relatively large number of veterans compared with nonveterans living in rural areas. Of the 924 VHA facilities nationwide, 404 have more than 60 percent of patients who are rural, with 298 of these facilities reporting more than nine out of ten of their patients being from rural areas (Weeks et al. 2004; 2006; MacKenzie, Wallace, and Weeks 2010).

There are multiple challenges for health-care providers working in rural areas. For instance, they are often overburdened because of scarce resources and a higher patient volume. They also have fewer opportunities than nonrural providers to form collegial relationships with peers and to receive continuing education in specialized fields such as geriatrics (Arora et al. 2011).

The Institute of Medicine concluded in its landmark report, "Retooling for an Aging America: Building the Healthcare Workforce," that all prior initiatives to promote geriatric specialization have been generally insufficient to produce an increased number of geriatrics specialists, and that "immediate and substantial action is necessary by both public and private organizations to close the gap between the status quo and the impending needs of future older Americans" (IOM 2008: 30). One approach to providing health care to the growing older population is to provide primary care providers with the skills and knowledge to deliver quality care to older adults. The Institute of Medicine report notes that in order to meet the need for flexibility, health-care professionals should have distance learning opportunities to increase skills and knowledge in geriatrics and to take on expanded roles in caring for older adults, such as inclusion on interdisciplinary health-care teams.

Over the years, several strategies have been developed and refined to increase the competency of the workforce to provide care to older adults. All have aimed to "geriatricize" providers and trainees to competently provide health care to older people (IOM 2008). In this chapter, we describe the Geriatrics Education Rural-Urban Alliance (GERA), which provides a group of education programs aimed at increasing knowledge and skills among primary care providers and trainees in the VHA system. We then provide an overview of five tested approaches to increase workforce competency in geriatrics: (1) education in geriatrics for primary care providers, (2) distance learning, (3) expert consultation to remote and rural providers, (4) exposing trainees to geriatrics, and (5) continuing professional education. The chapter concludes with a description of five GERA programs that includes evidence of each program's impact based on preliminary evaluation data.

THE GERIATRICS EDUCATION RURAL-URBAN ALLIANCE

The foundation of education and clinical programs sponsored by the Mount Sinai Medical Center, the James J. Peters VAMC, and the VA Greater Los Angeles Healthcare System has enabled the creation of what is referred to as the Geriatrics Education Rural-Urban Alliance (GERA). This alliance (as shown in Figure 10.1), created in 2012, is made up of the Health Resources and Services Administration-funded Geriatric Education Center and programs funded by the VHA which include Rural Interdisciplinary Team Training, Rural Provider and Health Care Staff Training and Education Initiative (RPSTI), Rural Health Training and Education Initiative, and the Geriatric Research, Education and Clinical Center (GRECC) program, GRECC Connect. GERA is a multimodal education initiative which has increased competency in geriatrics on the continuum from preprofessional to seasoned providers.

GERA builds on several evidence-based strategies in its partnership between urban-based medical centers and medical centers with satellite rural clinics. Within a framework of proven models, the aim of GERA is to increase competencies in geriatrics among primary care providers as it is not feasible to increase the geriatrics specialist workforce in the near future (Peterson et al. 2011). Partnering rural and urban health-care systems and universities is a proven method for increasing health-care options for rural residents and increasing opportunities for knowledge and skill acquisition for health-care providers, faculty, and students prac-

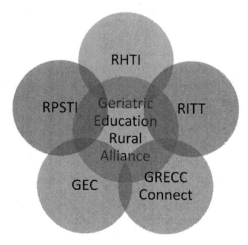

Figure 10.1: Geriatric Education Rural Alliance (GERA) Schema

ticing or preparing to practice in rural areas (Spies 2012). As depicted in Figure 10.1, there are multiple ways in which the programs discussed in this chapter overlap and intersect to create a rural geriatrics experience that can stretch across the career life course of rural providers.

The Rural Provider and Health Care Staff Training and Education Initiative and GRECC Connect both offer opportunities for rural primary care providers to learn about geriatrics and gerontology through online learning and telehealth facilitated by geriatrics specialists. The Geriatric Education Center provides specialized training, both online and in person, in geriatrics and geriatric mental health to meet the health-care and educational demands of the growing older adult population in New York State and beyond. Rural Interdisciplinary Team Training provides team-based, geriatrics in-person accredited training to providers and staff at VHA rural clinics throughout the United States, while the Rural Provider and Health Care Staff Training and Education Initiative sponsors a virtual learning community (VLC) that fosters online interaction among health-care providers nationwide by building relationships based on life and work experiences. GRECC Connect also uses online technology through tele-health consultation for complex geriatric cases and case-based training to rural VHA clinics throughout the country. The Rural Health Training and Education Initiative is a multimodal learning and teaching community which prepares future health-care providers to work with older rural veterans through an in-person and web-based rural immersion experience. Our hope is that the Rural Health Training and Education Initiative graduates will continue their professional development through participation in the VLC in order to stay abreast of developments in evidence-based geriatrics practice.

Current Models for Rural-Urban Partnerships

Geriatrics Education for Primary Care Providers

The Geriatric Scholars Program, funded by the VHA Offices of Rural Health and Strategic Integration, delivers intensive core training in geriatrics to primary care providers and associated health professions that work in primary care (i.e., social work, pharmacy, advanced nursing, physician assistant, and psychology). It is a longitudinal program with opportunities to individually tailor additional education in geriatrics for continuing professional development, including self-directed web-based learning, clinical practice, and quality improvement projects. A national collaborative of ten GRECCs is a nationally recognized model for training primary care providers in geriatrics to better manage the care of medically complex older patients. Initiated in 2008, the Geriatric Scholars Program has educated scholars from 185 facilities. A recent evaluation of the program demonstrated its effectiveness in improving core competencies in geriatrics and improving the care that veterans receive at rural community-based outpatient centers (Tumosa et al. 2012). The Rural Interdisciplinary Team Training Program, an elective component of the Geriatric Scholars Program, brings team-based geriatrics education to primary care providers and staff at rural clinics and is geared to practice change within the existing clinic infrastructure. Organizational change to improve the care of older persons has been found to be very effective at the clinic level (Ganz et al. 2008). The Rural Interdisciplinary Team Training action plans enable providers to develop a team-based project to bring about organizational change. Through a structured brainstorming process, clinical and nonclinical staff work together to create a project aimed at enhancing care for older patients in their clinic. For example, in Hilo, Hawaii, health-care professionals and staff implemented a system of using geriatric syndrome and red flag reminder cards in order to identify at-risk older patients. After 1 month, almost 90 percent of staff reported using the cards as a regular part of their practice.

Distance Learning

A VLC is based on Knowles Model of Adult Learning, which promotes a climate of openness, collaboration, competence, creativity, and success (Knowles 1976). A VLC, which fosters interaction among learners by building relationships based on life and work experiences (Woodland, Szul, and Moore 2007), includes dynamic content and reflects the heterogeneity of the learners. In the case of the Geriatric Education Rural-Urban Alliance, the VLC meets the needs of rural providers by creating an online space to change knowledge, skills, and attitudes about health care for older rural veterans (Salmon 2000). Some advantages of this type of learning include increased flexibility in accessing information, ease in updating content, tailored and self-directed instruction, ability for widespread distribution, standardization of content, automated tracking of learners, and accountability (Ruiz, Mintzer, and Leipzig 2006). The Rural Provider and Health Care Staff Training and Education Initiative, which is discussed in more detail below, sponsors a VLC that is being developed to meet the needs of rural health-care professionals throughout the United States.

Expert Consultation to Remote and Rural Providers

Telemedicine has significantly expanded in the last decade to assist veterans in rural areas, often far from a medical center or clinic, to access patient-centered care (Spies 2012). The VHA Office of Rural Health and the Office of Specialty Care Transformation collaborated to bring the VA Specialty Care Access Network-Extension for Community Healthcare Outcomes (SCAN-ECHO) model to clinical specialists and primary care providers within underserved communities (VHA 2013; Spies 2012). This model is focused on expanding knowledge for primary care providers and increasing expertise in a particular area. The virtual clinics of SCAN-ECHO are case-based and offer an opportunity for primary care providers to share the cases they encounter, solicit specialist input, and receive education on evidence-based practices in order to provide the best possible care. GRECC Connect, with its geriatric teams based at GRECC, draws on the SCAN-ECHO model in its approach to engage rural primary care providers.

Exposing Trainees to a Field

There is evidence that students who were raised in rural areas or have significant exposure to rural life are more likely to practice in rural areas (Burrows, Suh, and Hamann 2012). One model, based at Indiana University and Indiana State University, incentivizes academically qualified rural high-school students to practice in rural areas after medical school through offering full tuition and acceptance into medical school. During their education, students have the opportunity to train with rural physicians in rural clinics and hospitals. In Utah, there are residency programs that bring residents to rural areas to train, live, and practice rural medicine (Burrows et al. 2012). Similarly, the Office of Rural Health-funded Rural Health Training Initiative, described later as a GERA program, integrates rural geriatrics into training programs for future health-care professionals.

Continuing Education

There are significant barriers to geriatric workforce development that include lack of trained faculty, inadequate curricula, and limited educational opportunities (IOM 2008). In particular, there is a need for primary care practitioners, who care for the bulk of older persons in the United States, to have targeted and practical knowledge and skills in geriatrics and palliative care. The IOM report also underscores the need for "geriatricizing" nurse practitioners, nurses, social workers, and other health-care professionals through continuing education opportunities. The Geriatric Education Center meets this need by providing continuing medical education (CME)-accredited education in geriatrics and geriatric mental health to current and future primary care providers. Similarly, the VHA-funded GERA programs offer continuing professional development through the array of educational offerings described in this chapter.

GERA Programs and Impact

The next section of the chapter will describe each GERA program in detail and its impact as measured by preliminary evaluation data.

GRECC Connect

Through GRECC Connect, geriatricians and educators at seven GRECCs and one affiliated VHA medical center provide ongoing consultation, education, and support to rural primary care providers in their vicinity through a number of modalities including case-based conferences based on the SCAN-ECHO approach and telephonic and electronic consultation. The early evaluation results from the pre- and post-program survey indicate that this approach is enhancing providers' knowledge about geriatrics. As shown in Table 10.1, respondents to the preprogram survey included 21 physicians and nurse practitioners, who reported that the majority of their patients were aged 65 or older. Preprogram results revealed that providers were strongly interested in geriatric consultation via telemedicine if it became available at their rural clinics. Fourteen clinical case conferences were implemented across all sites from February to September 2013. Providers brought cases to the clinical conferences on topics such as dementia, chronic disease, heart failure, and recurrent hospital admissions. For the post-program survey, more than half of the

Table 10.1: Rural Health Training and Education Initiative 2013 Demographic Data by % (n = 25)

(n = 25)		
Age	n	%
20–25	9	36
26–30	10	40
31–35	4	16
36+	2	8
Total participants	25	100
Race/Ethnicity		
White	16	64
Asian	4	16
Black or African American	2	8
Hispanic/Latino	2	8
American Indian or Alaskan Native	1	4
Total participants	25	100
Gender		
Female	18	72
Male	7	28
Total participants	25	100
What degrees do you hold?		
BA	12	48
BS	5	20
MA	5	20
PharmD	4	16
BSN	2	8
BSW	2	8
MS	1	4
Where is your VA training placement located?		
VA Hudson Valley HCS	17	68
James J. Peters VAMC (Bronx)	8	32
Total participants	25	100
In which of the following areas have you had clinical experiences?		
Urban (50,000+ people)	13	52
Rural (non-urban)	1	4
Both	6	24
No prior clinical experience	5	20
Total participants	25	100

14 providers reported an increase in knowledge in managing older adults in their practice and almost 80 percent reported an increase in skills.

Rural Health Training and Education Initiative

The Rural Health Training and Education Initiative (RHTI), initiated in 2012, trains future health-care providers in rural geriatrics and gerontology, as depicted in Table 10.1. The curriculum for psychology, social work, pharmacy, medicine, and physician assistants at JJP and Hudson Valley Healthcare System weaves in components of rural geriatrics in order to prepare students for careers in the field of rural aging. The RHTI model includes integration of rural geriatrics in didactics (e.g., journal clubs, case conferences, seminars, workshops), clinical experiences (e.g., longitudinal and intensive, short-term encounters with rural older veterans, teleconsultation, e-consults), integrative activities (e.g., journaling, book discussion), and focused mentoring and precepting. In order to assess knowledge, skills, and attitudes related to geriatrics and professional development, a preprogram questionnaire is sent to students that includes the UCLA Geriatrics Knowledge Test and the Interdisciplinary Education Perception Scale. At the end of the program, students are asked to commit to a quality improvement project related to rural geriatrics. All measures are then followed up on at 3 months, 6 months, and 1 year in order to maintain a connection with students and their career goals. Data are still being gathered and analyzed for this program.

Rural Provider and Health-Care Staff Training and Education Initiative

The Rural Provider and Health-Care Staff Training and Education Initiative (RPSTI), established in 2013 with 20 funded sites throughout the United States, develops training and education programs for rural-based providers and staff through easily accessible training sessions that eliminate the need for travel and time away from work (http://www.rural-health.va.gov/education/RPSTI.asp). The GERA program funded by this initiative has received the resources to develop a national VLC to increase knowledge and skills in geriatrics for rural primary care providers. For rural providers, in particular, web-based learning is ideal because of the lack of training opportunities in rural locations (Woodland et al. 2007).

Now in the beta testing phase (http://www.gerischolars.org/mod/forum/ discuss.php?d=8), it includes 12 interactive and multimodal courses on geriatrics topics such as dementia, caregiving, sexuality, and falls. The VLC will include an online journal club, virtual case conferences, discussion boards, clinical demonstrations, and a catalog of online opportunities in rural geriatrics. Ideally, health-care professionals will participate in multiple activities and become repeat users of the VLC. It is hoped that rural providers will increase their knowledge, skills, and attitudes in geriatrics. New members of the VLC are asked to complete the validated UCLA Geriatrics Knowledge Test (Lee et al. 2004) with a follow-up 12 months later to assess changes. Additionally, every webinar includes a pre- and post-training questionnaire to assess knowledge, skills, and attitudes gained for that specific topic. Additionally, webinars developed through the Rural Health Training and Education Initiative are posted on the VLC, which allows for synergies across programs and ultimately expands the reach of GERA. This project was recently funded and data collection is in the early stages.

Rural Interdisciplinary Team Training

The Rural Interdisciplinary Team Training (RITT) is a resource-intensive, team-based program where geriatrics specialists travel to rural VA community-based outpatient clinics (CBOCs) and provide training for rural primary care providers and staff. The RITT addresses this pressing national need, which also is a VHA priority, by enabling convenient training at the practice site and enhancing geriatrics knowledge and skills for primary care providers (VHA 2013). CBOC providers and staff participate in an interactive eight-hour training day consisting of short didactic presentations, case discussions, demonstrations of geriatric screening methods, DVDs followed by group discussion, and action plans focused on microsystem change at the CBOC. The goal of the RITT Program is for providers and staff to have increased knowledge about principles of effective teamwork and common issues facing older veterans. Between 2011 and 2013, the RITT trained 523 health-care professionals from rural clinics across the country, as shown in Table 10.2. A recent evaluation of the program demonstrated its effectiveness in improving core competencies in geriatrics and improving the care that rural veterans receive at rural CBOCs (Tumosa et al. 2012).

Table 10.2: Rural Interdisciplinary Team Training Program
2012 Demographic Data by % (n = 227)

(n = 227)		
Age	n	%
20–30	6	3
31–40	36	16
41–50	55	24
51–60	54	24
61–70	36	16
71+	2	1
Unknown	38	17
Total participants	227	100
Race/Ethnicity		
White	129	57
African American	36	16
Asian	11	5
American Indian	1	0
Other	9	4
No race or unanswered	41	18
Total participants	227	100
Hispanic	17	7
Not Hispanic	210	93
Total participants	227	100
Gender		
Female	159	70
Male	63	28
No response	5	2
Total participants	227	100
Profession		
Registered nurse	53	23
Allopathic medicine	33	15
Licensed practical nurse	30	13
Pharmacy	14	6
Nurse practitioner	12	5
Social work	11	5
Health administration	10	4
Nutrition and food services	8	4
Other	45	20
No response	11	5
Total participants	227	100

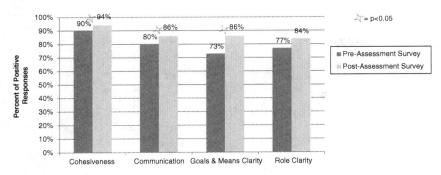

Figure 10.2: Rural Interdisciplinary Team Training Program (RITT) 2012 Changes in Team Development All Sites

In order to assess the performance of the rural CBOC teams, the Team Development Measure (TDM) (Salem-Schatz, Ordin, and Mittman 2010) is used as an evaluation tool to measure team cohesion, communication, and clarity of team roles and goals, and the means to achieve them over time. In 2012, there was a statistically significant increase in team cohesiveness, communication, and goals and means clarity across all sites among the health-care professionals from the beginning of the training when compared with 6 months after the training, as indicated in Figure 10.2. Additionally, an action plan is put into place by the team members to continue the momentum of the training day. Teams develop a plan related to geriatrics or team dynamics and identify challenges, resources, and strategies available to overcome barriers, benefits of the goal, data-collection process for monitoring activities, and a time frame for completing specific activities by individual team members.

Geriatric Education Center

The Consortium of New York Geriatric Education Centers (GEC), a partnership of the Icahn School of Medicine at Mount Sinai, New York University, Columbia University, GRECC at James J. Peters, Hebrew Home for the Aged, and Jewish Home Lifecare, educates providers, students, and faculty in geriatrics and gerontology through in-person and online training programs. In 2012, GEC offered full-day, in-person training programs in Montrose, Utica, and Binghamton, New York, all located in rural areas of the state. Each GEC training program includes a pre-, post-, and 30-day post-training questionnaire on the topics relevant to the particular day in order to assess providers' knowledge, skills, and attitudes. For

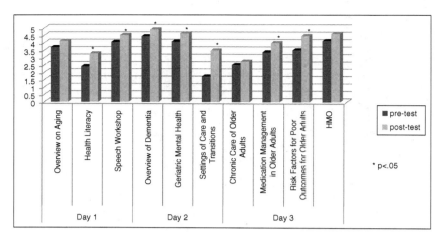

Figure 10.3: CNYGEC 2012 Rural Knowledge, Skills and Attitudes Assessment

all rural trainings, geriatrics knowledge, skills, and attitudes increased from the beginning to the end of the training day, as reflected in Figure 10.3. In March 2012, the RITT partnered with GEC and the Alzheimer's Association of Hudson Valley/Rockland/Westchester New York Chapter to present an eight-hour training on rural interprofessional teamwork in Harris, New York. The GEC, in collaboration with the VA Hudson Valley Health Care System and the Hudson Valley Rural Geriatric Education Collaborative, sponsored a three-day, 24-hour training series in Montrose, New York on working with older people, providing interdisciplinary geriatric care, and special considerations for older adults. A diverse group of health-care professionals, as shown in Table 10.3, reported on their knowledge, skills, and attitudes before and after the training. There was a significant increase in knowledge, skills, and attitudes related to the following topics: overview of aging, culture and aging, health literacy, effective communications/sensory changes with aging, speech workshop, overview of dementia, geriatric mental health, settings of care and transitions, medications management in older adults, risk factors for poor outcomes for older adults, and palliative care and ethical issues.

Discussion

Often, we, the urban members of the GERA collaborative, are met with some surprise from colleagues regarding our involvement in rural educa-

*Table 10.3: Consortium of New York Geriatric Education Centers
2012 Rural Demographic Data by % (n = 39)*

(n = 39)		
Age	n	%
30–39	2	5
40–49	3	8
50–59	19	49
60+	9	23
Unknown	6	15
Total participants	39	100
Race/Ethnicity		
White	23	60
Asian	9	23
Black	6	15
Hispanic	1	2
Total participants	39	100
Gender		
Female	34	87
Male	5	13
Total participants	39	100
What degrees do you hold?		
Associate	1	2
BSN	18	46
Masters	15	39
MD, PhD	5	13
Total participants	39	100

tion and training. Why, they ask, would we be delivering training in rural and remote regions of the United States? And what do the rural providers think of urban colleagues coming to their rural areas to deliver training? When we explain the rationale for programs that enhance geriatrics expertise among providers and staff and the need to incentivize trainees to work in rural areas, there is often an instant leap of understanding about what we are doing. GRECCs are strategically located within their respective Veterans Integrated Service Network (VISN) and are called upon to serve the needs of the VA nationally, which increasingly prioritizes the rural aging population. Moreover, GRECCs are located at richly resourced academic centers of excellence which further the reach of the VA mission to advance care for the entire United States. Our partners on the rural side of the collaborative understand that our expertise is enriching to their practice and patients and welcome our interest, resources, outreach, and solicitation of input. And we, the urban partners, many who grew up or have spent significant time in rural areas, are renewed by the opportunity to collaborate with rural providers and in the delivery of evidence-based health care.

The GERA program components are geared to improving care for older rural veterans with complex medical issues through a multimodal education and training collaborative. We work to enhance knowledge and skills in team-based geriatrics care through face-to-face and distance learning programs. GERA has been successful because of the strength of its academic partners in geriatrics and gerontology, the VHA network of medical centers, and CBOCs, supported by the GRECCs and, perhaps most importantly, funding from the VHA Office of Rural Health. Outcome measures are preliminary but promising in terms of the impact of the GERA programs on providers' knowledge and skills, clinical processes, and veterans' health care. While it is evident that GERA has an impact on VHA, the impact on the larger health-care delivery system may be more subtle. The VLC adds to the collective knowledge of rural geriatrics and is accessible to health-care professionals worldwide via the Internet. Long-term evaluation follow-up on the VLC has the potential to track how health-care professionals use their newly attained knowledge in daily practice. Through the Rural Provider and Health Care Staff Training and Education Initiative, younger generations of rural geriatric practitioners have the opportunity to take what they learn at the VHA and begin careers in other sectors. While the intention of training programs such as this is to attract future providers to the VHA, many in fact have careers in the non-VHA system and are sensitized to the health-care needs and issues of older veterans. The RITT program (see Figure 10.2) is geared to teams at VHA rural clinics but in fact has been adapted to non-VHA settings because of the relevance of the content to providers in the private sector. Through various presentations at national meetings, GERA has garnered interest among health-care professionals, faculty, and students throughout the United States who are interested in adopting the program in their health-care facilities or educational institutions. We have made the curricular materials for all GERA programs freely available through websites, SharePoint, and syllabi.

REFERENCES

Affordable Health Care for America. 2010. *Health Insurance Reform at a Glance: Rural America.* Washington DC: House Committees on Ways and Means, Energy and Commerce, and Education and Labor. Retrieved from http://docs.house.gov/energycommerce/RURAL.pdf.

American Geriatrics Society. 2014. *Current Geriatrician Shortfall.* New York: Geriatrics Workforce Policy Studies Center. Retrieved from http://www.americangeriatrics.org/files/documents/Adv_Resources/GeriShortageCurrentNumbers.pdf.

Arora, Sanjeev, Summers Kalishman, Denise Dion, Dara Som, Karla Thornton, Arthur Bankhurst, Jeanne Boyle, Michelle Harkins, Kathleen Moseley, Glen Murata, Miriam Komaramy, Joanna Katzman, Kathleen Colleran, Paulina Deming, and Sean Yutzy. 2011. "Partnering Urban Academic Medical Centers and Rural Primary Care Clinicians to Provide Complex Chronic Disease Care." *Health Affairs*, 30(6):1176-84.

Burrows, Elizabeth, Ryung Suh, and Danielle Hamann. 2012. *Health Care Workforce Distribution and Shortage Issues in Rural America.* Washington DC: National Rural Health Association.

Department of Veterans Affairs, Office of the Actuary. 2011. *Veteran Population Projection Model 2011.* Washington DC: Office of the Actuary. Retrieved from http://www.va.gov/vetdata/Veteran_Population.asp.

Gamm, Larry D. and Linnae L. Hutchison. 2004. "Rural Healthy People 2010: A Companion Document to Healthy People 2010." *The Texas A&M University System Health Science Center, School of Rural Public Health, Southwest Rural Health Research Center* 3:1-246.

Ganz, David A., Constance H. Fung, and David B. Reuben. 2008. "Key Elements of High-Quality Primary Care for Vulnerable Elders." *J Gen Intern Med* 23(23):2018-23.

Institute of Medicine. 2008. *Retooling for an Aging America: Building the Healthcare Workforce.* Washington DC: The National Academies Press. Retrieved from http://www.iom.edu/Reports/2008/Retooling-for-an-aging-America-Building-the-Health-Care-Workforce.aspx.

Knowles, Malcolm S. 1976. *The Modern Practice of Adult Education: Andragogy versus Pedagogy.* New York: Association Press.

Lee, Ming, LuAnn Wilkerson, David B. Reuben, and Bruce A. Ferrell. 2004. "Development and Validation of a Geriatric Knowledge Test for Medical Students." *JAGS* 52:938-88.

MacKenzie, Todd A., Amy E. Wallace, and William B. Weeks. 2010. "Impact of Rural Residence on Survival of Male Veterans Affairs Patients After Age 65." *Journal of Rural Health* 26(4):318-24.

Maiden, Robert J., Beverly P. Horowitz, and Judith L. Howe. 2010. "Workforce Training and Education Gaps in Gerontology and Geriatrics: What We Found in New York State." *Gerontology and Geriatrics Education* 31(4):328-48.

National Advisory Committee on Rural Health and Human Services. 2010. *The 2010 Report to the Secretary: Rural Health and Human Services Issues.* Washington DC: The National Advisory Committee on Rural Health and Human Services. Retrieved from http://www.hrsa.gov/advisorycommittees/rural/2010secretaryreport.pdf.

National Association of Social Workers. 2012. *Workforce Stats Show Social Work Field is Growing*. Washington DC: NASW News. Retrieved from http://www.social workblog.org/nasw-news-article/2012/06/workforce-stats-show-social-work-field-is-growing/.

Pachana, Nancy A., Erin Emery, Candace A. Konnert, Erin Woodhead, and Barry A. Edelstein. 2010. "Geropsychology Content in Clinical Training Programs: A Comparison of Australian, Canadian and U.S. data." *International Psychogeriatrics* 22(6):909–18.

Paradise, Julia, Cedric Dark, and Nicole Bitler. 2011. "Improving Access to Adult Primary Care in Medicaid: Exploring the Potential Role of Nurse Practitioners and Physician Assistants." *The Kaiser Commission on Medicaid and the Uninsured*. Washington DC: The Henry H. Kaiser Family Foundation. Retrieved from http://kaiserfamilyfoundation.files.wordpress.com/2013/01/8167.pdf.

Peterson, Lars E., Andrew Bazemore, Elizabeth J. Bragg, Imam Xierali, and Gregg A. Warshaw. 2011. "Rural-Urban Distribution of the U.S. Geriatrics Physician Workforce." *JAGS* 59(4):699–703.

Ruiz, Jorge G., Michael J. Mintzer, and Rosanne M. Leipzig. 2006. "The Impact of E-Learning in Medical Education." *Academic Medicine* 81(3):207–13.

Salem-Schatz, Susanne, Diana Ordin, and Brian Mittman. 2010. *Guide to the Team Development Measure*. Washington DC: Veterans Health Administration.

Salmon, Gilly 2000. *E-Moderating: The Key to Teaching and Learning Online*. London: Kogan Page.

Spies, Kate. 2012. "VA Aims to Revolutionize Veteran Care with SCAN-ECHO." *Government Health IT*. Retrieved from. http://www.govhealthit.com/news/va-aims-revolutionize-veteran-care-scan-echo.

Tumosa, Nina, Kathy Horvath, Terri Huh, Elayne E. Livote, Judith L. Howe, Lauren I. Jones, and Josea Kramer. 2012. "Healthcare Workforce Development in Rural America: When Geriatrics Expertise is 100 Miles Away." *Gerontology and Geriatrics Education* 33(2):133–51.

U.S. Census Bureau (2010). *The Next Four Decades. The Older Population in the United States: 2010–2050*. Washington, DC: Vincent, G.K. & Velkoff, V.A.

Veterans Health Administration. 2013. "Current VHA Legislative Priorities." Irving, TX: Veterans Health Affairs. Retrieved from https://www.vha.com/AboutVHA/PublicPolicy/Pages/CurrentLegisPriorities.aspx.

Weeks, William B., Amy E. Wallace, Stanley Wang, Austin F. Lee, and Lewis E. Kazis. 2006. "Rural-Urban Disparities in Health-Related Quality of Life within Disease Categories of Veterans." *Journal of Rural Health* 22(3):204–11.

Weeks, William B., Lewis E. Kazis, Yujing Shen, Zhongxiao Cong, Xinhua S. Ren, Donald Miller, Austin Lee, and Jonathan B. Perlin. 2004. "Differences in Health-Related Quality of Life in Rural and Urban Veterans." *American Journal of Public Health* 94(10):1762–7.

Woodland, Dawn E., Linda F. Szul, and Wayne A. Moore. 2007. "Virtual Learning Communities." *Business Education Digest* 16:70.

CHAPTER 11

THE SYNERGISTIC INTERPLAY OF PHILOSOPHY, PLACE, PROGRAM, AND POLICY

Learning the Art of the Possible from Small-House Nursing Homes

Rosalie A. Kane and Lois J. Cutler

INTRODUCTION

Developing and sustaining group residential settings that support autonomy and better quality of life (QOL) for older people with substantial disability and functional impairment is a persistent challenge. Fueled since 1995 by the Pioneer Network in Long-Term Care (Koren 2010), the culture change movement for nursing homes (NHs) has made strides in promoting individualized person-centered services in NHs and empowerment of both residents and direct-care unlicensed staff. But some critics lament the enthusiastic embrace of its vaguer tenets (Rahman and Schnelle 2008) and some question the evidence base for culture-change activities (Shier et al. 2014). Meanwhile, institutional living erodes residents' QOL and their sense of identity.

The more care seniors need, the fewer their options are for appealing, function-enhancing living quarters. Assisted living (AL) settings often are made up of comfortable, attractive apartments, yet state policies on the scope of AL practice, supply, and Medicaid rates as well as the providers' targeted market and prevailing rates for privately paying residents put most AL settings out of reach for seniors qualifying for NH levels of care. Another approach is to transform licensed and certified NHs into desirable homes. Here, we describe our cumulative research on a potentially transformative NH model, small-house NHs (SH-NHs) and the trademarked Green House® (GH) version.

BACKGROUND

Prevalent Ideas Incorporated into Green Houses®

Small Scale

Hospital-like facilities and their cavernous dining rooms are gradually being reconfigured into decentralized organizations. Much decentralization has aimed to make the nursing unit or wing, which typically houses 40–50 residents, the focal point of NH life. A further level of decentralization creates a *neighborhood* or *household* organization with smaller living units (perhaps with 25 or fewer residents) to make daily living more manageable and familiar and take on attributes of home (Grant and Norton 2003; Green 2014).

Private Rooms

The large stock of hospital-like NH buildings made up of double rooms (or even three- or four-person rooms) is resistant to change, even in new construction, because a double room is the basic Medicaid benefit. A multifaceted study of privacy preferences found that consumers and their families strongly prefer private bedrooms and bathrooms, regardless of race or ethnicity of respondents (Kane et al. 1998), debunking the notion that older people find pleasant companionship with assigned roommates in shared quarters. Further, Calkins and Cassella (2007) convincingly showed the health and social benefits of single occupancy. Moreover, the cost of building single rooms and bathrooms is negligible in new construction, and operational costs for single occupancy may even be lower than for shared rooms.

Individualized Person-Centered Services

Individualized approaches are embedded in the NH culture change movement, including in the Eden Alternative, as an approach to normal-

PHILOSOPHY, PLACE, PROGRAM, AND POLICY

izing NH life and dispel loneliness, boredom, helplessness, and lack of meaning (Thomas 1996). The Eden Alternative goes beyond its popularized incorporation of animals and plants to flattened hierarchies and empowerment of certified nursing assistant (CNA) staff so that they can empower residents. Common wisdom suggests that the permanent assignment of CNAs to residents is an important step in fostering individualized services.

Description of the GH Model

GHs are small, self-contained dwelling-places, which, as conceptualized by Thomas (2004: 222–35), require comprehensive systemic changes that deinstitutionalize NHs by simultaneously and substantially modifying three aspects of NHs: physical environments, staffing models, and the philosophy underlying care (Rabig et al. 2006).

Physical Environments

Scale initially was conceptualized as seven to ten residents, and later increased to up to twelve residents. Entry to the GH cannot be achieved through traversing other hallways; most GHs are literally separate houses but high-rise urban GHs have been developed, each as separate apartments with their entrances off elevator lobbies. GHs use residential materials and seek residential scale for common spaces (including in kitchens accessible to residents). The private rooms and bathrooms tend to be much larger (sometimes triple) the minimum federal NH square footage of requirements (a meager 100 square feet for single rooms). Each trademarked GH includes a dining table that seats at least 16 (ample for all residents and on-duty direct-care staff, and a few guests), a fireplace in the living area, inviting outdoor space, function-enhancing technology such as ceiling lifts in residents' rooms, resident-accessible laundry areas, spas with whirlpools, and beauty salon stations.

Staff

Staffing is built around CNAs who receive substantial additional preemployment training. They perform their usual personal care duties but also cook and serve meals and do light housekeeping and laundry. They may coordinate care planning meetings, act as rehabilitation aides (overseeing range-of-motion and other exercises), and serve as activity personnel. The term *shahbaz* (plural, *shahbazim*) is suggested but not required for CNAs in GHs; however, GHs must find a fresh term for those in the reconfigured CNA role. The shahbazim support the work of all professionals (not just nurses) and their most fundamental role is assistance to residents.

Typically, two to three shahbazim work on day shifts, two on evening shifts, and one or two at night. They work in house-specific self-directed teams across shifts and sometimes alternate leadership roles—for example, house coordinator, scheduler, food coordinator, cleaning coordinator, or activity coordinator. They are directly responsible to guides, who may be the NH administrator of record. All professional personnel (for example, nurses, medical directors, social workers, rehabilitation therapists, or activity directors) constitute a clinical support team that serves the GHs as home-care staff might serve its clientele. To be realistic financially, the model cuts back or eliminates cooks and dietary service workers, laundry workers, housekeepers, and even rehabilitation aides and activity assistants with the assumption that shahbazim will perform these functions. GH-NHs include all the positions and functions required under federal regulations, but the model disrupts the usual NH hierarchy in ways that the Eden Alternative did not.

Philosophy

Consistent with the culture change movement and Eden Alternative, the GH philosophy emphasizes QOL, resident autonomy, resident choice, and individualized service. Residents are likely to become well-known to the shahbazim and to benefit from informal interactions with each other, staff, and visitors through the entire day and week.

Importantly, these GHs are NHs. They must serve residents with the range of care needs found in NHs and draw on state NH reimbursement rates, which almost always far exceed AL rates. They thus present a groundbreaking chance to explore whether a social model with many attributes considered "amenities" can be provided to a typical high-acuity NH population within the constraints of the state's Medicaid rates and with levels of QOL atypical for most NHs.

Implementation of GH-NHs

In 2002, the Robert Wood Johnson Foundation (RWJF) funded William Thomas at the Center for Growing and Becoming to encourage NH providers to develop GHs. Project staff worked with about a dozen potential sponsors, including the sponsor of the first operational GHs in Tupelo, Mississippi. In 2005, the RWJF made a $10 million, ten-year grant to Capital Impact to spread the GH concept through technical assistance (but not construction funds) to interested providers. According to the GH Project website (see http://thegreenhouseproject.org/green-house-model/find-home), by early 2015, 18 organizations were sponsoring 20 separate GH projects in NHs in 17 states; the project scale ranged from 1 to 16 GHs and included some built on new campuses with GHs only and some that were an added "product line" to existing senior living campuses. Many more GH-NH projects were under development. Only one sponsor had a for-profit tax status.

CONCEPTUAL, EMPIRICAL, AND THEORETICAL BACKGROUND

Three-Legged Stool Framework

Keren Brown Wilson (2007) envisaged group residential settings as a three-legged stool, with each leg integral to quality (Figure 11.1). The first leg is the residential environment with its two prongs—the private and the shared environment. The second leg is the service capacity with its two prongs: the capacity for routine services to meet functional needs including routine nursing and medication management, and the capacity to marshal specialized health and other services as needed. The final leg is a philosophy of respect for resident control and choice, again on two dimensions: their care and their lives. The GH has high potential for realizing the elements of this model.

Physical Environments

Theoretical Models

Lawton's ecological model posits the concepts *of environmental stress* (which must be minimized) and *environmental press* (which must be present) in living settings for seniors with functional and/or cognitive

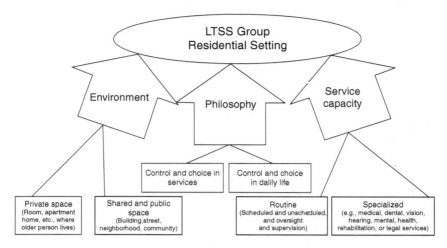

Figure 11.1: Schematic Model for Quality in LTSS Group Residential Settings. (Adapted from Wilson 2007)

impairments (Lawton and Nahemow 1973). With aging, control over one's environments is often compromised; environmental supports are needed to promote mobility and independence. Yet environments must pose sufficient challenge (or press) to engage and interest residents. Graham Rowles further took into account the access of individuals to various aspects of their near, mid, and remote environments (Rowles and Bernard 2013). In GHs, the private room is commodious with views to the outside, and access to inviting shared space is nearby. SH-NHs potentially can offer a better mix of environmental support and environmental press, and afford residents more chances to experience multiple environmental levels than can traditional NHs. In the latter, few residents benefit from special features such as restaurants, exercise facilities, or swimming pools—whether GH residents achieve such benefits will depend on how the staff models and philosophy work in practice.

Studying Environment and QOL

We examined the relationship between physical environments and QOL in a large multistate study of 2,000 NH residents. We used self-reported measures for 11 interrelated QOL outcome domains including comfort, security, autonomy, dignity, individuality, privacy, meaningful activity, relationships, enjoyment, functional competence and spiritual well-being. These measures were shown to be reliable for many residents with substantial cognitive impairment (Kane et al. 2003).

Environmental attributes were positively related to QOL self-reports on multiple QOL domains. For example, being in a private room was associated not only with QOL outcome measures for privacy but also with domains such as meaningful activity, relationships, enjoyment, and functional competence. To assess environments themselves, we developed detailed objective checklists completed by trained observers without special expertise for environmental assessments at the level of resident's rooms, nursing units, and entire NH. We then created composite conceptual measures to assess each resident's actual environment on constructs such as personalization, visual privacy, and amenability to resident control at the room level; function-enhancing features and enjoyment-enhancing features at each environmental level; dining experience; and bathing experience. We thus could zero in on a specific resident's environment—his/her room size, location, and view; the functionality of knobs, faucets, light switches, closets, mirrors, and other features for his/her condition; his/her dining and bathing experience; the distances he/she needed to traverse to get outside; and the common spaces he/she actually could access (Cutler et al. 2006). Although these tools need updating for SH-NHs, they point to an approach for future research.

Family Support and Residential Care Settings

Ethel Shanas (1979) and Elaine Brody (1985) long ago dispelled the myth that family members abandon their frail, elderly relatives. But much of the conceptualization and research on family caregiving roles is predicated on community-dwelling older people. The mechanistic and dehumanizing term "placement," for admission to an NH, encapsulates that the resident has been sent somewhere outside normal family life. When families are too conspicuously present, engage in actual care delivery, or give too much advice, NH staff tends to say family has overstepped proper boundaries, although family members often perceive advocacy for their relatives as part of their role (Bowers 1988; Hamann 2014). Zimmerman and colleagues (2013) conducted a group-randomized trial of a *Family Matters* intervention in NHs and ALs that culminated in family members signing on to a Family Matters Service Plan that specified their own roles to improve the residents' QOL. Despite modest benefits for residents, staff member enthusiasm, and family perceptions that their relatives in the demonstration had better QOL, family members in the demonstration experienced more guilt and burden and more conflict with staff. The Family Matters program, and others like it, underscore that the staff is in charge in NHs and family roles, even if promoting QOL, are typically ancillary and planned.

Though family members may be intensely involved and be frequent visitors, family tends to fit poorly into NH life. In contrast, GH-NHs usually welcome family participation, including that of minor children, in any way and time that residents and families chose, including being guests at meals or overnight. GHs potentially could mitigate family guilt about choosing an NH and allow families to function independently of staff-initiated care plans.

OUR RESEARCH ON SH-NHs

From 2000 to 2015, we completed four projects on GHs (two with longitudinal data collection from residents, family, and front-line staff and three entailing systematic environmental measures). In chronological order, we briefly review the goals, methods, and findings of each study.

Quasi-Experimental Study of First Operational GH

The Setting

In 2003, the Traceway Retirement Community in Tupelo, Mississippi, the flagship location for Methodist Senior Services (MSS), built four 10-person GHs in an undeveloped part of its residential campus and downsized the remaining, formerly 180-bed NH to about 100 beds. The first two GHs were occupied by 20 residents from the sponsoring NH's outdated dementia special care unit, and the other two by residents of the downsizing NH. Subsequent vacancies in the GH were filled from waiting lists of those already on campus.

Research Methods

Using a quasi-experimental design, we compared the GHs to the legacy NH on campus and to a smaller, newer NH at another MSS campus. We interviewed residents, their family members, and all shahbazim (CNAs in comparison settings) at baseline and at three subsequent six-month intervals. We used national quality measures derived from the NH minimum data set to determine whether any physical health detriments resulted from what some critics saw as a de-professionalized setting. We hypothesized that, compared with control settings, QOL for residents and satisfaction and involvement of families would be better in GHs; quality of care outcomes would be as good; and frontline staff would be more engaged, know their residents better, and be more satisfied with their work. We also conducted postoccupancy evaluations (POEs), a technique that combines qualitative and quantitative techniques and includes structured observation of how space is used, environmental tracers such as worn areas, and interviews with users of the space (Preiser, Rabinowitz, and White 1988).

Findings

The GH residents experienced better QOL. No quantitative quality indicators declined for GH residents and a few indicators (most notably, decline in late-loss functional abilities) favored the GHs, suggesting no deleterious health effects (Kane et al. 2007). Further, family members were more engaged with relatives in the GHs and more satisfied with services (Lum et al. 2008).

Compared with control groups, staff members knew their residents better and expressed more job satisfaction (Kane 2005). Open-ended comments from all groups were positive. Direct-care staff largely liked their new role and the new name. Some found the culinary skills challenging, a few were frightened working alone in the SH at night, and some complained that the self-managed team concept broke down if others failed to pull their weight. Most took pride in their new setting. Many commented that despite expanded duties, the pace was more relaxing with more time to interact with residents than in previous traditional NH jobs.

The longitudinal POE (Cutler and Kane 2009) showed that the designs facilitated resident function and well-being and that users—residents, visitors, staff—liked the settings. Informants made useful suggestions for change or incorporation into the next designs; examples included paved sidewalks to encourage family to wheel or walk with residents, automatic doors for patio access, more wall storage space near resident's rooms, and redesigned showers. Staff needed to be vigilant to avoid what was sometimes called *institution creep* in routines and to avoid clutter. Conscious effort was needed to ensure that the potential of the new environments was actualized (Kane and Cutler 2009a; Kane and Cutler 2007).

This study was more ambitious and controlled than any former or subsequent GH study but still had limitations, including an imperfect separation between the legacy NH and the GH on the same campus, a two-year span, and possible Hawthorne effects in a highly publicized program.

Evolution of SH-NHs in Three Large Firms

In 2008, we received a small grant from an operating consortium of nonprofit NH firms that were committed to developing and testing innovations such as SH-NHs, effective use of technology, and branching into home care. The goal was to explore issues in implementation of SH-NHs in three firms in the consortium, all faith-based, multicampus innovative firms: the organizations were MSS of Mississippi (henceforth Firm A), Otterbein Lifestyle Choices (Firm B), and Presbyterian Villages of Michigan (Firm C). (See Table 11.1 for a descriptive summary of the organizations.)

Research Method

We used semistructured interview guides to explore issues that the organizations took into account in deciding to develop SH-NHs; any development or regulatory challenges they faced; their decisions about staffing details, physical plants, programs, target populations, and desired case mix; issues that arose as the SH-NHs matured; and the business experience of running SH-NHs. At each SH complex, we probed whether and how the SHs were differentiated from each other— whether they developed a house personality due to their mix of residents and their particular staff. At site visits over 18 months, we talked to dozens of corporate personnel, including CEOs, CFOs, corporate personnel assigned to regulatory affairs, human resources, clinical services, marketing, and board members, and at the local level, we talked

Table 11.1: Comparison of AL Development in Three Firms

Firm (State)	Organization before Small-Houses (SHs) were Built	Summary of SH Experience
Firm A (Mississippi)	Ten campuses all over the state with independent housing duplexes, market-rate and low-income apartments, and assisted living (AL); nursing homes (NHs) were on just three campuses; 180 beds at flagship campus, and two smaller NHs.	Downsized 180-bed NH to 140 and, in 2003, opened four 10-person Green House (GH)-NHs in a residential section of campus for 40 beds. In 2005, opened six more 12-person GHs, leaving 38 beds in the legacy home, largely for postacute care. By 2006, partnered with a failing nonprofit NH to create a campus of six 10-person GHs, which became the eleventh campus. Also added two GH AL settings to another campus without an NH.
Firm B (Ohio)	Six campuses with senior housing and apartments, assisted living, and (on five campuses) existing NHs.	Obtained certificate of need and beds for planned SH development. Except for a single house on a campus with no NH, other SH neighborhoods were built sequentially, each with five 10-person houses. Four were operating when we started the study, and two more are now operating. The SH neighborhoods are each licensed as a separate NH. Other initiatives include development of hospice and home health system-wide within the firm, and investment in the existing campus.
Firm C (Michigan)	More than 25 continuing care campuses all over the state with mixes of market and low-income housing, assisted living, and memory care. Only a few campuses had NHs.	Built two ten-person GHs on a campus where an NH already existed. Redid a postacute care unit at the legacy home. No more NHs were developed. The firm expanded into low-income areas, community health programs, and PACE programs at various sites.

to administrators and other SH personnel, including some CNA-level staff and board members.

Findings

Firms A and B substantially expanded their SH-portfolios, convincing their boards to move to SH-NHs despite prior financial and emotional investment in existing models. Firm C did not expand beyond its two GHs on one NH campus. With the exception of the two original dementia houses in Firm A, no effort was made to group residents by cognitive abilities.

As described previously, Firm A had created the first operational GH model. Convinced that SHs were the path to better NH care and finding that managing both a conventional NH and GHs on the same campus was challenging, Firm A accelerated its expansion from four to ten GHs, bringing its GH capacity to 102. Its second wave of GHs on campus were built with 12 rooms each, a change that permitted staffing in each home by an extra 0.5 full-time equivalents (FTEs). In practice, the footprint of the new GHs was a bit large for coziness, and the half-time shahbaz disrupted the teams while being needed in both assigned homes during the same peak hours. With ten GHs on campus, administration became more complex—the number of guides increased, a *coach* role for peer support and advising of shahbazim was created, and the overall NH administrator no longer served as a guide.

To expand further, Firm A needed more beds. To that end, it acquired a near-bankrupt 40-bed nonprofit NH in a small town near the state capital and, with legislative action, was able to expand it to build a group of six 10-person GHs at a new location, which became Firm A's eleventh location. A guide from the original GH trained all personnel in the model, and all unlicensed personnel at the old home were trained to the CNA level and then as shahbazim.

Firm B was convinced of the merits of the SH concept and, through several CEOs and the development of all the homes, the Boards of Directors and leadership staff held to an idealistic vision. Often using the tagline "small house, big difference," the vision is articulated as a frontal attack on institutional care models, which limit both residents and staff. While inaugurating a new SH construction in 2013, CEO Jill Hreben expressed this vision as follows:

PHILOSOPHY, PLACE, PROGRAM, AND POLICY

> [Our] small house neighborhoods fulfill our call to create an environment
> that frees older persons, to ensure these people have what we can't imag-
> ine being without—control over our own lives. Some have called [FIRM B]
> radical. We prefer liberators on a mission ... to liberate the nation from the
> mindset of institutional care.
>
> *(Otterbein n.d.)*

Firm B planned carefully from the outset, acquiring beds largely by downsizing its NHs and assembling certificates of need for seven sites. In Ohio, bed supply is managed at the county level. Though beds were mostly drawn from downsizing a large flagship NH in nearby Dayton and a smaller one near Toledo, Firm B needed to purchase beds at a high price to expand at its northeastern campus without an existing NH; accordingly, it built just a single ten-person SH there. This one house bore all the required NH overhead because the state would not allow the director of nursing (DON) from the heavy-care AL located a few feet away to be shared with the SH. Operating a ten-person, long-stay NH was financially impossible. That SH became dedicated to Medicare-funded postacute care, which was needed in the region, and the project succeeded but could not test the SH model for living or the new staff roles. All other Firm B SH projects are five-house complexes and are located away from multilevel campuses.

Here, we summarize the highlights in Firm B's SH evolution:

- By the end of the study period, Firm B sequentially had built four SH-neighborhoods in residential areas, each with five 10-person houses; each configuration held a separate NH license. (Following the plan, two other communities were opened after the study period and at the time of writing other neighborhoods are being developed. Depending on location, the plan was that one or two houses per project would be dedicated to postacute services.)
- Like Firm A, Firm B developed a coach position, but in its model the coaches had administrative training and direct responsibility for overseeing CNA-level resident assistants—the term used rather than shahbazim.
- Rather quickly, the firm decided that the SH-neighborhoods should be operated as a separate division from the legacy cam-

puses (which themselves needed investment) for the benefit of both models. After some rebranding, the firm now has two major divisions: its Lifestyle Communities, i.e., multi-level campus with various types of housing, AL, and NHs; and Skilled Nursing Home and Rehabilitation Neighborhoods.

- Optimally, Firm B strived for a mix of payment sources, including private pay, Medicare, and Medicaid, and attempted to dedicate one SH or more to posthospital care for persons discharged from hospitals. Such houses had higher staff ratios. If long-stay residents developed a need for posthospital care (for example, after a hip fracture), they ordinarily returned to their own SH and either received rehabilitation there or were brought to the rehabilitation SH house to use the equipment and work with specialists.

Firm C, one of the earliest sponsors of a GH, created two houses with pleasing architectural features; the houses were more spacious than others previously developed and boasted garages and front hall closets. They had the advantage of being situated so that their front yards and porches faced a residential street so private homeowners were the neighbors. The shahbaz staff was assigned permanently to each house, but the charge nurses were not permanently assigned at the time we visited but rather were drawn from a part-time pool. The management was pleased with the GHs but was not planning to change all NH stock on the campus into SHs or to build GHs on its other campuses (most of which had no NHs). The legacy NH was remodeled to create a separate entrance for its postacute care section with an imposing entrance and all private rooms, a priority over redesigning the long-stay units there.

At the time of our visit, Firm C was developing outreach models to urban, low-income areas and the development efforts of the firm were in other directions. From the experiences of Firm C, we saw that it was possible to build a few SH-NH on a campus and add it to the choices available rather than adopt the format as the best way to deliver NH care through an entire system. We were unable to identify which system was used to allocate residents to the two GHs rather than the legacy home, and do not know whether, eventually, the state Medicaid program allowed a higher rate for the GH residents. In October 2015, Firm C sold the legacy NH and the two GHs, in keeping with its direction away from NHs and toward home care and low-cost housing. The new owner is retaining the GH model (personal communication, January 7, 2016).

From this small study, we learned that evolving and expanding SH-NHs was a difficult as well as rewarding task involving trial and error and much detail, though not all adopters pursued the model firm-wide. More specific conclusions that emerge from the case study derived from Firm A and B are summarized as follows (Kane and Cutler 2009a):

- Developing optimal staff mixes for SHs and determining what tasks should belong to the CNA-level personnel was an ongoing issue. The RN/LPN-to-resident ratios were higher than in most NHs, in part because of safety concerns of nurse leaders. Refining the CNA-level role entailed determining pay levels for SH CNAs compared with CNAs elsewhere in the firm, and determining the specific boundaries of the elder assistant role.
- Freestanding SH-NH communities of five houses could end up with a heavy management and professional structure. Firm B's 50-bed NHs each had four senior positions—an administrator, a DON, a minimum data set (MDS) coordinator, and a coach, a costly overhead for a 50-bed NH. (We note that, in 2016, two pairs of nearby houses share an administrator, which seems a good idea both for cost savings and to add interest to the position.)
- The original GH model gave little attention to the roles of required positions in NHs such as DON, social service director, activities director, in-service educator, or dietary consultant; the first adopters had to develop the details, deciding whether and how to combine positions or share them between nearby SH communities. At the time of our study, Firm B had decided to combine some positions between two closely located SHs and had decided to maintain the separate MDS coordinator role rather than offer it to the DON or charge nurses. (We would guess the model has evolved further in subsequent years in both firms.) Unconstrained by the GH trademark, Firm B tended to develop approaches that worked in a particular geographical area based on the other organizational resources and personnel in the locality rather than imposing them on all their SHs.
- Involuntary relocation of residents between SHs was inconsistent with the model, though on request residents could relocate.

Strategies to managed higher acuity in an SH included adding personnel from in-house temporary pools or temporary agencies, or bringing in hospice services, which were being heavily marketed to NHs in the state at the time.

- In general, 12–18 months seemed to be required for an SH-NH to hit its operational stride. We could discern differences in the SH sites that had been operating longest.
- The activity function largely fell to the CNA-level staff, supported by a half-time activity director; the former had care duties that made planning off-site activities difficult and the latter were still working out their roles. Volunteer functions were not well developed, and vans tended to be shared and available on limited schedules only.
- The initial GH rhetoric about empowering the CNA level left nurses feeling dispossessed and devalued, as well as worried about quality of care. Yet nurses were vitally needed to teach and model to direct-care staff. Integrating licensed nurses into SH operations and establishing their unique roles without undermining the autonomy of front-line staff was a challenge. The GH project incorporated self-directed, cross-shift teams of shahbazim into Thomas's original model early in its evolution with the intent that teams manage their own scheduling and that professionals would attend team meetings by invitation only. In practice, the teams sometimes floundered, and self-scheduling failed. Exclusion of licensed staff from self-managed teams was meant to develop CNA leadership, but accentuated the divide between CNA-level staff and nurses.
- Handling food and meals was an ongoing theme because menu planning, food ordering, food delivery, cooking, and actual meal service needed reinvention in SHs. SHs on a campus could order raw foods from central kitchens, sometimes with some prior preparation. In Firm A's second NH-GH project, which consisted of six SHs without a large NF on the campus, the food vendor refused to divide the orders among the houses without prohibitive added costs; therefore, all the boxes were off-loaded on the dining room table of one house SH for redistribution. Other issues included negotiating with food service vendors with their own menus and models, minimizing but providing as-needed special diets; pur-

chasing fresh food from local stores; managing waste; and trying to implement house-specific menus.

- We were unable to isolate costs of SH-NHs compared with legacy NHs and other entities when both were on the same campus, as in Firms A and C. Determining differential costs for each SH in a project (relevant for all three firms) was even more difficult because labor, raw food, and supplies were not clearly allocated to houses and our grant budget did not permit us to further disentangle the costs.

- Regulatory issues were a constant concern and regulators were unpredictable in ways that varied within states. State regulatory agencies might have been enthusiastic about the potential of SH-NHs but local inspectors were unprepared for what they found. Federal look-behind inspectors could create havoc by requirements for expensive changes that had already been approved by the state in the construction phase. For Firm B, the state originally required that each house to be occupied by a few private-pay residents before the complex could be certified, leading to high initial costs and a nonoptimal start to implementing the new staffing models.

Dementia in SH-NHs

The Settings

With funding from the Alzheimer's Association, we studied how SH models worked for people with Alzheimer's disease or substantial cognitive and communication impairment. The study took place in Firm B. At that time, Firm B had three operating SH projects, each located in residential neighborhoods, with 50 residents in five SHs. For comparison, we sampled cognitively impaired residents in Firm B's three legacy NHs, two of which had dementia units.

Method

We used MDS diagnosis and/or MDS cognitive performance scores to identify all residents with dementia or related conditions in the SHs and the comparison settings, and followed their trajectory over a year. Data collection included interviews with residents and a direct assessment of cognition, interviews with a resident assistant who knew that resident, and phone interviews with a family member. Open-ended questions tapped care strategies, if any, for this resident, and what the resident assistant had determined gave the resident pleasure or upset the resident. We also conducted key informant interviews with major staff— guide, coach, activities and social work personnel, MDS coordinators, and some charge nurses—to elicit respondents' impressions about how the SH settings worked for dementia and evaluated the physical environments. A year later, we repeated the resident-level data collection, often with a different staff respondent, and, if the resident had died or relocated, we obtained information about the circumstances.

Findings

We identified 67 cognitively impaired residents from 120 long-stay SH residents, and a comparable number from the comparison NHs. The sample included three married couples, where one or both spouses were in the study. Among the sample were residents with strokes and cognitive impairment due to trauma or drug reactions. A side observation was that the record systems prohibited a clear identification of the etiology of the dementia; this was particularly true in the comparison sites where many residents had dwelled for decades and a few might have originally been mislabeled as having cognitive impairment.

The participating residents largely did well in the SHs (Kane et al. 2011). In one SH, a group of five residents with dementia relocated there from the dementia special-care unit of the legacy NH along with a staff member. The latter reported that several residents regained functional abilities in the new setting. In general, staff stated that wandering and exit-seeking were minimized. We noticed considerable interaction such as chatting and joking among the residents, including those with dementia. For example, one resident whose dementia advanced more quickly than the others was interacting with a life-like animated dog, and another resident with dementia commented that an additional advantage of that dog was that it ate very little. One resident with dementia was engrossed in gardening, a hobby she shared with a cognitively intact resident; each had a labeled box for their tools on the patio. Some residents gravitated to particular staff members, regardless of their role; for

PHILOSOPHY, PLACE, PROGRAM, AND POLICY

example, a male resident bonded with a maintenance man. One resident exercised his preference to remain in his room most of the day and come to the common living space at night. Contrary to expectations, residents with dementia tolerated long meals, though one resident was noted to get up and down from the table frequently during meals.

The sample included three couples with one or both spouses cognitively impaired. Because public policies prohibited sponsors from adding residents to a house or from giving price breaks to spouses who shared rooms, the marital pairs received two rooms. All couples in the sample chose to share bedrooms. In one instance, in which the husband was very disabled with stroke and the wife had mild dementia, they used the extra room for their computer and a wide television; the extra room was a place where they watched old movie channels, a playroom for their visiting grandchildren, and a place where the wife (one of the above-mentioned gardeners) started plants for the GH patio garden in the extra shower. For couples, the second room worked best if they were contiguous, but in another case, the couple had a second room across the hall, which they used for a sitting and TV room. One couple, both with dementia, who were not part of the study due to refusal by the family guardian, occupied separate rooms at the behest of that guardian who believed it was better for them. We noticed them constantly together in the shared spaces. (In future developments, perhaps rooms can be designed with connecting doors, in the manner of adjoining hotel rooms or with an easily knocked-out wall, so that contiguous rooms need not be entered from the central area.) One husband died just before we returned for our follow-up visits and his widow received enormous support from the group. Many residents went to the funeral, and the family opted to have the postfuneral reception at the SH where their mother still lived. In another situation, a resident's wife remained in her own home but spent long hours at the SH almost every day, usually having lunch and often dinner there. To preserve her husband's dapper appearance, she posted detailed instructions in her husband's closet about maintenance of his wardrobe and placed her chosen outfits for each day of the week on labeled hangers in the closet. The SH-NH seemed to support husbands and wives well in the face of dementia.

According to our observations and discussions, cognitively intact residents who were in houses where more than half of the residents were cognitively impaired experienced no problems related to being with so many residents with dementia. The former enjoyed their private space and their time with staff and their own families and several told us they preferred the SH greatly over more traditional NHs where they had been. Often these were younger residents below age 75, who kept their own hours and were up well into the evenings. On several occasions when one of us made late evening visits to interview an evening staff member after their peak work time, it was a resident who answered our knock on the door.

Only two residents in our sample left the SH for a more typical NH, one at the request of management and one at the initiative of a daughter. (We were told of a third situation of an involuntary departure that just predated our study.) In all three cases, the residents manifested behavior that staff could not manage. A resident who was quite functional with a walker emitted loud noises, called *vocalizations* in the medicalized term, that resounded through the SH day and night; this seemingly involuntary noise ceased when she began speaking. Another resident was anxious and hyperactive and needed to be engaged almost continuously—a task staff thought should be performed by family. The third resisted care and seemed to be in pain—she was calmer with one of the morning staff. (This last situation occurred in the first year of the home's operation; the guide told us that they would have been able to manage the situation given current staff capability). In the case of the resonating noise, night nurses did not intervene with suggestions for mitigating the problem because of boundaries that they saw as intrinsic to the model. Again, with greater maturity of the setting, such a problem might be managed.

The SH resident assistants were empowered to look at the health records (not permitted in the comparison settings), but only a few took time to do so. The resident assistants reported high familiarity with likes and dislikes of the residents about their past work or interests and their family structure, but were not familiar with the residents' health conditions, including the etiology of the dementia and the nature of coexisting illnesses.

Family members were generally pleased with the friendly atmosphere of the SHs, though they mentioned a few concerns. One otherwise-satisfied daughter recounted "the episode" when SH staff phoned her for permission to transfer her father to a hospital for observation because he seemed more than usually belligerent and a small army knife was found

PHILOSOPHY, PLACE, PROGRAM, AND POLICY

among the memorabilia in his room. Reconstructing the incident, it seemed another sample member with mild dementia was annoyed by the resident with the disruptive vocalizations, and her father gallantly and aggressively sprang to the first lady's defense. The respondent took her dad for a visit to her own home and brought him to her family doctor (who thought he posed no threat whatsoever) and the crisis blew over. Her confidence was a bit shaken and she wondered what would have happened had she been unreachable at that moment. She believed he would have declined during an observational stay in a psychiatric hospital and that the situation should have been de-escalated and the combatants distracted. The daughter of the resident with the disturbing vocalizations was a retired early childhood specialist who was generally unsatisfied with what she thought was an underdeveloped activity program. She suggested and led spelling bees, which the residents loved. Staff was surprised by the suggestion, assuming that residents with dementia—and especially one with a piercing verbal tic—would be unable to spell. Such examples illustrate the need for more dementia training; in this example, staff might learn about abilities that are often retained despite substantial dementia.

These few "failures" notwithstanding, we were impressed with the successes possible in normal environments. Families generally expressed satisfaction with their relatives' situation. We observed family members, including small children, coming in and out of the homes, sharing meals at the SH, and interacting with other residents besides their own relative. We were repeatedly told that family no longer dreaded visiting in the NH, and that they were comfortable bringing minor children into the setting because it was not fearsome. The most frequent family concern, oddly, was that their relatives were receiving *too much* choice. Examples centered on choices family members believed their relative could not and should not be asked to make—for example, about whether they want to get up in the morning or stay in bed most of the day, missing two meals (Shippee et al. 2011). Training could have helped staff distinguish between having residents choose rising and retiring times and times for breakfast based on habitual personal rhythms, and helping residents with dementia get themselves started in some pattern consistent with their preferences. Staff told us that when residents rolled over and waved them off, they saw that as a resident choice to be honored. Again, more just-in-time training could mitigate those issues.

A year later, most of the residents were stable or had declined cognitively and functionally. But a few improved, one dramatically so. On our first visit, she was completely unresponsive and her son, who was making his daily visit, said that was the way she had been for months. But at follow-up, she was much more alert and talking a little.

Our general conclusion was that SH-NHs are not only feasible but preferable NH locations for many people with dementia because of their scale, familiarity, and individualized philosophy, but that staff training was needed for optimal realization of the potential in the model. From the comparison sites, we learned that once already established in an NH, some families were reluctant to try a more normalized mode. Families from comparison settings told us they were aware of SH options but that such settings would "never work" for a person like their relative—this despite the fact that others like their relatives had successfully relocated as part of the downsizing.

SH-NH Typology

Aims

Between 2011 and 2013, we conducted a multistage study of SH-NHs with the following aims: (1) describe the prevalence and location of SH-NHs in the United States; (2) collect detailed information about the identified SH-NHs and empirically derive a classification system; and (3) conduct in-depth studies of ten SH-NHs along the categories derived.

Method and Findings by Aim

For aim 1, we began with a working definition of SH-NHs that was less restrictive than GHs. To qualify, the setting needed to be self-contained, housing no more than 18 residents; be comprised of private bedrooms and bathrooms; use permanently assigned front-line staff; and prepare and serve meals in the SH itself. Besides identifying operating GH-NHs from the GH project, we telephoned multiple informants per state—the state licensing and inspection agency, the state ombudsman office, the state NH trade associations, a culture change coalition (if there was one), and even culture change consultants who worked in the state. Using this triangulation method and confirming the facts from facility websites and phone calls, in 2011 we identified 45 operating SH-NHs that met

PHILOSOPHY, PLACE, PROGRAM, AND POLICY

our definition, 21 of which were GH projects. About twice as many SH projects were under development. We also identified 18 look-alikes—that is, NHs with small units that missed the SH definition by just one criterion (Cutler, Kane and Henning Smith 2011).

For aim 2, we conducted systematic telephone interviews with administrators of each identified SH project to describe staff composition, CNA-level roles and staffing, and the development of each required element of NH regulation. We included questions about areas suggested in earlier research, that is, food procurement and preparation, activities development, and clinical nursing. As needed, we interviewed a corporate official to comment on development issues, business models, and expansion plans, if any. Selected conclusions from aim 2, many consistent with our previous work, are briefly described as follows (Henning-Smith et al. 2013):

- When SH-NHs were part of a campus with an existing NH, many shared personnel and purchasing functions were used and the patterns of staffing and expenditure for the SHs collectively or for each SH were hard to discern. The layers of administration tended to be more complex.

- Developing the expanded role of the direct-care staff was an ongoing effort. (Besides the term shahbaz, we found almost 20 different names, including versatile workers, compassionantes, and sharaths, among the more unusual terms.) The issue was to accentuate autonomy and increase communication and clinical skills of CNA-level staff while evolving meaningful coaching and modeling roles for professional leaders, especially nurses.

- The business model for many SH projects was predicated on planned proportions of Medicare and private-pay clientele. Success in attracting a Medicare population depended on proximity to hospitals, the nearby competing postacute services, and their prior experience. Veterans Administration (VA) certification was highly valued because of the enhanced payment rates in the VA contract NH program. The SH-NHs had an advantage on the revenue side because of their competitive appeal.

- The major variable that separated SH-NHs into "types" was whether they had another form of NH on campus. If the only NHs on campus were SHs, the transformed CNAs were likely to have broader roles. Our classification system was based on

195

the variable of having a traditional NH or campus, modified by the related factor of the number of SHs in the project, a number ranging from 1 to 18 and which we cut off at 1–4 and more than 4.

For aim 3, we selected homes that varied in scale and in whether they were on a campus with other NHs. Of the ten SH projects, all with different sponsors, half were GHs. They were located in seven states, with two homes each in Ohio, Texas, and New York and the others in Arkansas, Kansas, Massachusetts, and Nebraska. The group included an urban high-rise SH project, an SH project consisting of two dementia SH on a campus with a legacy NH, a for-profit SH project, a two-house project in a new senior housing development, and a 16-house development that replaced a large and respected NH. During site visits, the second author (LC) took numerous photographs to capture unique features and to compile a photo essay of the same shot at each site visit. Conclusions from this part of the research include (Kane and Cutler 2013):

- The SH-NHs looked and felt qualitatively different from traditional NHs. They sometimes seemed quieter and more serene, perhaps because many residents used their private spaces. We saw residents moving on their own initiative in the shared indoor and outdoor spaces. Family members and other guests were often present and even children of staff members frequented the SHs and became known to residents.
- The SH model was not relegated to the well-to-do; some of the projects were succeeding financially with large Medicaid populations. It was also not a model for those with lesser needs; SH-NHs could and did serve the full range of nursing-home residents with all diagnoses, functional and cognitive impairments, and high-care needs such as managing feeding tubes and tracheotomies, intravenous fluids, and sliding-scale insulin.
- The small-scale design of these NHs encouraged experimentation with innovative ways that NH residents could exercise control, choice, and autonomy in their lives. For example, an *Independent Traveler* program was developed in one 16-house GH complex whereby some residents were able to use a protocol to leave the house on their own recognizance to experience the

PHILOSOPHY, PLACE, PROGRAM, AND POLICY

larger outdoor community.

- While realizing that simply living in a SH offered more natural opportunities for activity and alleviation of boredom, every project expressed frustration with how to encourage sufficient and meaningful activity. The traditional activity program of group events, classes, and games fits poorly into an SH model, and yet organizing to make meaningful individualized activity possible both on the SH project premises and in the larger community is challenging, given the lean staffing models. Sometimes more impaired residents temporarily stayed in other houses so that the majority could take an excursion.
- The food was only as good as the person cooking it and not everyone was equally talented in the kitchen. Some projects added staff devoted to and experienced in food preparation, which also freed up CNA-level staff to socialize with or assist residents.
- State regulations and policy influenced the model development. Some state regulatory agencies were supportive and others were skeptical; sometimes intrastate variation was present or regulatory reactions changed over time. In states with support at the top (notably Arkansas and Kansas), the stance was less of a regulatory adversary and more of a partner working together for a success. Federal regulation and policy were also relevant. In one upstate New York community, local and state regulators were initially supportive of integrating two-house GH projects into housing neighborhoods using the general staff at the downsized legacy NH for some key roles, but federal regulations did not permit leadership staff to be located at a central *mothership* location, so the growth of that model is unlikely to continue. In the same setting, federal surveyors were insensitive to the changed culture during their first surprise inspection, proceeding to remove food and supplies from kitchen cabinets and piling them on the floor while visibly upset residents were lunching in the room. (In traditional NHs, such spaces would be largely invisible to residents.)

The photo essays proved a helpful method and product in at least three ways (Cutler 2013): for educational purposes in classrooms and for groups of professionals; for advocacy purposes, because pictures of residents in private quarters and shared spaces that look dramatically different from NH stereotypes—even bedrooms with double or queen beds—make a strong impression, as do photos of an elder struggling because of poor design; and for research purposes. A research project can entail careful examination of photos showing different kinds of problem-solving to compare their features, and even generate a better or more tailored solution. Pictures proved powerful for positive and negative messages. A sweater draped over a living room chair or a resident in a dressing gown going into the kitchen for coffee signifies home. A yellow cone announcing a wet floor (which itself is a tripping hazard), a tea-cart doubling as forbidden medications care, or a line of unused chairs piled against a wall signifies institution.

DISCUSSION

Developing Evidence of Benefit

From our own cumulative work and that of others on SH models of NHs, we discern great promise from SH-NHs. Not only do they improve NH life, but we see potential to expand their insights back to more traditional NHs and to heavy-care ALs. Our original evaluation posited effects on QOL only, but others have suggested better care outcomes are associated with GHs and culture change in general (Grabowski et al. 2014a). Development of a scientific basis for SH-NHs is confounded by selection effects, as pointed out by studies of adaptors of GHs or other culture change (Eliot et al. 2014; Grabowski et al. 2014b). Because the SH-NHs entail multiple simultaneous changes, including private bedrooms and bathrooms, transformed meals, and reorganized staff models, pinpointing which changes led to which effects was nearly impossible.

Implementation Issues

Often the divide between clinical health-related care and the personal care and attendant services seemed too wide. The original model may have overcompensated for medical dominance over resident lives by minimizing the need to work out the health-care aspects of NH. The role of GH nurse, and of other professionals, had been initially described as a visiting model analogous to home health care, an approach that

PHILOSOPHY, PLACE, PROGRAM, AND POLICY

nursing leaders believed marginalized nurses (Bowers 2011; Bowers and Nolet 2014). Also, the role of the direct-care worker needed further development and nurturing. Sharkey and colleagues (2011) studied roles and time use of CNA-level personnel in GHs and traditional NHs operated by the sponsoring organization and reported sufficient coverage. Although the ratio of direct CNA staff to residents was slightly higher in GHs than in the traditional NHs, overall staffing of nursing and non-nursing departments (excluding administration) was a little less than in traditional NHs. Even though shahbazim did indirect care (such as cleaning, laundry, and food preparation), they interacted with residents while doing those tasks, and researchers had difficulty distinguishing when the shahbazim were engaging residents and families as a specific activity rather than as a joint function with other tasks. The GH model was designed to be more natural, without the need to code arbitrary moments as *socialization*. Such accounting for time is almost antithetical to the GH model while at the same time useful to know and be able to cite to skeptics.

Creativity within a Trademarked Entity

Premature orthodoxy for GHs and other SH-NHs is a risk. A pro forma provided for the first GHs somewhat anchored the way staff has been deployed, yet multiple routes are possible to the desired bottom line (Jenkens et al. 2011). Certain elements such as the hearth and the long table and the requirement that shahbazim must exclusively cook the food have become hallmarks of GHs without any real evidence for them (Zimmerman and Cohen 2010). The impetus to control the nature and, thus, the quality of the trademarked organizations is understandable, yet experimentation is needed to experience the potential of the SH.

The GH has its own vocabulary—residents are elders (even the rare child, or residents many decades younger than 65). The language of guides, coaches, sages, and shahbazim (or alternative terms) has been described. In a study of AL in Oregon, Carder (2002) argues that the constant use of new language to reflect a social rather than medical AL model (such as tenants, not residents; move-in, move-out, and eviction rather than admission and discharge, or service plans, not care plans) legitimized the new approach, even if some personnel had not fully accepted it. Similarly, GH language might help legitimate a new type of NH, though possibly the somewhat contrived vocabulary would not resonate readily with consumers.

Person, Place, Program, and Philosophy

Can generic SH-NHs and trademarked GHs live up to their ambitious goal of deinstitutionalizing NHs? In other work, we identified five criteria, each viewed on a continuum, that render a setting more or less institutional, namely residential scale and materials; privacy; control and choices by residents while in the setting; control and choice by residents to move freely in the larger community; and resident control over moving in, remaining in, or leaving the setting (Kane and Cutler 2009b). We argue that physical environments, so often downplayed by the culture change movement because of the slow pace and high costs of changing them, are crucial, even if insufficient. Organizational staffing, care philosophy, and policies are also pivotal for any resident control and integration with the broader community. Perhaps, as Green (2014) argued, residents have a richer array of opportunities if they are part of a larger campus community and if they are enabled and encouraged to use the broader amenities. For NH residents to really use campus-wide opportunities, purposeful staff action is needed.

To turn an NH into a real home without the stigma so often perceived in any all-senior group housing (Hrybyk et al. 2012) is an enormous challenge. We noted how easily an SH-NH can become cluttered, or relapse into institutional appearance. We also noticed the limitation of the slogan that "if you don't have it in your own home, you should not have it in a SH" (Shield et al. 2014). These arguments were applied against exit signs, dedicated off-street parking, entertainment rooms, and even an activity program. Yet such features are present in multi-family housing complexes where many old people live. Seniors can and do maintain activity calendars at gyms, clubs, and religious organizations located outside their homes. The elusive goal is to keep the living unit small while expanding activity to the community at large.

We hope for synergism of philosophy, place (that is, physical environment), program, and policy in an idealized model of residential care for seniors. All four components need to work together for a more satisfactory whole for residents' QOL. Cantor's social model of

PHILOSOPHY, PLACE, PROGRAM, AND POLICY

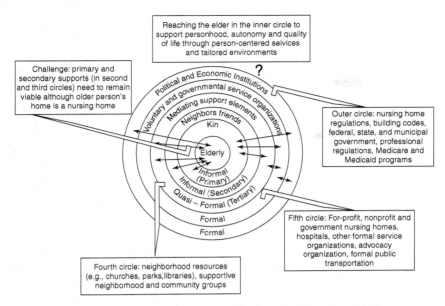

Figure 11.2: Cantor Model of Social Support for Older People Applied to Small House NHs: Source for concentric circle model: Cantor 1991 © Oxford University Press. Used with permission.

support for older people shows this complexity (1991). She envisaged seniors and their families at the center of concentric circles of influence on their well-being, starting with close family members, radiating to neighbors and friends, then formal organizations, and finally public policies. She posited a "systems model" to encompass "the intricacies involved in providing social care to older persons (Cantor 1991:338)." In Figure 11.2, we transposed SH-NH challenges into Cantor's concentric circles.

Despite the involvement of family members with relatives living in NHs, the institutional setting—with its rules and timetables—may attenuate the strong ties of kinship and friendship, the two inner circles of the diagram. Cantor stressed the interactive and changing nature of the spheres of family, community, social agencies, and government, all components of her model. The SH has the potential to create a setting that fosters rather than disrupts the primary roles at the heart of the social world of older people by situating GHs in real neighborhoods where seniors or their adult children live, by welcoming family and friends into GH life, and by encouraging primary friendships between elders and resident assistants. Could an SH truly have the lure of grandma's house to visiting children, serve as a real household where grandma lives, yet, equally importantly, be a setting that promotes and sustains grandma's ties to her own community, including family, religious, leisure, civic, and even professional groups?

The organization of voluntary and governmental agencies (i.e., the SH-NHs themselves) and the political and economic institutions in the outer concentric circles need attention for this ambitious vision to be actualized. Even public attitudes must change if neighborhood and community resources in the third circle from the center are to be engaged.

Finally, reimagining nursing-home care in any substantial way requires accommodating or changing a large number of federal and state regulations, which in turn strongly influence staff roles, opportunities offered to residents, and even physical facilities—that is, the program agenda. It requires working within or changing entrenched public policies and complex ways that care is funded—that is, the policy agenda. It requires trying to improve physical designs in dramatic ways that, in turn, will modify resident opportunities and staff behavior—that is, the agenda related to place. It requires connections to the immediate neighborhood and the worlds of each resident, with kin and friends being freed to play normalized roles as sons and daughters, nieces and nephews, and grandchildren, without being constrained by the settings—that is, the social agenda. It requires a new vision for what constitutes a good and safe enough life for older people needing NH levels of care—that is, the generativity agenda.

In this chapter, we used the example of SH-NHs to explore profound issues in long-term services and supports. The SH-NH is difficult to implement, test, and bring to scale. After following it and studying it for a decade, we consider it enormously promising and advocated for some policy changes to further its evolution (Kane and Cutler 2015). Yet we also see it as a way-station, a source of ideas and experiences that can be applied to a wide variety of senior housing and group residential settings where people with NH-level needs can live. Long ago, Elaine Brody (1973) referred to the NH sector as "a million procrustean beds"; Procrustes was a mythic innkeeper who stretched or chopped his guests to fit his one-size beds. This chilling metaphor still encapsulates how

PHILOSOPHY, PLACE, PROGRAM, AND POLICY

difficult changing NHs will be, requiring as it does changes in physical plants, programs, attitudes, and public policies for payment and regulation.

ACKNOWLEDGMENT

This chapter draws from our research on SH-NHs and other residential settings for seniors over almost 20 years. We thank the Commonwealth Fund for support of our initial GH evaluation in Tupelo, Mississippi; the Alzheimer's Association for support of our studies of SH-NHs for people with dementia in Ohio; and the Maurice and Hulda Rothschild Fund for support of our comparative analysis of state NHs and AL regulations, including environmental regulations. We particularly thank the Retirement Research Foundation (RRF), which provided two seminal grants to the University of Minnesota—one to develop practical strategies to improve physical environments in NHs and a second to classify and study SH-NHs national-wide—as well as a grant to the Pioneer Network, which furthered Lois Cutler's development of Design on a Dollar, a resource for NHs. Nancy Zweibel and Julie Coffman at the RRF were particularly supportive. Thanks also to Robert L. Kane, Minnesota Chair of Aging and Long-Term Care and director of the Minnesota Center on Aging, who consistently supplemented our work during the last decade. Finally, we thank three organizations that opened their doors to our earliest research: Methodist Senior Services, Inc. headquarters in Tupelo, Mississippi, CEO Stephen L. McAlilly; Otterbein Senior Lifestyle Choices headquarters in Lebanon, Ohio, past and current CEOs, Donald Gilmore and Jill Hreben, respectively; and Presbyterian Villages of Michigan, headquarters in Southfield, Michigan, CEO Roger L. Myers. An earlier and much briefer version of the chapter was presented at an invitational conference, "Social Support and Service Provision to Older Adults: Marjorie Cantor's Legacy to Gerontology," held at Syracuse University, January 16, 2014.

REFERENCES

Bowers, Barbara J. 1988. "Family Perceptions of Care in Nursing Homes. *The Gerontologist* 28(3):361–8.
Bowers, Barbara J. 2011. "Empowering Direct Care Workers: Lessons Learned from the Green House® Model." *Senior Housing and Care Journal* 19(1):109–20.

Bowers, Barbara J. and Kimberly Nolet. 2014. "Developing the Green House Nursing Care Team: Variations on Development and Implementation." *The Gerontologist* 54(S1):S53–64.

Brody, Elaine M. 1973. "A Million Procrustean Beds." *The Gerontolgist* 13(4):430–516.

Brody, Elaine M. 1985. "Parent Care as a Normative Family Stress." *The Gerontologist* 25(1):9–29.

Calkins, Margaret and Christine Cassella. 2007. "Exploring the Cost and Value of Private versus Shared Bedrooms in Nursing Homes." *The Gerontologist* 47(2):169–83.

Cantor, Marjorie H. 1991. "Family and Community: Changing Roles in an Aging Society. *The Gerontologist* 31(3):337–46.

Carder, Paula C. (2002). "The Social World of Assisted Living." *Journal of Aging Studies*, 16:1–18.

Cutler, Lois J. (2013). "Photo Essays of Selected Small House Nursing Homes: Tools for Education and Research." (Paper at Symposium, "Small-House Nursing Homes in the United States: Learning About Them and From Them," Gerontological Society of America, New Orleans, LA, Nov. 20-4). *The Gerontologist* 53(S1):388–39.

Cutler, Lois J. and Rosalie A. Kane. 2009. "Post-Occupancy Evaluation of a Transformed Nursing Home. The First Four Green House® Nursing Homes." *Journal of Housing for the Elderly* 23(4):304–34.

Cutler, Lois J., Rosalie A. Kane, Howard B. Degenholtz, Michael J. Miller, and Leslie A. Grant. 2006. "Assessing and Comparing Physical Environments for Nursing Home Residents: Using New Tools for Greater Specificity." *The Gerontologist* 45(1):42–51.

Cutler, Lois J., Rosalie A. Kane, and Carrie Henning-Smith. 2011. "Variation in Small-House NHs in the United States." (Paper at Symposium, "Small House Nursing Homes: Findings & Futures," Gerontological Society of America, Boston, MA, Nov. 18-22), *The Gerontologist* 49(SII):252–3.

Elliot, Amy, Lauren W. Cohen, David Reed, Kimberly Nolet and Sheryl Zimmerman. 2014. "A 'Recipe' for Culture Change? Findings from the THRIVE Survey of Culture Change Adopters." *The Gerontologist* 54(S1):17–24.

Grabowski, David C., James O'Malley, Christopher C. Afendulus, Daryl J. Caudrey, Amy Elliot, and Sheryl Zimmerman. 2014a. "Culture Change and Nursing Home Quality." *The Gerontologist* 54(SI):25–45.

Grabowski, David C., Amy Elliott, Brigitt Leitzell, Lauren W. Cohen, and Sheryl Zimmerman. 2014b. "Who are the Innovators? Nursing Homes Implementing Culture Change." *The Gerontologist* 54(SI):S65–75.

Grant, Leslie A. and Laverene Norton. 2003. "A Stage Model of Culture Change in Nursing Facilities." (Paper at Symposium, "Culture Change II: Theory and Practice, Vision and Reality," Gerontological Society of America, San Diego, CA, Nov. 22, 2003). Retrieved from http://www.leadingageny.org/home/assets/File/n00002611.pdf.

Green, David A. 2014. "Conceptualization and Development of the Household/Neighborhood Model for Skilled Nursing Facilities: A Case Study." *Frontiers of Architectural Research* 3(3):228–37.

Hamann, Darla J. 2014. "Does Empowering Residents' Families or Nursing Home Staff in Decision Making Improve Quality of Care?" *Journal of Applied Gerontology* 33(5):603–23.

Henning-Smith, Carrie A, Rosalie A. Kane, Lois J. Cutler, and Greg Rhee. 2013. "Describing Patterns of Variation in Small-House Nursing Home Programs." (Paper at Symposium, "Small-House Nursing Homes in the United States: Learning About Them and From Them,"Gerontological Society of America, New Orleans, LA, Nov. 20–4.) *The Gerontologist*, 53(SI):398.

Hrybyk, Regina, Robert L. Rubinstein, J. Kevin Eckert, Ann C. Frankowski, Lynn Keimig, Mary Nemec, Amanada D. Peeples, Erin Roth, and Patrick J. Doyle. 2012. "The Dark Side: Stigma in Purpose-Built Senior Environments." *Journal of Housing for the Elderly* 26:(1–3):275–89.

Jenkens, Robert, Terri Sult, Newell Lessell, David Hammer, and Anna Ortigara. 2011. "Financial Implications of the Green House® Model." *Senior Housing and Care Journal* 19(1):3–22.

Kane, Rosalie A. 2005. "Overview of Green House Effects on Residents, Their Families, and Caregiving Staff." (Paper at Symposium, "Multifaceted Study of the Green Houses of Tupelo, MS and Implications for Replication: De-Institutionalizing Nursing Homes," Gerontological Society of America, Orlando, FL, Nov. 18–20). *The Gerontologist* 45(SII):371.

Kane, Rosalie. A. and Lois J. Cutler. 2007. "Evolving and Sustaining Culture Change in Small-House NHs. (Paper at Symposium, "Beyond Culture Change: Creating Caring Communities by Promoting Capacities of Elders," Gerontological Society of America, San Francisco, CA, Nov. 16–20.) *The Gerontologist* 47(SII):507.

Kane, Rosalie A. and Lois J. Cutler. 2009a. "Successes and Challenges in Implementing Small-House Nursing Homes. (Paper at meeting of the Gerontological Society of America in Atlanta, GA, November 18–22.) *The Gerontologist* 49(II):257.

Kane, Rosalie A. and Lois J. Cutler. 2009b. "Promoting Home-Like Characteristics and Eliminating Institutional Characteristics in Community-Based Residential Care Settings." *Senior Housing & Care Journal* 17(1):15–37.

Kane, Rosalie A. and Lois J. Cutler. 2013. Learning from In-depth Studies of Small-House Nursing Homes. (Paper at Symposium, "Small-House Nursing Homes in the United States: Learning About Them and From Them," Gerontological Society of America, New Orleans, LA, November 20–24). *The Gerontologist* 53(SI):388-339.

Kane, Rosalie A. and Lois J. Cutler. 2015. "Re-Imagining Long-Term Services and Supports: Towards Livable Environments, Service Capacity, and Enhanced Community Integration, Choice, and Quality of Life For Seniors." *The Gerontologist* 55(2):286–95.

Kane, Rosalie A., Mary O. Baker, Jennifer Salmon, and Wendy Veazie. 1998. *Consumer Perspectives on Private versus Shared Accommodations in Assisted Living Settings.* Washington, DC: AARP.

Kane, Rosalie A., Kristin C. Kling, Boris Bershadsky, Robert L. Kane, Katherine Giles, Howard B. Degenholtz, Jason Liu, and Lois J. Cutler. 2003. "Quality of Life

Measure for Nursing Home Residents." *Journal of Gerontology: Medical Sciences* 58A (3):240–8.

Kane, Rosalie A., Terry Y Lum, Lois J. Cutler, Howard B. Degenholtz, and Tzy-Chyi Yu. 2007. "Resident Outcomes in Small-Group-Home Nursing Homes: A Longitudinal Evaluation of the Initial Green House Program." *Journal of the American Geriatrics Society* 55(6):832–9.

Kane, Rosalie A., Lois J. Cutler, Terry Y. Lum, and Laura Peterson. 2011. "Small-House Nursing Homes and Dementia Care." (Paper at Symposium, "Small House Nursing Homes: Findings & Futures," Gerontological Society of America, Boston, MA, Nov. 18–22.) *The Gerontologist* 49(SII):252–3.

Koren, Mary Jane. 2010. "Person-Centered Care for Nursing Home Residents: The Culture Change Movement." *Health Affairs* 29(2):312–7.

Lawton, M. Powell and Lucille Nahemow. 1973. Ecology and the Aging Process. P. 619–74 in Carl Eisdorfer and M. Powell Lawton (eds.) *Psychology of Adult Development and Aging*. Washington, DC: American Psychological Association.

Lum, Terry Y., Rosalie A. Kane, Lois J. Cutler, and Tzy-Chyi Yu. 2008. "Effects of Green House® Nursing Homes on Resident Families." *Health Care Financing Review* 30(2):37–51.

Otterbein. n.d. "Otterbein Senior Lifestyle Choices breaks ground in Gahanna on new small house neighborhood." Retrieved from https://www.otterbein.org/news-events/archive/anderson-otterbein%E2%80%9Ss-person-centered-care-%E2%80%9Ccutting-edge%E2%80%9D.

Preiser, Wolfgang, Harvey Z. Rabinowitz, and Edward T. White. 1988. *Post Occupancy Evaluation*. New York: Van Nostrand Reinhold.

Rabig, Judith, William Thomas, Rosalie A. Kane, Lois J. Cutler, and Stephen McAlilly. 2006. "Radical Re-Design of Nursing Homes: Applying the Green House Concept in Tupelo, MS." *The Gerontologist* 46(4)543–39.

Rahman, Annie N. and John F. Schnelle. 2008. "The Nursing Home Culture-Change Movement: Recent Past, Present, and Future Directions for Research." *The Gerontologist* 48(2):142–8.

Rowles, Graham D. and M. Bernard. (eds.) 2013. *Making Meaningful Places in Old Age*. New York: Springer Publishing Company.

Shanas, Ethel. 1979. "Social Myth as Hypothesis: The Case of Family Relationships of Old People." *The Gerontologist* 29(1):3–9.

Sharkey, Siobhan, Sandy Hudak, Susan D. Horn, Bobbie James, and Jessie Howes. 2011. "Frontline Caregiver Daily Practices: A Comparison Study of Traditional Nursing Homes and the Green House Project Sites." *Journal of the American Geriatrics Society* 59(1):126–31.

Shield, Renee R., Denise Tyler, Michael Lepore, Jessica Locze, and Susan C. Miller. 2014. "Would You Do That in Your Own Home? Making Nursing Home Home-Like in Culture Change Implementation." *Journal of Housing for the Elderly* 28(4):383–98.

Shier, Victoria, Dimitry Khodyakov, Lauren C. Cohen, Sheryl Zimmerman, and Debra Saliba. 2014. "What Does the Evidence Really Say About Culture Change in Nursing Homes?" *The Gerontologist* 54(S1):6–16.

PHILOSOPHY, PLACE, PROGRAM, AND POLICY

Shippee, Tetyana, Rosalie A. Kane, Laura Peterson, and Lois J. Cutler. 2011. "Family Perspectives on Dementia Care in Nursing Homes. (Paper at Symposium, "Small House Nursing Homes: Findings & Futures," Gerontological Society of America, Boston, MA, Nov. 18-22.) The *Gerontologist* 49(SII):252-3.

Thomas, William H. 1996. Life Worth Living: How Someone You Love Can Still Enjoy Life in a Nursing Home: The Eden Alternative in Action. Acton, MA: VanderWyk & Burnham.

Thomas, William H. 2004. *What are Old People For? How Elders Will Save the World.* Acton, MA: VanderWyk & Burnham.

Wilson, Keren Brown. 2007. "Historical Evolution of Assisted Living in the United States: 1979 to the Present." *The Gerontologist* 47(SIII):8-22.

Zimmerman, Sheryl and Lauren W. Cohen. 2010. "Evidence behind the Green House and Similar Models of Nursing Home Care." *Aging Health* 6(6):717-37.

Zimmerman, Sheryl, Lauren W. Cohen, David Reed, Lisa Gwyther, Tiffany Washington, John Cagle, Philip Sloane, and John Preiser. 2013. "'Family Matters' in Long-Term Care: Results of a Group-Randomized Trial." *Senior Housing and Care Journal* 21(1):3-20.

INDEX

AARP, political clout of 33
Acquaviva, K. 80
activities of daily living (ADLs) 34, 45, 156;
 see also instrumental activities of daily
 living (IADLs)
Addis, J. R. 86
advance directive documents 83
Affordable Care Act (ACA) 109
AIDS Service Organizations (ASOs) 58, ,73
Ainsworth Strange Situation 10–11
Ajrouch, K. J. 19
Alzheimer's disease or a related dementia
 (ADRD) 124
American Community Survey (ACS) 112
Americans' Changing Lives survey 2
Angel, J. 4, 38
antiretroviral therapies (ART) 54
Antonucci, T. C. 2, 4, 8, 17–20
Assisted living (AL) settings 173; *see also*
 small-house nursing homes
attachment, behaviors *see* Ainsworth
 Strange Situation

baby boomers 3–4, 20, 34–5; aging and 28–9;
 Latino baby boomers 30–1, 33, 41; sexual
 and gender identities 96
Behavioral Risk Factor Surveillance
 Surveys (BRFSS) 112
Bengtson, V. L. 11
Berkman, L. F. 17
biomeasures 21
Birditt, K. S. 17–19
Boerner, K. 5, 136

Bott, E. 11
Bowlby, J. 10
Brennan, M. 59
Brennan-Ing, M. 5, 54
Brody, E. 147, 179, 202
Brownstein, R. 32, 35

Cagle, J. 179
California Health Interview Survey
 (CHIS) 101
Calkins, M. 174
Cantor, M. H. 1, 4, 6, 8–9, 12–13, 16, 18,
 23, 55–6, 59, 71–3, 78, 91, 136, 200–1,
 203
Carder, P. C. 199
caregiving in later life 118–32; background
 119; caregivers of older relatives and
 grandparent caregivers 121; factors
 conducive to caregiver well-being 120–1;
 foster care payments 128–9; housing,
 finding 126; reasons for caregiving
 119–20; subsidized guardianships 129;
 successful coping 120
CaringBridge 92
Carstensen, L. L. 2
Casella, C. 174
Center for Epidemiological Studies
 Depression Scale (CES-D) 59, 69–70
Center on Halsted (COH) 58
Centers for Disease Control and
 Prevention 96
certified nursing assistant (CNA) 175
Chambers, D. B. 57

209

Chesney, M. 57
Civil Rights Act (1964) 111
Cohen, L. W. 179
Connidis, I. A. 2
continuing medical education (CME) 162
convoy model 2
Cox, C. 5, 118
Cutler, L. J. 6, 173

Demko, C. M. 4, 27
depression: caregiver 43, 121; forgiveness
   and 19; HIV and 54, 59; in LGBT older
   adults 103
de Vries, B. 77, 80
differences, group and individual
   8–23; assessment 9; caregiver burden
   20; classic findings 13–18; conflict
   within and across generations 12;
   documentation 18; family structure
   20; forgiveness, health and 19;
   friends 16; gender equity in network
   membership 15; new developments
   21–2; non-adjacent generations 11–12;
   recent findings 17–18; siblings 15–16;
   stress 18; subgroup differences 19;
   widows 11
Dream Act 32
Durbin, K. 79

Emlet, C. A. 107
employed caregivers 124–5
epigenetics 22
Equality Act 111
Erosheva, E. A. 107

Family Matters Service Plan 179–80
Family and Medical Leave Act (FMLA) 123–4
family structure: changing 20; trends in 3
Fingerman, K. 2
forgiveness, health and 19
foster care payments 128–9
Fostering Connections to Success and
   Increasing Adoptions Act 128–9
Fredriksen-Goldsen, K. I. 5, 95, 107

Gay Care Co-Op 92
gender: dysphoria 100; equity in network
   membership 15; role segregation
   (marriage) 11
geographic mobility 40, 141
"geographic privacy" 146
Geriatric Education Centers (GEC) 167–8

Geriatrics Education Rural-Urban Alliance
   (GERA) 157–8, 161–2, 164–5, 168, 170
Geriatric Scholars Program 159
Gil, F. T. 4
Goldsen, J. 107
grandparent caregivers 121, 125–8
Greatest Generation 96, 98
GRECC Connect 158–64
Green, D. A. 200
Green Houses® (GH): description of 175–6;
   implementation 177, 198; prevalent ideas
   incorporated into 174–5; three-legged
   stool framework 177; see also small-house
   nursing homes
Griffith, J. L. 5, 155
Gwyther, L. 179

Harmon, D. K. 147
Hayes-Bautista, D. 33, 35
Health Equity Promotion Model 99
Health and Retirement Study (HRS) 2, 112
hierarchical-compensatory model of social
   relations 1, 6, 13
Hierarchical Compensatory Theory 55
Hispanic Established Population for
   Epidemiologic Study of the Elderly
   (H-EPESE) 4, 44
"Hispanic Paradox" 50
HIV/AIDS 5, 12, 81
HIV, impact of 54–74; analysis
   60–1; antiretroviral therapies 54;
   demographic profile 58; depression
   54, 59; HIV status and morbidity 58–9;
   methods 58–61; multimorbidity 55;
   program implications 73–4; purpose
   and rationale 57; results 61–70; sample
   and procedure 58; sociodemographic
   characteristics 61–3; support
   perceptions and relation to mental
   health 57; theoretical perspectives 55–6
HIV and social networks see social
   networks, of older adults with HIV
HIV and social support: availability and
   adequacy of 60; kin support resources,
   activation of 71; multivariate analyses
   of instrumental and emotional support
   sufficiency 68–70; negative social
   support 65–7; network supports,
   functionality of 73; perceptions of
   social support availability and adequacy
   67–8; types and frequency of assistance
   from family and friends 60

INDEX

Hoffman, C. 147
Horn, S. D. 199
Horowitz, A. 5, 136
Howe, J. 5, 155
Howes, J. 199
Hoy-Ellis, C. P. 5, 95, 107
Hudak, S. 199
Hung, W. 5–6, 155

immigration reform 32
Institute of Medicine (IOM) 96, 155
institution creep 182
instrumental activities of daily living
   (IADLs) 45
Internet-based support groups 150

James, B. 199
Jennings, L. K. 147
Johnson, L. M. 57
Jorge Chapa, J. 33, 35

Kane, R. A. 6, 173
Karpiak, S. E. 5, 54
Kim, H.-J. 107
Kleban, M. H. 147
Kramer, B. J. 6, 155

Larson, B. 5
Latinization of the United States, aging
   and 27–36; common concerns and
   investments 33–6; diversity and
   Latinos 29; economics, assets, and
   investments 35; generational mismatch
   32; inclusiveness and acceptance 36;
   long-term care and caregiving 34;
   national security 35–6; taxpayers and
   entitlements 34–5
Latino family, role of in late-life caregiving
   38–50; background 40–1; caregiving
   burden, concentrated 50; culture
   and family caregiving 41–3; data and
   methods 43–5; difficulty to maintain
   cultural tradition 40; financial
   tasks 47; health security 42; late-life
   immigrants 39, 46; likelihood of decline
   39; lost wages 40; social capital 44;
   socioeconomic resources 41; strain in
   social ties 43; stressors 42; trends 38
LEGACY (Living Equitably, Grandparents
   Aiding Children and Youth) 130
lesbian, gay, bisexual, and transgender
   (LGBT) older adults, health disparities

100–2; background characteristics 107–8;
differences by race and ethnicity 108;
education levels 108; health behaviors
105–7; implications for services, policy,
and research 108–13; informal care 110
lesbian, gay, bisexual, and transgender
   (LGBT) older adults, risk and adversity
   104–5; barriers to health care 106;
   discrimination 107; gender dysphoria
   100; interventions needed 108, 112;
   social isolation 105; sociopathic
   personality disorder, homosexuality
   as 96; statistics 95; stigma 104, 107;
   suicidal ideation 109
lesbian, gay, bisexual, and transgender
   (LGBT) older adults, resilience and
   resources 102–4; disclosure of sexual
   orientation or gender identity 102;
   group identity 103; partners and
   spouses, benefits provided by 102
lesbian, gay, bisexual, and transgender
   (LGBT) older adults, preparations for
   later life care among 77–93; absence
   of community 87; discussions about
   receiving care 88; document completion
   81; fear of isolation 80; finances,
   concern about 84; focus groups 83, 85;
   funeral arrangements 80; intentionality
   78; likeliness to live alone 78; marriage
   77; MetLife study 79, 81; offspring 78;
   qualitative findings 83–90; source of
   caregivers 90; survey findings 79–83
Lifespan Respite Care Act 122–3
Lifetime Respite Program 132
Litwak, E. 1
living will 80–1
long-distance caregiving 136–52;
   challenges 143–8; communication 147–8;
   definitions and prevalence 138–9;
   future directions 150–2; identification
   of long-distance caregivers 139–43;
   interested family members, absence
   of 148; service needs and service/
   technological options 149–50; sibling
   networks 143; sources of stress 144–5;
   see also "geographic privacy"; "moving
   closer" decision
Longitudinal Study of Generations
   (LSOG) 2, 9, 11–12
Lopata, H. 11
Lüscher, K. 2
Lynch, F. 33, 35

Mahalik, M. E. 86
Manalel, J. 4, 8
Markides, K. 4, 38
Martin, S. S. 147
Mason, A. 80
McMullin, J. A. 2
Midlife Development in the United States survey 2
minority group status, forgiveness and 19
mixed feelings in supportive relationships 2
"moving closer" decision 146-7
Muraco, A. 107
Myers, D. 33, 35

National Family Caregiver Support Program (NFCSP) 121-2, 132
National Health Interview Survey 112
national security 35-6
National Survey of Families and Households 2
nursing homes *see* Green Houses® (GH); small-house nursing homes (SH-NHs)

Obergefell v. Hodges (2015) 111
older adults, social support and service provision to 1-6; ethnic diversity 4; family structure, trends in 3; hierarchical-compensatory model of social supports 1, 6; lesbian, gay, bisexual, and transgender older adults 5; methodological advances 3; mixed feelings in supportive relationships 2; policy and program needs 5; shifting costs 4; statistical techniques 3; surveys 2;

Parker, M. W. 147
Petry, H. 107
Pillemer, K. 2
Pioneer Network in Long-Term Care 173
postoccupancy evaluations (POEs) 181
Preiser, J. 179
Public Health Service Act 123

quality of life (QOL) 173, 176, 178-81, 198, 200
Quam, J. 80

Reed, D. 179
replacement rates 30

residential care settings, family support and 179-80
Robert Wood Johnson Foundation (RWJF) 177
Roff, L. L. 147
Rote, S. 4, 38
Rural Health Training and Education Initiative (RHTI) 164
Rural Interdisciplinary Team Training (RITT) 165-7
Rural Provider and Health Care Staff Training and Education Initiative (RPSTI) 158
rural veterans, improving access to geriatrics care for 155-70; continuing education 162; current models for rural-urban partnerships 159-62; distance learning 160-1; expert consultation to remote and rural providers 161; exposing trainees to a field 161; primary care providers, geriatrics education for 159-60

Schink, W. 33, 35
Schoonover, C. B. 147
Seidel, L. 5, 54
Shanas, E. 179
Sharkey, S. 199
Sherman, C. W. 20
sibling networks 143
Silent Generation 96, 98
Silverstein, M. 1
Sloane, P. 179
small-house nursing homes (SH-NHs) 173-203; background 174-7; dementia in 189-94; evidence of benefit 198; evolution in large firms 182-9; family support and residential care settings 179-80; federal regulations 202; neighborhood organization 174; person, place, program, and philosophy 200-3; physical environments 177-9; privacy preferences 174; research 180-2; typology 194-8
smoking and drinking 106, 108-9
social capital 44
social isolation 105
social networks: among aging gay men 56; among lesbian, gay, bisexual, and transgender (LGBT) older adults 103; components 63-5; empirical evidence describing 16; informal 59-60; of older adults with HIV 56-7

INDEX

social relations: early perspectives 8–13; hierarchical-compensatory model of 13; negative 9, 17; practical/practice perspective of 12–13
socioeconomic status (SES) 16; SES-health model 16–17
socio-emotional selectivity theory 2
subsidized guardianships 129
Syme, S. L. 17

task-specific model 1
Taylor, J. M. 57
Team Development Measure (TDM) 167
Temporary Assistance to Needy Families (TANF) 129–30
Thomas, W. H. 175
Tighe, L. 18
Torres-Gil, F. M. 27, 35

UCLA Geriatrics Knowledge Test 165
U.S. Department of Housing and Urban Development (HUD) 130
U.S. Supreme Court ruling on marriage equality 80

VA Specialty Care Access Network-Extension for Community Healthcare Outcomes (SCAN-ECHO) model 161
Veterans Health Administration (VHA) 6, 155
Veterans Integrated Service Network (VISN) 169
virtual learning community (VLC) 159
vocalizations 192

Washington, T. 179
Washington State Behavioral Risk Factor Surveillance System (WA-BRFSS) 100
Webster, N. 17–18, 20
widows 11
Wilmoth, J. 1
Wilson, K. B. 177
Wisconsin Longitudinal Study 2
Within-Family Differences Study 2
World Health Organization (WHO) 105

Zimmerman, S. 179